CW01391055

TRIUMPH

TRIUMPH

THE STORY OF THE
LEGENDARY
MOTORCYCLE

Mike Armitage

Michael O'Mara Books Limited

First published in Great Britain in 2025 by
Michael O'Mara Books Limited
9 Lion Yard
Tremadoc Road
London SW4 7NQ

EU representative:
Authorised Rep Compliance Ltd
Ground Floor
71 Baggot Street Lower
Dublin D02 P593
Ireland

Copyright © Michael O'Mara Books Limited 2025

All rights reserved. You may not copy, store, distribute, transmit, reproduce or otherwise make available this publication (or any part of it) in any form, or by any means (electronic, digital, optical, mechanical, photocopying, recording, machine readable, text/data mining or otherwise), without the prior written permission of the publisher. Any person who does any unauthorized act in relation to this publication may be liable to criminal prosecution and civil claims for damages.

A CIP catalogue record for this book is available from the British Library.

This product is made of material from well-managed, FSC˚-certified forests and other controlled sources. The manufacturing processes conform to the environmental regulations of the country of origin.
For further information see www.mombooks.com/about/sustainability-climate-focus

Report any safety issues to product.safety@mombooks.com and see
www.mombooks.com/contact/product-safety

UK edition:
ISBN: 978-1-78929-752-2 in hardback print format
ISBN: 978-1-78929-764-5 in trade paperback format
ISBN: 978-1-78929-772-0 in ebook format

US edition:
ISBN: 978-1-78929-801-7 in paperback print format
ISBN: 978-1-78929-814-7 in ebook format

1 2 3 4 5 6 7 8 9 10

Front cover photograph: RapidEye/Getty Images
Back cover photograph: Heritage Image Partnership Ltd/Alamy Stock Photo
Cover design by Natasha Le Coultre
Designed and typeset by Ed Pickford
Printed and bound by CPI Group (UK) Ltd, Croydon, CR0 4YY

www.mombooks.com

MIX
Paper | Supporting
responsible forestry
FSC
www.fsc.org
FSC® C013604

To my wife Jane and sons Edward and Lyle, for their
ongoing tolerance of all the two-wheeled silliness.

CONTENTS

'WHAT IS IT, MATE – A TRIUMPH?'

No other motorcycle brand is as well known, instantly recognizable or resonates so widely as Triumph. Through their record-breaking antics, benchmark engineering, race success, active service in two world wars and by being the wheels of choice for a stream of celebrities – and, crucially, through creating bikes that are simply fabulous to ride – the firm has rightly gained legendary status.

Not just among riders, either. When you arrive home riding a new machine and your nosey non-biking neighbour wanders over for a gawp, they'll nod at your shiny bike and ask if it's a Triumph. When work colleagues catch a glimpse of the Triumph logo on your T-shirt, they immediately know it's the two-wheeler. Head over to the pub quiz and any 'name a make of motorcycle' question will bring a bundle of answer sheets with the same name at the top.

Triumph's products have achieved something else too. They've become brands on their own. Tell someone you ride a Bonneville, Daytona or Thunderbird, and there's no need to bother with any more detail. Everyone knows you're talking about a Triumph. Few products and creations can do this, let alone others within motorcycling. You can probably count them on the fingers of one hand. E-type, iPhone, Walkman, Beetle … erm, that's about it. And the iconic, evergreen bike models have such standing because of the British brand's legendary status.

Marking 140 years since the company was founded and 120 years since their first proper all-Triumph machine – the 1905 Triumph 3hp Motor Bicycle – this book takes a celebratory stroll through the amazing story of an icon. The remarkable individuals, landmark moments and influence on popular culture. From misfortunes, harsh times and disruption, to world records and being the star of the silver screen. And, of course, the inspiring, bestselling, exemplary motorcycles. Set against the fashions, events, technology and changing tastes of the times, it's quite a ride.

CHAPTER 1

THE START OF SOMETHING EPIC

THE MAN BEHIND IT ALL

There's a compliment made in the automotive world when something is particularly smooth and quiet. Wheel your new motorcycle out of the garage to show inquisitive friends, fire the engine into life to impress them with its polite whirring, smooth running and subtle sound – and it's almost guaranteed that someone will mutter, 'Ooh, it runs like a sewing machine.'

Which is rather fitting when the bike in question is a Triumph because the founder of the legendary British company started out flogging machines for stitching your clothes together.

Siegfried Bettmann was born in Nuremberg, Germany, on 18 April 1863, the son of a wealthy timber merchant named Meyer and his wife, Sofie. Educated at university, Siegfried arrived in Great Britain in 1883, aged 20. Victorian Britain was flourishing: manufacturing was booming off the back of the Industrial Revolution, there was an ever-expanding network of steam railways and shipping routes and London – centre of the empire – was seen by the rest of the world as being the finest of cities. British traders and investors dominated overseas markets and it was desirable to have 'Made in England' stamped on your shiny new products. There was also huge intellectual progress being made, with rapid advances in technology, medicine and science. Quite a lot to shout about, in other words. The lure for the bright, ambitious young German was obvious.

Dropped into the middle of bustling Victorian London, Bettmann splashed out on a few nights at a hotel before finding somewhere more financially attractive to stay on Church Road, Islington. He found work for Kelly & Co., publishers of a trade directory, which contained all the tradespeople, companies, landowners, charities and other notable characters in a particular British town – a bit like a Victorian paper version of Google. Bettmann used his language skills to create their foreign versions. He also befriended another German, who'd been in London for a few weeks after seven years in Holland. His new buddy Mauritz Schulte would play a key role in Triumph's story.

Within a year, Bettmann had changed course and was working for White Sewing Machine Co., a move that would be pivotal in his future. The market for sewing machines was thriving with everyone keen to be able to make and then also repair their own things, rather than pay someone else. Bettmann travelled across Europe on behalf of his employers and soon decided to kickstart his own sideline business. The year was 1885. He set himself up as the British agent for German-made Biesolt & Locke sewing machines, but also carried on working for the White Sewing Machine Co. – his manager at White even invested in the new venture, which was called S. Bettmann & Co.

Something important also happened. Siegfried Bettmann got into the two-wheeled scene, selling British-built bicycles at home and overseas.

TRIUMPH IS BORN

Karl von Drais is the bloke responsible for getting humans onto two wheels. In 1817, he cobbled together two cart wheels with lengths of timber to invent the 'running machine'. You perched yourself on top, grabbed hold of conveniently placed handles, and propelled yourself along with your feet. It was much like a full-size version of the balance bikes that children use nowadays to terrorize pedestrians in parks. In June that year, he scurried the respectable distance of eight miles in less than an hour. This was clearly far quicker (and cooler) than walking, and the design of his 'Draisine' was rapidly copied across Europe and America. These first commercially successful two-wheelers were commonly known as a 'dandy horse', after the nickname 'dandy' given to the preening well-heeled men of the era who rushed out to buy the things.

Draisines were all the rage with such gents in London in 1819. Everyone who was anyone had to be seen rolling along. However, riding a Draisine wasn't quite as natural as walking and accidents were common. Fines started to be issued to anyone riding on the pavement and some cities started to ban them.

Risk-averse inventors decided three wheels might be better. Or even four. These contraptions could hold themselves up on their own, minimizing embarrassing meetings between the rider and the ground, and you didn't need to do any of that bothersome balancing. The middle decades of the 1800s saw a boom in these tricycles and quadracycles. Hand cranks and treadles (where you swing your legs back and forth, a bit like on those strange exercise machines in a gym) were used to usher the machines along, although their weight and rolling resistance made it a sweaty affair.

A couple of pioneering French chaps called Pierre Lallement and Ernest Michaux invented a 'velocipede' in 1861, which featured pedals and a crank to directly turn the wheel. These contraptions started to look like something we might recognize as a bicycle. Suddenly, you didn't have to trudge about on foot – with some simple twirling of your limbs, you could scoot along merrily at running pace or even keep up with a cantering horse. It was marvellous. Not yet having brakes was less marvellous, resulting in lots of what were known as 'headers', where out-of-control riders careered into things. After a few more years of rather questionable designs (including the famous and comically unstable penny-farthing, with its huge front wheel and tiny rear one), a logical chap by the name of John Kemp Starley designed a bicycle with equal-sized wheels, a chain drive from the crank to the rear wheel, steering, brakes, mudguards … it even had a sprung saddle to give your behind a nicer time. The year was 1885 – the same year that Bettmann set up his business.

Starley hit the jackpot with his 'safety bicycle': the modern bike as we know it had arrived. Almost overnight, it went from being a toy for the wealthy to effective, efficient transport. It was immediately a huge success, and bicycle manufacturers sprang up across the globe.

One such company serving the demand was William Andrews Ltd, based in the British manufacturing city of Birmingham in the Midlands – one of the city's very first cycle companies. Their bicycles were innovative and high quality, featuring their own in-house, purpose-made parts, rather than cheaper, bought-in components. William Andrews had a background in sewing machines – he'd worked for Singer, the brand that dominated the market, and had filed patents for his own designs, which is probably how he crossed paths with sewing salesman Siegfried Bettmann. As part of his new business venture, Bettmann started to distribute William's high-quality bicycles and tricycles. Having 'Bettmann' on his products didn't really tally with cycles marketed as being British and promoted as coming from London, though. Siegfried needed a more English-sounding name … and the first Triumph two-wheelers were born.

RAPID PROGRESS

Mauritz Schulte had been travelling around Europe peddling pottery and had managed to save £250 – almost £28,000 in today's money – which he invested into Bettmann's new company, becoming a partner. The duo's Triumph-branded cycles were proving extremely popular, not just in Britain but in mainland Europe too, with the firm displaying their wares at trade fairs and advertising in several countries. The name Bettmann and Co. disappeared, the sewing machines were all but forgotten and The Triumph Cycle Company strutted forwards.

The set-up with William Andrews was straightforward. Triumph specified what they wanted, Andrews supplied the bicycles and they were finished and plastered with Triumph stickers at Bettmann and Schulte's London premises. The cycle world was evolving at a breakneck rate, however. Not only were the bikes themselves becoming better, but they were becoming quicker, easier and cheaper to manufacture. Machinery and tools had rapidly been designed that could mass produce key components like frames to feed the worldwide demand for cycles, and the standardization of parts, processes and practices brought a greater supply. This was good news for would-be cyclists, as it meant that bicycles became cheaper and more accessible, with more and more companies able to easily and cheaply start producing and selling. Remember how when the mobile phone was first launched, we all wondered how normal folk would ever have such a miraculous thing, but now they're commonplace? A bit like that.

Seeing this swift progress, Schulte convinced Bettmann that Triumph's future lay in making its own products. Manufacturing, not middlemen. Trying to come up with a bicycle from scratch that could follow on seamlessly from the high standard set by their advanced William Andrews products would be tricky, though. Both had forged their careers selling stuff, not actually making it. They were in no way engineers.

Schulte had the solution. He spent two months working at the Andrews factory in Aston, Birmingham – not in the offices or just floating around observing, but at the workbenches, twirling tools. Proper hands-on learning. With Schulte's newfound knowledge and experience, in 1888, the enterprising pair both borrowed money from their families, which Bettmann used to buy a site on Much Park Street in Coventry – the heart of the industrial Midlands – where they could build their machines. Helpful relations weren't the only people who spotted a bright future for the duo. John Boyd Dunlop had invented the world's first pneumatic tyre in the same year. The first bicycle tyres had been iron bands encasing wooden wheels, followed by solid rubber on the penny-farthing; wrapping bicycle wheels with air-filled rubber brought comfort and smooth running to those pedalling to work every day, and was also a way of getting a much-needed edge in the increasingly popular sport of cycle racing. And the Dunlop Pneumatic Tyre Company invested in Bettmann's new operation. The Much Park Street facility started churning out Siegfried and Mauritz's own Triumph cycle in 1889.

Although high-quality bicycles were still something of a luxury item, the Triumph Cycle Company made money. Proper money. The products were popular, demand was increasing, and so Bettmann decided to create another factory in his hometown of Nuremberg, Germany, in 1896. It carried the catchy title Deutsche Triumph Fahrradwerke Aktiengesellschaft. Going from strength to strength, Triumph was a busy business. And Bettmann was a busy man. First, he moved with his business partner to Coventry to be close to the blossoming factory, lodging with a watchmaker with German roots called Marks Baum. In 1895, Bettmann became a naturalized British subject while living at the Craven Arms in Coventry, and the same year married Annie Meyrick (known as Millie) from Shifnal in Shropshire. Two years later, he'd also become a director for Robert Bunting and Sons, a Sheffield-based company churning out steel, tooling, machinery and, notably, various cycle components – and one of Triumph's suppliers. The man behind Triumph also joined the city council in 1907. He would go on to be Coventry's mayor and was twice visited by British Prime Minister Ramsey MacDonald during the 1920s. Siegfried became the president of the Coventry Liberal Association too, and was a founding member of the Coventry Chamber of Commerce, a Justice of the Peace and president of the

Godiva Harriers athletic club (the Bettmann Cup, a competition to win the trophy donated by Mr Triumph, still runs to this day).

There's more. He formed the Annie Bettmann Foundation with his wife in 1914, for young folk who wanted a helping hand in starting a business, and which extended its remit to also provide grants to assist with further education.

Quite the guy, our Siegfried.

FROM PEDALS TO PETROL

While dandies were still whizzing around London impressing themselves on their self-propelled contrivances, something far more advanced was being developed. Something that would completely revolutionize travel and change the world beyond recognition.

Humans had been trying to harness energy to cause motion for centuries. Even the ancient Egyptians and Greeks had very basic devices that used steam or compressed air. There were steam-powered and even clockwork (yes, wind-up) carriages invented during the 1600s, and various self-propelled vehicles powered by electric motors and vast batteries appeared during the late 1700s and early 1800s. Those Teslas queuing at your local charging point really are nothing new.

However, things got serious from the early 1800s, thanks to the fascination with using controlled explosions to move things. An engineer from France by the name Nicéphore Niépce invented something called the 'Pyréolophore' in 1807, an engine fuelled by a cocktail of lycopodium powder and gaseous resin that was ignited by an electrical spark. In the 1860s, Belgian engineer Étienne Lenoir patented the first practical internal combustion engine, which used coal gas as fuel, and found some commercial success in stationary applications (bolted down and driving something else to make it move, rather than as an engine inside a vehicle). But it was forward-thinking German Nicolaus Otto who came up with the internal combustion gamechanger in 1876.

His cunning 'Otto cycle' engine used four strokes of a reciprocating piston, with a mixture of gasoline vapour and air as its fuel, with an electric spark to ignite the explosion. The four strokes were: intake (a falling piston draws fuel into the cylinder through a valve); compression (the piston rises and squashes the fuel charge); power (the spark makes it go bang and the expanding gases push the piston back down, turning a crank) and exhaust (the rising piston pushes the waste gas out via another valve). Or: 'suck, squeeze, bang, blow'. As the first truly practical, efficient and reliable four-stroke internal combustion engine, the design set a new standard and is still the foundation for today's petrol engines. The engines in your motorbike, the family car and that old Suffolk Punch mower at the back of the shed? They're thanks to Nicolaus Otto.

Karl Benz invented the first petrol-powered automobile using the new engine in 1885, inspiring folk to immediately start feverishly bolting them into their bicycles too. The idea of a powered two-wheeler was nothing new, but the various designs and patents of the preceding years used unrealistic electricity or steam for motivation. Compact, efficient, workable, this new-fangled four-stroke internal combustion engine made wind-in-hair, bugs-in-teeth dreams very much a reality.

Or it did once the concept had been nailed. In the same year as Mr Benz was finishing his car, Gottlieb Daimler and Wilhelm Maybach fitted an Otto engine into their two-wheeled Reitwagen. Yes, it was the first petrol motorbike ... but being configured like the old dandy horses (and needing outriggers to stay upright) and with only one prototype built, it hardly caused a step-change. British engineer Edward Butler tried his hand with an Otto-cycle tricycle in 1888, built by the Merryweather Fire Engine Company (obviously), but with a lack of funding and a disappointing lack of interest the Butler Petrol Cycle went nowhere. It was another German company, Hildebrand & Wolfmüller, who got the recipe right with the world's first mass-produced motorbike. Their 1489cc, two-cylinder, liquid-cooled device was the first powered two-wheeler to use the moniker 'motorcycle' (or actually '*motorrad*', given they were German), made 2.5hp (horsepower) at a plodding 240rpm (revolutions per minute) and trundled along at 28mph.

Hildebrand & Wolfmüller's wondrous machine went on sale in 1894: just nine short years after the first modern configuration pedal bike had been invented. Just imagine if the Wright brothers' first controlled, powered, sustained flight in 1903 had been followed up by a jet-powered repeat just nine years later. Or if the first telephone had been invented and then people were swanning around with mobiles less than a decade later. Amazing, really.

Seeing the future, bicycle manufacturers around the world instantly started shoehorning the new burbling, petrol-slurping lumps into their products. Triumph was among the first. In 1901, Bettmann and Schulte strengthened the frame of one of their bicycles and attached a 2.5hp engine from Minerva. Based in Belgium but founded by a Dutchman, Minerva had started out manufacturing their own 'safety bicycles' in 1897, but immediately jumped on the internal-combustion bandwagon. Just three years after they started making bicycles, Minerva were churning out lightweight cars and motorcycles, plus an extremely lucrative line of 'clip-on' engines. Attached in a sort of 'that'll do' fashion beneath the frame's downtube and driving the rear wheel via a belt on the left-hand side, they were initially designed to add petrol-power to the company's own pedal cycles. But they were also available in kit form for you to tack onto your own bicycle, and they were supplied to other manufacturers for use on motorcycles. More than 100 other companies would make use of Minerva's motors, which introduced features such as mechanically opened valves and efficient carburettors, bringing much-needed refinement to these early petrol-burners. The motors were exported to France, Germany, Australia – and, of course, to Britain.

Aside from its strengthened frame, the clip-on Minerva power unit and a fuel tank nestling in its middle, Triumph's very first motorcycle was just like their regular bicycle. It had pedals, rod-operated brakes and a nice little rack on the back for carrying your packed lunch. They displayed the bike a few times to gauge reaction and to generate interest in a Triumph motorcycle ... and it was, of course, fabulously well received. The new Triumph No.1 motorcycle went on sale in Britain in 1902, with production for the European mainland starting at the German plant the following year.

Remarkably, the original prototype was unearthed almost 120 years later. A brand aficionado was contacted by the friend of a collector who had passed away with details of what he had – which included an official letter from Triumph from the 1930s confirming the bike's details and its provenance, supported by documentation from engine supplier Minerva. With prototypes and concept models usually broken for parts or simply destroyed, it was a remarkable discovery. Restored to its original splendour, as shown in 1901, the actual No.1 Triumph went on display at the Triumph Factory Visitor Experience at the current Hinckley factory.

ALL THEIR OWN WORK

The rate of motorcycle development was blindingly fast at the start of the twentieth century. A new engine or fresh model would be introduced to the eager and rapidly expanding market, and almost immediately be superseded by something bigger, quieter, faster, better equipped or more comfortable.

And comfort was important. Tarmacadam, a mixture of tar and macadam (crushed stone and sand) as the name suggests, is today used all over the world as the surface for roads, and better known simply as tarmac. But it wasn't invented until 1902, and so most of the roads travelled by pioneering motorcyclists were little better than mud and stone. Farm tracks, essentially. Macadam roads had been introduced in the early nineteenth century, but without the magic ingredient of tar they were prone to developing bothersome ruts and were notoriously dusty. As such, piloting your new, exciting, fast but also unsuspended, vibrating and noisy motorcycle could be like being inside a tumble-drier on its fast-spin cycle. Rolling down a hillside.

Competition during this phase of hand-over-fist advancements was fierce. In France, the Werner brothers Michel and Eugene (originally from Russia) had been tinkering with motorized bicycles that had the engine precariously attached to the steering, and managed to sell quite a few before making a breakthrough in 1900. Their 'New Werner' placed the engine at the bottom of the frame, where the crank and pedals would usually be on a bicycle. It was a bespoke frame design, rather than a bicycle that had been butchered and bent to suit, and Werner's patented design would become the blueprint for the motorcycle for decades. By this time, the ground-breaking brothers were also manufacturing their own engines rather than buying them in from other factories; by 1903, they'd come up with a parallel twin (two cylinders standing next to each other) 500cc engine at a time when everyone else was using thudding single-cylinder units. They were a deserved success across Europe.

Seeing the Werners making a fair bit of money, rival French firm Peugeot waded in too. They'd been making powered trikes and quadracycles since 1898, using De Dion-Bouton engines, but then swapped to making motorcycles in 1900, using Swiss-made Zürcher and Lüthi motors. They'd become extremely successful (and would also be a well-known scooter manufacturer, far before the likes of Vespa and Lambretta made the scooting scene cool). Over in America, the Hendee Manufacturing Company set up their Indian motorcycle brand in 1902, claimed the motorcycle land-speed record within a couple of years, and would become the world's largest motorcycle company within a decade. Their arch-rivals Harley-Davidson went to market with their first engines and complete motorcycles in 1905, and rapidly grew into a motorcycling force.

More of a concern for Triumph was that they had opposition closer to home as well. Bicycle makers Royal Enfield had also moved into using spark-ignition engines for motivation, rather than the rider's flailing legs, but they'd done so even earlier. They set up their motorbike business in 1901 and were quickly earning a reputation for fine machines. And they were in Redditch, just down the road from Triumph. Other rivals were even closer. James Lansdowne Norton had established his company in nearby Birmingham in 1898 and was making the Norton Energette with a 143cc Clement engine by 1902. And the Birmingham Small Arms Company (BSA) had also created a motorcycle branch by 1903 – and, as the name suggests, BSA were also Bettmann's neighbours.

However, in these pioneering days of the motorcycle there was something of a shortage of sturdy, robust machines. The spark-ignition internal combustion engine was still new technology, metallurgy was still something of a dark art and in many cases thorough testing was conspicuous by its absence. Anybody could get hold of a proprietary clip-on engine from Europe, whack it onto the downtube of a bicycle and thrust the undeveloped result into the hands of soon-to-be-disappointed customers.

So, despite the advances in design, and despite a motorcycle still being an expensive item, motorcyclists were still required to have tolerance and a certain strength of character. And strong legs too. Hills of a steeper persuasion required you to dismount and push, and roadside breakdowns and punctures were common – and if you couldn't bodge the bike back together yourself, you were pushing your pricey, complicated, non-complying, 'luxury' item home.

By 1904, the boom in powered two-wheelers had turned into a decline, these troublesome and costly contrivances falling out of favour with vexed buyers and failing to attract 'average' riders. Normal folk had better things to do than sit on a grass verge with oily fingers and the prospect of an hour or two trudging home.

Engineers, therefore, fell over themselves to make their latest motorcycle – or 'single track', as opposed to a car, which was double track – as advanced, polished and pleasant as possible. Partly to make their machines stand out, but mainly to prove that motorbikes weren't a foolish folly for those with swollen bank accounts. And also – which was crucial if motorcycles were to flourish – to further widen the appeal of these glorious devices.

Mr Bettmann and Mr Schulte understood the importance of quality and dependability from their sewing machine background. They had also discovered the advantages of being able to create everything themselves in house with their hugely successful pedal cycles. Having experimented with a JAP engine from the Tottenham manufacturer and a unit from Belgian outfit Kelecom, and having been disappointed with both, Triumph realized that what they needed to stand out was what excitable marketing types with jaunty haircuts would these days call a no-brainer: a bespoke, purpose-made, all-Triumph motorcycle.

Schulte was responsible for designing the all-new model. It featured a frame that was, according to Triumph's period adverts, a 'new registered design, long wheel-base' and twin front down tubes, one behind the other. A girder front fork carried a 'new pattern very powerful front rim-brake'. Riders would be cossetted by the 'Rideasy' saddle which was 'large size, very comfortable' and Triumph made a point of mentioning that 'efficient foot-rests are fitted, giving a most comfortable position'.

This freshly designed chassis mounted the engine centrally at the bottom, as had been established as a Very Good Idea by our friends the Werners. It was a single-cylinder 398cc (78mm cylinder bore diameter and 76mm stroke, the distance the piston travels up and down in the cylinder) side-valve unit chock-full of modern features. It boasted 'very large heavy fly-wheels' and a 'special economical carburettor', had inlet valves that were opened mechanically rather than relying on the suck of the descending piston, and had a drive pulley that turned in ball bearings. It churned out 3hp at 1500rpm. There was no clutch or gears, the power being transmitted straight to the rear wheel by a large rubber V-belt. A bicycle-style crank was fitted behind the engine so you could pedal along to start the bike, waggling the fuel tank-mounted levers for fuel, ignition and all the other complicated things required to stir pioneer-era motorcycles into life and keep them functioning.

Triumph's name was proudly cast into the crankcases and their advertising frothed about the engine being 'made at our works'. It's unlikely that the engine's major components were sketched out by Schulte, however, or made in the Much Park Street works. Pouring molten metal into moulds to cast the crankcases required expensive foundry facilities and people with specialist skills. This would have been mildly problematic, given there weren't either of these things in the Triumph factory. The crankcases and the cylinder – two major and pricey components – used for the engine were the same as found on a few bikes from other manufacturers; they could literally be interchanged between the models. Triumph had been using engines from Fafnir through 1903 and 1904, and it's likely that they were involved with these significant parts for the new 398cc engine; partly because they were a German manufacturer, and partly because they had a convenient London-based office. Their engines also had a remarkable visual similarity …

Triumph either paid extra to have their crankcases manufactured with their name proudly emblazoned on them or they confidently ordered such a large quantity that it was simply put on by default. The 'made at our works' boast referred to these significant parts being assembled with all the other spinning, whirring and sparking bits. Triumph could use their own choice of bearings, tappets, ignition, carburettor, drive belt and all the engine's other necessary components – some would have been bought in, but many would have been designed and created in house. Schulte was involved, though other Triumph employees of a more mechanical persuasion were responsible for deciding what all the hot and oily bits should be like, and works foreman Charles Hathaway, who'd been with the company since 1890, was the man behind finalizing the motor.

Unlike most of the motorcycle manufacturers that had sprung up, Triumph was now no longer relying on proprietary engines with a reputation for questionable durability; someone else may have knocked up the large bits for them, but it was their creation.

An early example of the new Triumph 3hp Motor Bicycle was given to the publication *Motor*, who gushed in their 25 October 1904 issue: 'We have been putting the first of the new models through its paces for the last week or two, and can say that up till now a more speedy, comfortable, and easily-controlled single tracker, we have never had the good fortune to drive.'

This first, proper, genuinely Triumph motorcycle went on sale as a 1905 model. You could putt-putt-putt away from a dealer on a shiny new 3hp model for a 'net cash' price of £43 – around £4,500 in modern money (2025). Though not an insignificant amount, it was in the bounds of what was broadly affordable for many. And the impact was huge.

SETTING A NEW STANDARD

Triumph had created the first British-made motorcycle for the masses. Here was a powered two-wheeler that was accessible for 'average' folk; a machine that could be used for trundling to work, popping to see the in-laws or for the simple pleasure of a sunny evening excursion. And you didn't need to be landed gentry to afford one.

The new 3hp model and the own-brand engine halted the decline of the fledgling British motorcycle industry and paved the way for British-built bikes to utterly dominate the market for decades.

Strong words? Over-excited hyperbole? Not a bit of it. Well thought-out, neatly designed and finished to Triumph's usual high standard, Schulte had devised a machine that was desirable, achievable and that was far less inclined to throw a tantrum when asked to negotiate a bit of a hill.

Gushing publicity helped the bike's reputation and attracted further buyers. The go-to biking publication was *The Motor Cycle*, which contained articles written by a famous journalist of the era known as 'Ixion'. This was the pen name of Canon Basil H. Davies. An Anglican priest and extremely keen motorcyclist, Ixion was known for organizing trials and reliability tests for these fashionable new internal-combustion devices. He carried out a pioneering ride the entire length of the country, from John O'Groats to Land's End, thereby establishing a test for machines and riders that's still undertaken to this day. Helpfully, Ixion and Schulte were first-name-terms friends and would occasionally go riding together … So there really was nobody better to demonstrate why the new Triumph was indeed a triumph.

The factory gave Ixion a bike – registration number DK43 – with the idea being that he would cover 1,200 miles in six days. (Incidentally, the registration number is still in use today, though it's now attached to a diesel Land Rover Discovery. I bet the owners have little idea of its historical significance.) Two hundred miles a day is nothing these days, but on an early-1900s motorcycle on rough roads, this was a serious test for any machine. And any rider. The trial would use Oxford as the base, with a different there-and-back destination each day: Taunton, Ludlow, Shrewsbury, Derby, Grantham and Bournemouth. The epic undertaking started in welcome sunshine at 6 a.m. on Monday 26 June, and the story '1,279 Miles in Six Days' appeared in the 10 July 1905 issue of *The Motor Cycle*.

I ran down to Box for breakfast … the chief annoyance was the number of domestic animals on the road; pigs, sheep, and cattle

*made the hill-climbs exciting ... no involuntary stops were made
all day ... Tuesday's destination was Derby ... lunch at Kegworth,
and tea at Leamington ... no stops of any kind with the machine ...
breakfast in Stratford ... the machine did some extraordinary hill-
climbing, considering it had fifteen stones up ... passing the seventh
milestone from Oxford I concluded the 200 for the day, and went
off the map for tea on a riverside lawn at Sandford.*

Clearly fond of his food, Ixion stated that he climbed seven pounds
in weight during the week of riding, but also that he only experienced
discomfort on two occasions where the route was particularly bumpy.
The Triumph drank 13 gallons of fuel over 1,279 miles, which was over
98 miles per gallon. Four 'involuntary' stops were reported: one for a
bad puncture and three for broken piston rings (the essential items
that seal the piston within the cylinder). Such a mechanical woe would
be headline news today, but in the early 1900s was an annoyingly
run-of-the-mill incident – and one that was breezily dismissed. 'The
ring trouble is unique,' wrote Ixion, 'and at present unaccounted for,
but they were speedily replaced by a duffer like myself ... Mr Schulte
assures me that no other Triumph engine has ever behaved thus.'

The test did exactly what Triumph hoped, the story providing the
1905 equivalent of celebrity endorsement – it'd be like having Jeremy
Clarkson gush about a car or Simon Cowell praise a new young singer
today. 'I am, of course, well aware that a trained rider on a high-
powered machine could probably cover 2,000 miles in the time I
occupied in doing 1,279,' concluded the bike-loving priest. 'But the ride
was intended to prove four things – the reliability, the economy, the
comfort and the radius of a good modern motor bicycle; and I venture
to say it has amply fulfilled its purpose.' Ixion was the 'influencer' of his
day – and his article did what the factory had wanted: his endorsement
of the performance of DK43 cemented the new Triumph's position as
the motorcycle of choice.

Triumph's marketeers were straight on the ball, running adverts trumpeting about the new model's success in the test. However, while the new bike undoubtedly had great performance, it seems that the reporting may have been a little, erm … let's say economical with the truth.

Nowadays, we're all very aware of influencers. Social media overflows with over-sincere youngsters pouting into phone cameras while telling us how the latest coffee machine, dog food, running shoes or whatever else they've acquired for free is the greatest thing in the world, ever. We know they've either been given the products or are being paid to say lovely things. And it seems that in his role as Ixion, Schulte's friend Canon Basil H. Davies may not actually have been that much different …

Ixion wrote for *The Motor Cycle* from the turn of the twentieth century until into the 1960s. In 1950, he published his 'Motor Cycle Cavalcade' and revisited the famous endurance test from 1905. Turns out, it had been a bit more eventful than originally reported. Ixion talked about how his leg muscles ached from all the pedalling required to help the Triumph on climbs. The engine had been losing power gradually through the first 1,000 miles and poking around inside revealed a tired-out cylinder bore and heavy pitting to the exhaust valve, as well as the worn piston rings. A replacement valve was fitted and ground-in on every remaining evening of the test. More worryingly, the frame snapped and a replacement had to be rushed into use.

Would it have mattered or made a difference if there'd been full disclosure at the time? Probably not. Early adopters of the motorcycle were well used to spark plugs that lasted ten minutes, fickle carburation, dragging their machine up inclines and even bits from inside the engine making an unplanned appearance in the fresh air. The new 1905 model was also something of a step-change for British motorcycles and set a new benchmark. And anyway, Triumph was very aware of any potential shortcomings and remedied the flaws in short order. Schulte and his engineers quickly introduced superior materials, stopped making valves out of what modern-day metallurgists would call cheese and introduced a series of improvements. Anything that could cause criticism was addressed and confidence in Triumph among the buying public soared. The bike was a success, with 250 sold in the first year – a number worth shouting about at the time. The Coventry firm was staking its claim as the country's leading producer of those exciting new motorcycle things.

BIGGER, FASTER, MORE

It may have all started in 1905, the year embossed into the history files as the first 'proper' Triumph, the first bike that was truly their own. Yet there was something equally important just two years later, in 1907. Three things, in fact.

With demand increasing year-on-year and Triumph's bank manager doubtless chuffed with the state of the company's accounts, the first major happening for 1907 was that Bettmann relocated motorcycle manufacture to a new premises on Priory Street, Coventry. The Much Park Street premises was simply no longer capable of feeding the public's insatiable appetite for two-wheelers carrying the Triumph badge, whether powered by busy legs or petrol-fuelled explosions. The expansive and impressive Priory Street factory gave the necessary space to keep up with production – they were selling 1,000 motorbikes a year by 1907 – and the capacity to allow the firm's blinding rate of expansion to continue.

The Much Park Street site stayed in Triumph's hands, though. Another company, Gloria Cycles, had started producing bicycles in 1898 and became a subsidiary of Triumph; manufacture of their cycles and sidecars carried on at the old factory, which was known as the Gloria Works, and Triumph also used it as the motorcycle business's service and competition department.

The second significant event of this year was the arrival of a new and improved flagship model. Building on the solid foundations of the much-admired 3hp model, Triumph increased both the diameter of the bore (and hence piston) and the length of the stroke, taking it to 82 x 86mm. This increased capacity from 398 to 454cc. With a fancy new jet carburettor, more ball bearings used throughout the engine and more reliable magneto ignition, the new motor supplied a 17 per cent hike in power. This new 3.5hp engine was tacked into a redesigned frame that was lighter and initially used a sloping design to give a lower seat height.

Triumph's adverts shouted about how the new 3.5hp model provided a far more comfortable ride than rival motorbikes and the unprecedented reliability thanks to the reworked engine. Not only was the bike faster and better at getting up hills, but it was also far less inclined to leave you stranded at the side of the road looking enviously at anyone on horseback. Triumph had, at last, proved once and for all that the motorcycle was not only a hoot and made you look cool, but was also a reliable way of getting about. Ixion was a fan (truly, it seems), later writing that it was probably the first really excellent motorcycle ever built. The Coventry firm and its imposing new factory had set a new standard for the way a motorcycle should be built, how it should look, the way it should perform – and how infrequently it should necessitate delving into your tool roll.

And the third major occurrence was Triumph stamping their authority in competition. The year 1907 marked the inaugural running of the international Tourist Trophy (TT) races, held on the Isle of

Man. Designed as a way of testing and proving the performance and robustness of touring motorcycles, and to further their development and bring advances in design, the race was over ten laps of a gruelling, rough, unpaved course that was over 15 miles long, with a total race distance of 158 miles. There were 25 riders split across two classes: one for single-cylinder bikes (18 starters) and one for twin-cylinder machines. There was a compulsory ten-minute rest stop for all competitors. This was due to the physical effort required to pilot the complicated bikes and provide pedal assistance on the more stubborn ascents, and because of how arduous the course was. In the wet, there were deep puddles and sloppy, muddy sections, and when it was dry the dust created by the bikes was almost unbearable. Organizers decided that spraying some parts of the course with acid would control the dust. It didn't. But it did burn holes in the riders' clothes. Even the fastest riders would take over four hours to complete the event, while some wouldn't see the chequered flag for almost six. Assuming they didn't dissolve.

Triumph expected to do well in the singles class. The previous year, they'd entered the Dashwood Hill Climb, where machines were timed up a twisting, rising course, with a prototype of what would become the new 454cc, 3hp customer model. Ridden by successful racer Frank Hulbert, the bike had beaten the course record. Triumph had more up their sleeve for the TT. The bikes entered in the first 1907 event had a 475cc version of the engine and were in the proven hands of Hulbert and local Coventry rider Jack Marshall. A little terse, Marshall had the cool head required of riders in the early years of motorcycle sport. No good hurling your toys out the pram if a tyre swallows a nail or the engine's spark plug decides it can't be bothered any more.

Riders started the time trail in pairs, and the two Triumphs were the first away in chilly, overcast conditions at 10 a.m. on 28 May 1907. Practice sessions (run early in the morning on roads open to other traffic, horses, meandering sheep and stray chickens) indicated that the greatest challenge for Marshall and Hulbert would be from brothers Harry and Charlie Collier on their JAP-engined Matchless machines, and so it proved.

Marshall initially led the race on his Triumph. He tipped off his bike on the second lap, however, and had to continue with a twisted ankle. With further time lost to a puncture, he couldn't make up the time gap on Charlie Collier, who won on his Matchless at an average speed of 38.21mph and received the grand trophy donated by the Marquis de Mouzilly and £25. Marshall finished second at 36.60mph (and won £15), with Hulbert third (winning a tenner). Without the time lost, it's likely that the Triumph would have won.

Rem Fowler won the twin-cylinder class on a Norton powered by a 671cc Peugeot engine. As the twins were generally larger, more powerful and faster than the singles, his victory is the one that most people hold in their memory. However, though Fowler's total race time of 4 hours, 21 minutes and 52.8 seconds was an almost incomprehensible half an hour quicker than the second-place finisher, it was still two minutes slower than the race time achieved by Marshall on the smaller and less grunty Triumph single. (Fowler did, admittedly, have all kinds of grief with punctures and broken parts, and was going to retire from the race until a spectator happened to mention how ridiculously enormous his lead was. But Marshall fell off, so let's call it evens.)

Clearly a tad miffed at having come so close to victory, Triumph strutted back to the Isle of Man for the 1908 TT with a dedicated racing machine – what is now considered possibly the world's first purpose-built race bike, rather than a hopped-up version of a customer model. Schulte had convinced Bettmann of the merits of duffing up rival brands in competition. The bespoke racer featured a 499cc (88 x 85mm) engine with a posh new carburettor and no pedals – some of the reason was to save weight, but it was also to prove that the bike didn't need pedals and was a 'proper' motorcycle rather than a motorized bicycle. The frame, seat and handlebars were all lower, and the wheelbase was reduced to make the bike more agile and responsive. Wheel rims were stronger to resist the TT's component-breaking surfaces and anything deemed unnecessary, such as lighting, was left off the motorcycle to keep weight down.

Marshall won the single class easily at the 1908 meeting, with an average race speed of 40.5mph and a quickest lap of 42mph. His overall race time was almost a quarter of an hour quicker than Collier had managed on his Matchless the previous year. Triumph had proved their superiority in competition as well as on the road and, just as Schulte had predicted, the victory brought a surge in sales.

The company was keen to capitalize on this success and a sporty, stripped-down TT Roadster model was introduced to the model line-up, sharing the racer's go-faster alterations – and, to reinforce its sporting prowess, it wasn't fitted with pedals either. It cost £50 in 1908, which was two quid more than the regular touring model. And the sales kept on surging. In 1909, the Priory Street factory produced 3,000 motorcycles.

Triumph was on a roll.

CHAPTER 2

TRUSTY TRIUMPH

HAND OVER FIST

Had you wanted to buy yourself a nice horse in 1910, it would most likely have been tantalizingly cheap. In fact, they were possibly doing two-for-one offers or throwing in freebies as part of the deal. Some hay, perhaps. Or maybe you'd get a free cart to hang from the back of your bargain-priced nag, taken from the large stock of disused traps, carts and carriages that were cluttering everywhere up.

Horses had long been filling cities around the world. They dragged waggons, carried folk about their business and deposited their byproduct on the roadways (keenly scooped up by householders desperate to have their street's finest roses). But the decline in horse numbers was clear for everyone to see. In the September 1910 issue of their esteemed publication, *The American Review of Reviews* reported that the number of horses trotting around London had dropped by 75 per cent in just six years, from 450,000 to 110,000. It was a similar story in other major cities across the planet. The article went on to say that 'a serious problem is presented to the farmers and market gardeners by the scarcity of manure which must inevitably follow the supersession of the horse.'

The reason behind this equine decline was of course the miraculous, world-shrinking, life-changing internal combustion engine. The steam train and its network of railways that had zigzagged their way across the country over the preceding century had caused something of a revolution. But the effect of Nicolaus Otto's four-stroke engine was far, far greater. Motorization was in flat-out overdrive, taking over the world with bewildering pace. Think the internet has changed things? It's nothing compared to the ginormous effect of suck, squeeze, bang, blow.

The status of the motor car had changed rapidly. It was no longer something rare and highly unusual that was occupied by people in top hats and brought excitement and wonder when it chuffed through your village. By 1910, the automobile was something commonplace; our obsession with the private vehicle had started. After registration and numberplates became mandatory thanks to The Motor Car Act in 1904 – which also raised the speed limit from walking pace to a decidedly heady 20mph – the number of cars chugging their way along UK roads had quadrupled by 1910. There were over 85,000. And there were more than five times as many in the USA, with a staggering half a million cars tearing up the still-unpaved roadways.

And it wasn't just all the new automobiles. Britain was leading this embracing of petrol power, and in addition to the cars there were 15,000 industrial vehicles – trucks, tractors and the like – and some 9,000 vehicles used for public transport. Some of these were taxi cabs, but most were buses. The London General Omnibus Company (LGOC, the company whose red livery became the signature of the city) used almost 30 different types of petrol-engine buses, including double-deckers, and was the single largest bus operator in the world by 1910. They'd had 7,000 horses dragging their buses around just four years previously, but now they had … well, none. Just large sheds full of discarded tack and nothing to encourage the roses.

There was even the rumble and drone of internal combustion coming from the clouds. Already holding records for altitude and flight duration, French aviator Louis Paulhan won the *Daily Mail* prize for completing the first flight from London to Manchester in less than 24 hours. Only two landings were allowed during the trip and Paulhan just made one overnight stop in Lichfield to conclude his flight in 12 hours, with just over a third of that spent looking down on rooftops and making small children whoop with joy. And a certain Charles Rolls – yes, the man behind the car brand – became the first person to do an eastbound crossing of the English Channel, the first to carry out a non-stop double crossing to France and back, and was also the first Englishman to complete the crossing in a plane screwed together in Britain. (He was, sadly, also the first British aviation fatality when his French-made Wright aircraft failed during a competition in Bournemouth later in the year.)

All this was terribly exciting – especially as the motorcycle was smack bang in the centre of it all.

Powered two-wheelers were massive news. There were nigh-on as many bikes kicking up dust clouds and rutting-up British roads as there were cars. As a nation, we couldn't get enough of the thrill-bringing motorbike, especially as reliability had come on leaps and bounds in just a few short years. You knew you'd get to work on time and without having to remedy some sort of mechanical malady at the side of the road. Hills could be gambolled up and over without the assistance of those awfully old-fashioned pedals (that was just *so* 1800s). Proper touring excursions could be undertaken on two wheels in the confidence that you would reach your destination. Probably. Might even make it back, too.

At the Cycle and Motorcycle Exhibition at London's Olympia from 4 to 12 November 1910, there were 57 companies exhibiting their smashing new motorcycles. And Triumph was the headline attraction. Lots of the very many rival machines had effectively copied the designs of Bettmann and Schulte; their 3.5hp Roadster model from 1905 and the Coventry firm's famous TT success had established them as the market leaders, and lots of opposing engineers considered Triumph's designs as something that couldn't be bettered ... so they simply bashed out what were little more than replicas. However, few offered anything as finely crafted or using such top-grade components.

Reporting on the Olympia event, the *Daily Telegraph* newspaper gushed about how Triumph's bikes were the classiest: 'The entire exhibit was marked by the beautiful workmanship for which this firm has attained a world-wide reputation.'

But despite prospering, and despite being the favoured brand, Bettmann and Schulte couldn't afford to sit back and count the money. This was a time not only of much market competition but also the rapid introduction of new technology. Today's mobile phone 'upgrades' are nothing compared to the engineering strides being made back then. And in among all the Triumph-alike models sparkling under Olympia's lights were several rival designs showcasing ever-smarter ways of making motorcycles more accessible, efficient and advanced – and, crucially, even more fun to ride.

CONFIDENCE

When deciding to set out on a motorcycle journey, you'd fill the bag strapped to your machine's rear rack with essentials. These would include: a tool roll, spare innertubes for the easily holed tyres, probably some engine oil ('total loss' lubrication of the time required oil to be pumped around the motor, usually by squeezing a hand pump every mile or so, with most of it ending up burnt by combustion or drifting off into the atmosphere) and some sandwiches for a nice relaxed lunch under the riverside shade of a silver birch. Egg and cress on white, perhaps. Maybe with a slice of pork pie.

The bundle would include drive belts and pulleys as well. Partly because the belts wore out with disappointing predictability, and partly so that you could perform roadside alterations when chugging into particularly hilly terrain. To get the engine to turn the wheel, pioneering bikes had a small pulley on the end of the engine's crankshaft (the spinning-round bit rotated by the flailing pistons) and a massive pulley on the rear wheel. The former was tethered to the latter using a belt. Some had a simple flat section, some were riveted together from lots of small pieces and others had a V-shaped profile that nestled into a groove on the pulleys. This meant the engine was positively linked to the wheel. You pushed or pedalled the bike into action, bump-starting the motor, which then cut out when you stopped at the roadside to discuss the upcoming village fete with the chairman of the horticultural society. There was no clutch and only a single speed. Changing the size of the drive pulley on the engine and playing with the belts allowed you to alter the bike's gearing. When presented with, say, the towering topography of the Peak District, you could sacrifice top speed for more acceleration and thrust by exchanging drive parts. Our old friend Ixion spent almost as much time discussing belt changes during the report on his 1905 Triumph road-test as elaborating on each day's menu.

Cars had been using frictional clutches since before 1900. These allowed the drive between the engine and the wheels to be disconnected, making the engine 'free'. This meant that the engine didn't stall every time you came to a stop and even allowed the transmission to feature a selection of different speeds, or gears, selected while the clutch was deployed. However, seeing as how they had evolved from bicycles, the fact that you needed to pedal a motorcycle into life had seemed entirely natural. It was just what you did. But all this was changing by 1910.

Engine design was galloping forwards. Most of the headline machines at the Cycle and Motorcycle Exhibition featured low-friction ball bearings throughout their engines, rather than simple bushes. Valve gear was mechanically operated, rather than crudely relying on the engine sucking the valves open, for increased performance and efficiency. Ariel – yet another motorcycle manufacturer from

Birmingham, just up the road from Triumph – had a natty widget on their camshaft that could be used to hold the exhaust valve open slightly on the compression stroke; what would become widely adopted and known as a decompressor, this made the engine easier to turn over and allowed the new Ariel de Luxe model to be started at a walking pace in less than 10 feet. Or so they said. No more sweaty huffing when leaving the factory after a ten-hour shift.

There was more. Much more. Automatic lubrication was becoming a thing, so riders didn't have to remember to tediously pump in oil to avoid calamitous engine failure. Engines were sprouting extra cylinders too. Norton had been selling an engine with two cylinders arranged in a 'V' since 1907, and in the same year, Bristol-based firm Douglas had released a fresh-from-the-drawing-board 'flat twin' engine (or 'boxer', with opposed cylinders, one sticking out either side ready to bump your shins). Now at Olympia, the handsome V-twin engines from British firm JAP were seemingly wedged into bikes on every other stand. Enfield also had a 344cc V-twin engine in their machine, supplied by Swiss manufacturer Motosacoche.

Power outputs for these larger twins were climbing into unknown territory too. With promises of an arm-wrenching 8hp and scorching 50mph, these more complex engines produced more than twice what Triumph's 500cc single-cylinder, fixed-drive engine was chugging out. Think about that for a minute. It only felt like ten minutes since the 'safety bicycle' had been devised, allowing you to whizz past the village green as briskly as someone running after their errant dog. And yet here were wild creations that drank whiffy fluid, did all the work for you and travelled at 50mph. Five times the velocity of a trotting horse, this could let you potentially blast from Wolverhampton to Leicester in 60 minutes. It must have been incomprehensible. Surely such extremes would give you a nosebleed at the very least …

(Mind you, Schulte was probably glad he wasn't competing directly with overseas firms. Belgian arms and ammunitions company FN had released a 363cc four-cylinder bike in 1905, and in America, the 1909 Pierce Four had a 696cc four-pot motor, giving an eye-streaming top speed of 60mph. That was a good 30 per cent swifter than the quickest Triumph. Luckily for the British firm, you were unlikely to see either of these streaking through Royal Leamington Spa.)

Riders no longer needed to rely on a convenient passing breeze to whisk excess heat away from their steed's engine either. Yorkshire company Scott had developed water cooling with a cutting-edge twin-cylinder two-stroke engine the previous year, and now London's Green Motor Co. offered water cooling on the market-dominating four strokes. Already known for powerboat and aircraft units, Green displayed an overhead valve inline twin which had the cylinders wrapped in copper water jackets and two honeycomb radiators. Space-age stuff in 1910.

All this stretching-for-the-horizon stuff wasn't lost on Triumph. They hadn't been afraid of fresh technology and had already introduced a variable pulley on the 3.5hp model in 1908. This let you alter the gearing without the need to unroll the tools; instead, you pulled over and 'simply' swapped the belt between pulleys by hand. It was one of the brand's standout attractions and part of the reason for their continued expansion – in 1910, the Priory Street works would screw together more than 4,000 bikes.

However, now, other brands, including Excelsior (also from Coventry) and BSA, all had models that boasted a variable pulley. And yet it was already old hat …

Bike designers had been dabbling with clutches and gears without much commercial success, but now they were very much the Thing To Have – and Triumph's competition were all over it. Ariel, Bat, Excelsior, Calthorpe, Matchless and more had bikes offering a 'free engine'. These used a clutch either located on the bottom bracket by the crank or, more commonly, housed in the hub of the rear wheel. The hub is also where they'd stash the two different speeds for the transmission. London-based Chater Lea were really pushing onwards, the bike on their 1910 display featuring a posh multiple-plate clutch and a three-speed transmission – yes, a befuddling three gears to decide between. Their new model also had a strong and reliable chain drive, instead of a flappy, unreliable belt.

All very glitzy and attention grabbing. Especially as headline act Triumph still had their same Roadster model, pottering along with the old single-cylinder engine as before. Mauritz Schulte and right-hand man Charles Hathaway weren't fussed, though. They had what Blackadder's right-hand man would call a cunning plan.

Firstly both Schulte and Bettmann knew that technology and designs might have been changing, but that workmanship was still key. Just like Levi Strauss, they understood that quality never went out of style. Years of experience in the sewing machine industry had taught this. Employing the same strict measures, insisting on superior materials and manufacturing in house to avoid shoddy bought-in parts had given their bicycles – and now their motorcycles – a class-leading reputation. They were luxury, premium, desirable. Better still, they were trusted.

Triumph had utter confidence in their design and high-quality approach. And now the bikes were getting better still. Though it looked pretty much the same when you nosed around it, the 1910 Triumph Roadster had undergone significant changes. Little things that you didn't see, but that made a difference in ownership. The engine's magneto (the widget that sent the spark to the plug) was now driven by a chain that was secreted away behind an aluminium cover. The bits that made the valves open and close were redesigned so that there was less of a clattering racket, and there were strainers fitted to the taps for the oil and petrol to extract the filth that had snuck in from refilling with a mucky funnel (or that was worryingly present in low-grade fluids). The pedal set-up was improved too, so starting the engine needed little more than a good kick from one hoof, rather than a frantic back-and-forth past the windows of your bemused neighbours. There was also a stand for the front wheel, which doubled-up as an additional mudguard stay when retracted. And so on, and so on … Sticking to this approach to quality, and refining and applying a deeper gloss to their esteemed 3.5hp bike, would work a treat. By the end of the following year, Triumph's production numbers would have increased by a sizeable 20 per cent.

Secondly, there was a teasing hint that Triumph had grander things on the horizon, with the announcement of a clutch and hence a free engine. Unlike fancier rival machines, the bike was still single speed. But thanks to the clutch tucked away in the rear hub, you could now get the engine to splutter into life on a stand before smoothly departing (or at least departing slightly more smoothly than by pedalling into action; the action of early clutches wasn't the slickest). Patented by Schulte back in 1908, the Triumph design was controlled by your foot – as with a car, and unlike modern hand-controlled bike clutches – and would be available as an option on 1911 versions of the Roadster. You could have it on the new TT model as well, which was based on the same 3.5hp bike but with the lower stance and shorter wheelbase of the firm's Isle of Man racer. Just the job for those of a sporting nature.

And thirdly, there were some very grand things happening in a secret corner at the Priory Street works. Schulte had got hold of a 616cc parallel-twin engine – two cylinders stood vertically, side by side – from a Belgian company called Bercley, designed by an inquisitive chap called Gustave Kindermans. After debuting at the Stanley Show at London's Royal Agricultural Hall in 1905, Bercley motorcycles were only in production until 1909. However, a key member of the enterprise, Hugh Mason, would establish NUT motorcycles in Newcastle-upon-Tyne in 1912 and win a TT. They knew how to build a motorcycle. And Schulte must have been impressed by the engineering and performance of the Bercley motor, as he slung it into a prototype Triumph.

Yet, as exciting as testing twin-cylinder concepts undoubtedly was, it was a distraction from what Schulte and Hathaway were really up to. They were getting ready to make some lengthy strides – and to direct a floodlight onto Triumph's superiority with one of the most significant machines of all time.

JUST LIKE A GRIFTER

If you grew up in the UK during the 1970s and 1980s, then you'll have scoffed candy cigarettes while watching Johnny Morris present *Animal Magic* on your Matsui portable black and white. You probably argued with your mates over whether Queen were better than Fleetwood Mac. And there's every chance you'll have pedalled to school on a Grifter, Denim or Chopper made by Nottingham-based cycle company Raleigh.

These three iconic kids' bikes featured three-speed Sturmey-Archer gears housed in the hub of the rear wheel. They were controlled by a sliding lever or twistgrip on the handlebars that yanked a wire to drag the required gear into position. You'd have gone everywhere in second gear: first was only good for wheelies outside school and third was so tall you only used it when careering down massive hills. And the gaping void between second and third ensured whacking your knees on the handlebars.

These limb-grazing gear systems are what brought flexibility to early motorcycles. Like Raleigh, Sturmey-Archer was from Robin Hood territory and started flogging their patented three-speed rear hubs for pedal cycles in 1902. The design of these was epicyclic, which is even harder to explain than it is to spell; all we really need to know is that by moving the 'planet' gears rotating around the central 'sun' gear, the gear ratio was altered internally without the need for variable external whatnots that interfered with the drive chain. Complex on the inside, yes, but all very clean and elegant on the outside.

Some manufacturers were experimenting with 'countershaft' gearboxes. These used a mainshaft driven by the engine's crank and a secondary countershaft to direct the drive to the required gear.

In 1911, the medals and plaudits in the gruelling International Six Days Trial (ISDT), a staggering test for rider and machine held over intentionally hideous terrain, were taken by Douglas and P&M motorcycles featuring two-speed countershaft gearboxes. They simply had the option of low or high. The new transmissions basically operated just like every gearbox you've ever used on your own bike, car, van or truck etc.; these metal boxes full of spinning shafts and splashing oil were the future.

Which was great, except that the countershaft gear bundles were expensive to make and largely unproven. With the average engine wheezing out just 3 or 4hp, they were probably over-engineered, too. Like using a 50-tonne crane to shift a couple of bags of sugar.

And so most motorcycle manufacturers went for the three-speed hub option. Affordable, neat, proven on thousands of bicycles being pedalled in countless countries across the world ... why wouldn't you? There was also the fact that most countershaft gearboxes offered two speeds – slow and not quite as slow – where the three-speed offered ... well, the clue is in the name.

Armstrong and Sturmey-Archer were the established firms, and it was the latter that rapidly became the go-to brand across motorcycling. 'The Sturmey-Archer Patent 3-Speed & Free Engine Gear' trumpeted the brand's advertising. 'THE Standard Gear for all Motor Cycles.'

It was certainly the obvious choice for Schulte, Hathaway and the rest of the decision-makers in Coventry. Not just because most of their rivals were using Sturmey-Archer, but because Triumph already had a rock-solid relationship with the manufacturer. They'd been merrily fitting their hubs and other cycle parts to their bicycles for years.

Triumph's proper stride into the world of clutch-controlled multi-speed transmissions came in 1913. This was a significant year for the Coventry factory (and not just because Bettmann was elected as the mayor of Coventry). Yet again the focus was on standards and workmanship – their established 499cc four-stroke single received further refinements and improvements in material, and it was the first year of Triumph's distinctive long exhaust pipes. There were updates to the proven, patented sprung front fork – the mildly bothersome springs used for the front suspension swapped for a much better single spring. Along with a toolkit for roadside remedial activity, this year's Triumph's also came with a neat bound-leather book which included an insurance coupon, tips on how to ride and assorted other useful titbits. Most considerate.

But the big news was of course the Sturmey-Archer three-speed hub, as proven on the factory race bikes that had barrelled around the TT course the previous June. No longer just the nicest-made motorcycles on offer, Triumph's products now stood wheel to wheel with the most feature-laden bikes on the market.

There was a whole swarm of the things for you to choose from in 1913. There were half a dozen 499cc four-stroke models of assorted transmission and style. There were three Roadster variants: Model A, the free engine example with a clutch; Model B, which was the same but with a fixed drive; and Model C, which used the blingy new three-speed hub and a clutch. There were two sporty TT models for those who regarded the UK's 20mph speed limit as more of a suggestion than a law: the Model D with the fixed engine and the model E with the free engine, both of which had two sets of footpegs giving the choice of comfort or a more attacking riding position. And then there was the Type F – the Racer – for anyone eager to make a name for themselves on track.

As if that wasn't enough, Triumph also launched a new lightweight two-stroke model. Two-strokes don't use valves to let the charge of fuel into the cylinder and control the expulsion of waste gas. Instead, they work like this (bear with me): as the engine's piston rises and compresses the fuel, it sucks the next charge into the crankcases beneath it. There's a spark and explosion, pushing the piston down the cylinder and turning the crankshaft, and at the same time pushing this next charge through transfer ports (little tunnels leading to holes in the cylinder wall) and into the cylinder, above the piston. This incoming charge also shoves the exhaust gas from combustion down the exhaust. The piston rises again, covering the intake and exhaust ports, and compressing the charge ready for combustion – and at the same time sucking in the next load of fuel. And round we go again.

With the engine firing every time the piston goes down and then back up (every two strokes) the design can make roughly twice the power of a similar size four-stroke engine. There are also fewer moving parts, making them simple and light. But they also need oil to be mixed with the petrol to lubricate the crank and cylinder as it passes through, and this oil is burnt. So, two-strokes are a bit smelly and dirty. Hence the nickname 'stinkwheels'.

Anyway, Triumph's new 225cc stroker was designed by Hathaway. It had a decompressor so that you could paddle it into action (there were no pedals) and could buzz along at 35mph, leaving a subtle smoky trail. Called the LW Junior (LW standing for 'light weight'), it was easy to manage, had a low saddle and was the first motorcycle designed specifically for women. Finding popularity with church ministers bored of pedalling, district nurses and kids from well-heeled families (you could ride one at 14 years old), it immediately became known as the 'Baby Triumph' (and from 1916 it would be made under licence in the USA under the Excelsior name by Ignatz Schwinn, of the bicycle fame). Notably, the Junior also had a tiny two-speed transmission; a proper little countershaft gearbox mounted behind the engine. But it didn't have a clutch, meaning that swapping speeds required nifty deployment of the engine's decompressor, perfect timing on the gear lever and no shortage of good old-fashioned luck.

In 1913, Triumph also built their own 600cc twin-cylinder engine. This was ground-breaking as it featured horizontally split crankcases. Normally, the two halves of these cases, which are a main chunk of the engine and hold everything in place, would have a left and right, with a vertical join. This made engines easy to manufacture and assemble, but it also meant that oil tended to sneak through the join and allowed your bike to mark its territory on your mother-in-law's garden path. The new twin didn't make it into production, but it was evidence of the firm's ambition – horizontally split cases wouldn't generally feature on engines until the late 1950s.

With newfound flexibility and usability, more sophistication than ever and even a new lightweight two-stroke, Triumph's popularity yet again increased. Around 7,300 bikes were produced in 1913 and there was still more to come. Further refinements arrived for 1914 and a new 550cc engine boasting a super-reliable Bosch high-tension magneto was launched for the Model A, taking power to 4hp. This meant that Triumphs increasingly became the choice for those wishing to fit a sidecar, turning their bike into an 'outfit' and giving a cheaper and far more entertaining family-transport alternative to a boring car.

Something else significant happened. Late in the summer of 1914, Sturmey-Archer started making a new gearbox called the CS. It was what we'd now call a game-changer. And when paired with the latest Triumph, that's exactly what it became.

THE MODERN BIKE IS BORN

'The new Sturmey-Archer countershaft gear is a revelation,' declared an advert in the 1 December 1914 issue of *Motor Cycling*.

Adopted for 1915 by the leading Moto-cycle Manufacturers. 3-speed & enclosed kick-starter. Suitable for Motor-cycles from 3 to 6/8hp. Gears constantly in mesh, and may be changed at any time without declutching or raising exhaust lifter. Clutch is of the cork inset type, operated from handle-bar, and very smooth in action. Kick-starter completely enclosed, constantly in mesh, with safety device to prevent injury should a back fire occur.

Advertising standards weren't quite as strict back in the early part of the twentieth century. You could essentially decide on any grand statement that you thought might encourage people to put their hands in their pockets and you were good to go. But Sturmey-Archer had every right to shout about their new transmission because it genuinely was a revelation.

Still writing as Ixion, Basil Henry Davies had started to see the advantages of a 'proper' gearbox, rather than the widely used and much-loved hub-based system. Earlier countershaft boxes were crude, noisy and unpredictable, their crashy action often providing stop-start progress and inciting colourful language from frustrated riders. Design and manufacture were taking huge strides, however. These latest countershaft units were still larger, heavier and more costly, but they also performed properly and functioned reliably. Changing gear sounded less like hurling a selection of hefty pots and pans down a flight of steel stairs. Ixion enthused over their benefits in articles published in *The Motor Cycle*, and they caused quite a bit of arm-waving and chuntering. At this time, manufacturers sold gearboxes as proprietary items – anyone could buy one to fit into their bike – and builders of hub gears started poo-pooing rival countershaft systems in their advertising. *The Motor Cycle* had printed a letter belittling Ixion's championing of countershafts from a man by the name of Harold Bowden – founder of the Raleigh bicycle company and chairman of Sturmey-Archer. And yet now here were Sturmey-Archer making one themselves …

Gearbox design really had turned a corner. The all-singing new CS (countershaft) gear system was a landmark moment, and the Nottingham firm's confidence that this was the way forward was obvious when you spotted something else in their advert: 'Write To-day for reduced prices of S.A. 3-speed Hub Gears … Send for descriptive booklet, post free.' Yes, the much-loved geared hubs were being sold off cheap.

Sturmey-Archer hadn't invented the countershaft gearbox but it was their design (and quality, pricing, reputation and status) that made it prevalent.

Triumph was one of the advertised adopters of this wondrous new bit of engineering. The Coventry cycle factory had a long-standing connection with the Nottingham gear company and so would have been very aware of the new transmission. But the CS box finding its way into a Triumph motorcycle was probably thanks to a man by the name of Claude Vivian Holbrook, who was nothing at all to do with either firm.

Something far more momentous happened in 1914 than all this faffing around with motorcycles. Austria-Hungary declared war on Serbia on 28 July, egged on by Germany. Russia and France waded in to support Serbia, and so Germany declared war on the former on 1 August and the latter two days later. Britain and its still-vast empire decided to get stuck in on 4 August. The world was at war.

Born in 1886, Holbrook worked for the British government's war office as a staff captain and was helping with the introduction of mechanical transportation. This included bikes. In 1914, there were around 200 different motorcycle companies operating in the UK, with another 200 in America, and the same again in the rest of Europe. So, a lot to choose from. Holbrook was a keen motorcyclist, and had owned three Triumph Roadsters. He knew first-hand that they were well screwed together and not prone to throwing tantrums, and so gained permission to select Triumph as the principal supplier of two-wheel transport for the British Army. On Saturday 6 August, just 48 hours after Britain had joined the war, he called Bettmann at home and said he'd quite like some motorcycles. Actually, the army would take as many as Triumph had. Bettmann said they had around 50 machines in stock, and was told to send them all to an army depot at Bulford – a village in England near Stonehenge – immediately.

These bikes were a jumble of Model A, B and C Roadsters, meaning some were fixed drive, some had a clutch and others used a three-speed hub. The military had bought Triumph's entire production of four-strokes but this still didn't satisfy demand, and so the army started hoovering up the two-stroke Junior model as well. Though dependable, strong and fine performers, the assorted Roadsters were being subjected to miserable conditions during the fighting and largely used by inexperienced riders with naff-all experience and even less mechanical sympathy. They were good, but not good enough for the rigours of conflict. So Holbrook told the Coventry bosses that they needed something more reliable and even stronger. The ideal bike should have a clutch for easier and more predictable control. Oh, and gears as well, please. One of those clever new kick-start things might also be more convenient in the middle of a muddy battlefield than trying to pedal the bikes into life.

Mauritz Schulte alluded to such a machine at Triumph's annual general meeting in October 1914. By the end of November, there were pre-production bikes floating about, and for 1915 there was a spanking-new Triumph: the Model H.

The first road-focused motorcycle from the Coventry factory without pedals and the first with a proper gearbox, the 550cc (85 x 97mm) single-cylinder engine was enhanced with an updated cylinder design, improved camshafts and valve actuation, Triumph's latest semi-automatic carburettor, a decompressor for less traumatic starting and various material changes. The exhaust had been redesigned as well. The power increased to 4hp, although claimed outputs of the era were nominal – in other words, what the engine could merrily churn out all day long in general use. Peak power when given a good seeing to was around 10hp, meaning the new bike could rattle along at 50mph.

All this oomph was transmitted by a new Sturmey-Archer CS three-speed gearbox, with an enclosed chain drive between the engine and gearbox, a regular V-belt sending the thrust to the rear wheel and the joy of breezy starting thanks to a kickstart lever.

The Model H also featured an updated chassis. The revised frame carried a 1.5 gallon fuel tank and was lower, putting the seat height at 762mm (30in) and meaning easy foot-dabbling for new riders (and for soldiers extracting the bike from muddy ditches). The Brookes saddle was adjustable and had a padded top to keep your bum cheeks happy, and the same company supplied twin toolboxes that mounted either side of the rear rack. There was a convenient hand pump mounted on the frame's top tube in case of incommodious punctures, too.

The Model H was a massive hit with the military. Other brands were used by the Royal Navy, Machine Gun Corps and Flying Corps – BSA, Enfield and plenty more – but the army called dibs on the Triumph and took as many as they could get. It was the despatch riders' favourite and by far the most popular two-wheeled transport of the war. Bettmann paid regular visits to Holbrook at the War Office and later the Ministry of Munitions; they had a strong working relationship and became friends, and during 1917, the ministry helped Triumph ramp up production to 100 Model H bikes per week – all for the army. Around 30,000 examples would be used by the allied forces during the conflict, with some two-thirds of this vast number being used by British forces. With the combination of Triumph's quality and Sturmey-Archer's innovative CS gearbox, they loved it.

So did the buying public. The Model H wasn't available until February 1915 and initial supply was slow due to limited availability of the exciting new gearbox. But, selling for £63, the new machine from the country's favourite motorcycle brand couldn't have been any more successful. With its brilliance demonstrated by its sterling service in the war and the sheer quantities knocked out, the Triumph became the go-to motorcycle for everyone – from leisure riders after a dependable tourer, to tradesfolk looking for reliable transport, to families who required a sturdy steed to lug a sidecar laden with children and all their clutter. At a time of rapid development and a barrage of new and updated designs, the Model H's engine and frame would provide the company's foundation for almost 13 years. They had most definitely got it right: Hildebrand and Wolfmüller had introduced the first mass-production bike 20-odd years earlier, but it was the CS-equipped Triumph Model H that set the blueprint for the modern motorcycle.

The company had been using the 'Trusty Triumph' slogan in their adverts since before 1910, and people who used their bikes as part of their work (despatch riders, district nurses, vicars in a hurry) had started referring to them with the 'Trusty' nickname. But it was the Model H and its solid contribution to the war effort that caused the tag to be firmly attached. Use the phrase Trusty Triumph today and it's the ground-breaking, market-changing Model H that instantly comes to mind.

CHAPTER 3

SETTING THE STANDARD

ALL CHANGE

Ah, the fabulous Roaring Twenties. A decade of financial growth, flamboyant fashion, cinema, social revolution, extravagant leg-tangling dances, art deco, and jazz cats tooting away in cool little clubs.

This was a period of a growing economy, increased prosperity and glamorous frocks. The misery of war had passed, and the world strutted headlong into recovery and exuberance. Construction worked overtime, electricity lines were draped across more and more of the country, consumer goods flew out of shops. If you had enough cash to splash out on a swanky new 'wireless' you could sit at home listening to all manner of programmes, with debates, news and music. And if you were *really* flush there was that amazing new electrical sound recording, allowing you to put a funny thin black disc onto a spinning thing on a 'gramophone' which then trumpeted music into your house. Goodness.

The role and perception of women in society changed radically through the 1920s, not least thanks to them at last gaining the right to vote across Europe and America, and finding new opportunities for further education and employment. Changing fashions introduced the phenomenon of the 'flapper', the term given to younger women who had short, bobbed hair and favoured knee-length garments that were generally considered shockingly short at the time. Shaking off Victorian shackles, they enjoyed wearing make-up, drinking booze, smoking cigarettes in public, driving cars – and riding motorcycles.

Sisters Nancy and Betty Debenham worked as stunt riders for the Olympia show, were successful bike racers, starred in BSA's adverts and wrote a book, *Moto-Cycling for Women*.

With the war over, civil aviation was permitted in Britain again in 1919. Avro Civil Aviation Service had jumped straight in with the first domestic airline service and Hounslow Heath was completed as the UK's first proper airport. It had a customs hall and everything, although thankfully no endless shops selling perfume, Toblerones and needlessly expensive luggage. By 1920, there were commercial flights to Paris. Handley Page fitted the first auto-pilot system in 1921. Commercial flights started at night, too. In 1927, American pilot Charles Lindbergh took to the sky above Roosevelt Field in New York in his custom-built single seat aeroplane, *Spirit of St. Louis*, and didn't come down again until he reached Paris-Le Bourget airport, becoming the first person to fly solo non-stop across the Atlantic. Lindbergh was in the air for a considerable 33.5 hours. He'd have been alone in the clouds for less time and still made the record books if he'd landed in the UK, rather than buzzing past to France, but hey ho.

Steam trains began to be replaced with diesel-electric locomotives, which used huge fuel-burning engines to generate electricity for the motors driving the wheels. Cleaner, more efficient and capable of hauling heftier loads, they also required less maintenance than chuffing steam trains and could travel further without having to stop to refuel (although they didn't smell as nice). This meant reduced fares and more accessible train travel.

And, of course, powered personal transport truly flourished. At the start of the twenties there were 200,000 cars registered in Britain, and even more motorcycles – over a quarter of a million (plus over three million bicycles sold every year). By the end of the decade, there would be more than 700,000 motorcycles scything across the land. And even more cars: by 1930, the quantity of registered four-wheelers topped the seven-figure mark for the first time.

The internal combustion engine was similarly growing reach around the globe. Over in the United States, Ford's revolutionary production line had allowed his company to build 15 million Model T cars by the time it was superseded in 1927, an almost incomprehensible amount. But Ford wasn't the only firm making automobiles and by the end of the decade, there were almost 27 million motor vehicles in the USA.

However, the 1920s didn't roar straight off the bat. In the UK, immediately after the war, there was a short depression, caused by the impact of the conflict on the British economy. The staple industries – ships, coal, steel – lost their lucrative foreign markets, causing a swift increase in unemployment. Many of the thousands who'd returned from active service found themselves unable to find a job, too. Later in the decade, those who did have employment found their wages were dropped and there was a general strike that involved millions of disgruntled folk. Largely thanks to social class divisions, the 1920s managed to both prosper and struggle at the same time.

The decade certainly started with testing times for Triumph. Siegfried Bettmann's partner and the factory's accomplished designer, Mauritz Schulte, left the company in 1919 following the sort of incident that a modern-day band would refer to as 'artistic differences'.

Perhaps noticing that the roads were increasingly clogged with cars, Schulte believed that the company's future lay with four-wheeled vehicles, rather than two-wheelers. Twin track, not single track. Although happy enough for Triumph to continue churning out motorcycles, he thought that they should ditch the pedal cycle side of the business. Bettmann, with his bicycle clips firmly attached to his tweed strides, strongly disagreed: bicycles were what had started his affluent business and the company's founder was still fond of a spot of pedalling. The pair argued, couldn't resolve their difference of opinion and so Schulte retired from Triumph in 1919. He was probably cheery enough as he departed the factory, though – he got a 'golden handshake' of £15,000, which would be over £650,000 in today's money.

With Charles Hathaway already working as the lead designer, Schulte's role as Triumph's general manager was taken by Claude V. Holbrook. You'll recall him as the chap at the War Office who had arranged for Triumph to supply bikes to the army and unintentionally gave birth to the Model H. Told you that he and Bettmann got along swimmingly.

The same year, Triumph had released a new top-of-the-range motorcycle. Called the SD, this featured a new frame with the firm's first brazed-on attachments to mount one of their Gloria sidecars, alongside special beefed-up steel wheel rims and reinforced spokes. There was a choice of bicycle-style rim brakes or car-style hub brakes with twin shoes. Putt-putting the bike along was the proven 550cc side-valve single-cylinder engine from the Model H, but refreshed with stronger big-end bearings and revised camshaft profiles. It also had a special spring-drive in the clutch assembly – hence the SD moniker. This mechanical widget was basically a shock absorber to eliminate engine snatch and provide a smoother, more controlled ride (the spring-drive system was devised by a man called Edward Middleton, who doesn't appear to be credited with anything else ever made by Triumph). Later variants of the bike also got an enclosed spring for the front suspension and a Pilgrim oil pump, so that the rider no longer needed to remember to squirt oil around the engine every ten miles or so.

Significantly, the SD also boasted all-chain drive (chains used for the primary drive, from the engine to the gearbox, and for the final drive to the rear wheel), rather than using belts. This was part of the reason for the spring-drive system, as the natural give in belts provided a smoother transmission than a metal chain biting into the teeth of a gear wheel. The SD also had Triumph's very first in-house designed gearbox, which was supplied with lower gear ratios for those wishing to lug all their family members into the countryside for a weekend picnic.

Before the new bike went on sale, *The Motor Cycle* gave the Model SD a glowing write-up in the 13 November 1919 edition. This included full details on the function of the gearbox and the new clutch system, all of which was extremely interesting and enlightening. Or it was to people like me who really need to get out more. All it's necessary to know is that – as well as waffling at length about three-faced cams, rotatable collars, phosphor bronze plates and dog gears – the tester was impressed:

> *It has long been an open secret that the Triumph Cycle Co. contemplated an all-chain driven model. Nine months ago we were permitted to make an extended trial of one of the early experimental models, which, we may say, demonstrated the advance made in single-cylinder machines for sidecar work. With characteristic caution and thoroughness, the Triumph Co. elected to try out every detail of the new model by continued and strenuous road tests before deciding to place it before the public as a finished article, and it was only on Monday last that the press were given an opportunity of studying the final design. The new Triumph gear box is a fine piece of work ... practically foolproof.*

The Model SD went on sale at the end of 1919, effectively as a 1920 model to kickstart the new decade. It cost £110, which was about six months' wages for the average UK worker and £18 more than the Model H. However, the only problem was that for all the 'improvements' and the trade press's glowing write-up, the SD wasn't particularly good ...

THE POWER OF STATUS

Stumer-Archer's critically acclaimed CS gearbox, as used in the Model H, was 'constant mesh'. This meant the various gears were all connected and spinning round, with the drive transmitted through whichever gears were locked to the gearbox shafts by things called sliding dogs. Triumph's own gearbox in the Model SD wasn't like this.

Patented by Schulte and colleagues back in 1916, the design was a non-synchronous 'crash' gearbox. His was the design commonly used early in the development of the car and for early countershaft bike 'boxes, like on that old two-speed Douglas. How this style of transmission behaved in use is what gave rise to its nickname – it doesn't take an engineering degree to understand that a gearbox called 'crash' won't be famed for its silky action and polite nature.

Shifting gears on the Triumph Model SD required the rider to deftly match the engine speed (revs) to the gearbox output shaft speed (driving the rear wheel) and balance the valve lifter to decompress the engine. And manage the clutch and stubby right-side, hand-operated gear lever – oh, and the throttle. All the time while dodging ruts and avoiding delinquent animals ambling down the road. Even with many miles of practice, a smooth gearshift was a rare thing; Triumph's three-speeder usually lived up to its 'crash' tag. Wincing was common among SD owners.

All this clattering and grinding of gears wasn't just unpleasant for the rider, it was unpleasant for the gears themselves. Back in 1920, understanding of the behaviour of metals was nowhere near what it is today, and the steel gears wore. And they wore quickly. It didn't help that the gearbox and primary drive shared their oil in Triumph's design – the primary ideally needed thin oil while the gearbox would have preferred something much gloopier, but both had to make do with the same grade. For added amusement, adjusting the bike's drive chain involved moving the entire gearbox. This caused oil leaks and much exasperation.

And yet, the Model SD sold well. Despite being their priciest bike to date, despite satisfactory gearbox operation requiring a degree in mechanical engineering and despite routine chain adjustment resulting in a slippery path outside your house, it was a success. Triumph's reputation and standing were so good that such 'niggles' didn't matter. The company's status and the quality of the rest of the machine made the SD popular. It was especially favoured by those who piloted outfits, the model's all-chain drive giving positive power transfer and more predictable performance than the belts on rival machines. Positive power transfer is favourable when you're chugging up a hillside, the sidecar chock-full of demanding family members, pets, luggage and supplies.

There were further tests of Triumph's reputation waiting just around the corner. The first came along in 1923 with the launch of the 345cc Model LS, the letters standing for Light Solo. The 350cc market was important – cheaper purchase prices, lower insurance costs and the perception of being less risky to control meant that rival firms were shifting plenty, but Triumph were firmly associated with the 'big' 500s that had defined the brand. Keen to make an entrance and do a bit of corporate flag waving, Triumph rustled up an advanced creation. The LS proudly carried their first in-house, engine-powered oil pump (away with you, pesky hand supply). There was an aluminium 'slipper' piston whizzing up and down the cylinder bore and the flywheel – large, weighty thing attached to the crank to provide inertia – was mounted outside the crank's bearings. But the massive news was that this was a 'unit construction' engine. Rather than the engine and gearbox being separate entities lashed together by a chain, all the cogs and shafts and oily reciprocating bits were housed in the same neat, compact, clean cases. With the drive transmitted by gears, the solution was neater, quieter and less likely to deposit oil all over your freshly polished brogues. Unit construction wouldn't become the default configuration on British bikes until the 1950s. The LS was cutting edge.

Unfortunately, it was also duff. Triumph's engine was decent enough, but the rest of the bike was below par. The front brake didn't have enough bite to hold the machine still on a modest incline. Worse, the overly wide handlebars clouted your knees when manoeuvring and the rear brake required you to lift a foot off the footrests, which themselves were positioned to only suit people with legs like stilts. Or maybe actual stilt walkers. Ungainly, unwieldy, uncomfortable and other words beginning with 'un', the LS struggled to find buyers. Triumph just couldn't shift them. It didn't stay in their line-up for long.

Their repute endured further trial just 24 months later. There was plenty of ambition, social change and roaring going on through the twenties, but all the issues with unemployment and falling wages were affecting machine sales. And not just for Coventry-built machines: the whole of motorcycling was in decline. Bettmann and Holbrook needed something that would keep Triumph afloat, so they devised a bike that retained the expected qualities – or that gave the usual Triumph impression of lofty standards – but that was built down to a price. And that could scurry down the production line in record time.

Their solution was the Model P. Using the slightly smaller 494cc engine, rather than the 550 unit from the H and SD, the P featured a three-speed gearbox and clutch, full chain drive rather than old-fashioned belts, the firm's well-known semi-auto carburettor and sprung front forks ... and so on. A proper Triumph, then. The difference was the P was cheap. Really cheap. First shown at the end of 1924 as a fresh model for 1925, it cost just over £42 (which would be around £2,150 today) and so was not just the cheapest big Triumph yet, but easily the most affordable on the market. Yet at a casual glance, the only real giveaway that it was the budget version was a flimsy tin cover over the engine's primary drive, rather than the fetching cast metal item used on bikes like the Model SD.

Penny-pinching corner-cutting was obvious as soon as you rode the Model P, however. Its cheapo clutch was shockingly crude. The front brake relied on you tugging a piece of asbestos rope and was as effective as a string vest in a monsoon. Far worse than this, to save time and expense, Triumph had machined holes for the valves to run directly into the engine castings, rather than fitting the usual hardened guides. Engines wore out and failed almost as soon as you started them up.

This could – should – have kicked a massive dent into the standing of the brand. Here was a Triumph that was disappointing, that was miles away from their luxurious and dependable reputation.

Yet it didn't. The buying public fell over themselves to get hold of a Model P. Sales were off the chart, with 20,000 finding buyers well before the end of the year despite the well-documented shortcomings. Sure, it wasn't the best ... but bikes always break down, don't they? And have you seen how cheap it is? When an improved and better-engineered Mark 2 version appeared in late 1925 and corrected (most of) the machine's flaws, any slight wobble in public faith was immediately banished. Their favourite brand soared: at peak demand, Triumph built 1,000 Model Ps in just one week. It completely reset the standard for value and forced rival brands to come up with their own affordable versions.

This was a step-change moment and a landmark in British motorcycle history. Disaster well and truly averted.

WHAT THEY WERE KNOWN FOR

These days, motorcycle manufacturers have flagship models which, in some cases, are loss-leaders. The company will offer a ludicrously powerful, staggeringly high-tech, teasingly exotic and eye-wateringly expensive sportsbike for sale in Europe. They'll spend a fortune racing it in the World Superbike championship so that it's seen on the world stage. But they'll barely sell enough to cover the cost. Sometimes they'll even lose a few quid on each one. It sounds like a stupid way to run a business; however, the existence of this high-end bauble will generate sales of small bikes in other markets. Riders in

Asia can't buy the 215hp Honda CBR1000RR-R Fireblade SP they fantasize about, so they splash out on an 18hp CBR150R instead. In their hundreds of thousands.

Triumph did something similar in the mid-1920s. They hurled thousands of the standard-setting Model P out the door because it was capable and cheap, sure – but there was something else at play. The Model P carried the same name on its fuel tank as another fast, advanced, expensive model that was an object of desire and being used to break world records. Just as today, people wanted to be associated with the go-getters and flashy brands.

The record-breaking antics came about thanks to a couple of intelligent types who were nothing to do with Triumph. Harry Ricardo was a Cambridge-educated engineer who was fascinated by internal combustion engines. He did endless research into combustion chamber design, the effect of mixture and different fuels, turbulence within the cylinder and flame speed, and much more. Before the First World War, he'd helped design a Vauxhall car engine for the RAC's 2,000-mile trial, come up with his own two-stroke motor and dreamt up an ingenious split-cycle engine. During the war, his Ricardo Engine Patents business devised a new engine for early British tanks that was 50 per cent more powerful and chuffed out far less smoke than the Daimler unit originally used, and he came up with a new 600hp flying boat engine. After the war, Harry then became technical director for the Air Ministry.

Changing name to Ricardo Consulting Engineers, Harry's company would work on buses, trucks, planes, trains and for almost every major car and motorcycle manufacturer around the world. You'll have ridden a bike or been in a vehicle that Ricardo had a hand in. Almost guaranteed. Ricardo are still leaders in automotive engineering; astoundingly, the innovative split-cycle engine that Harry designed back in 1909 was resurrected by a consortium in 2017 and its development is ongoing.

Ricardo's respected company was joined in the twenties by Major Frank Halford. A flight instructor before the war, and a skilled engineer who redeveloped and designed aero engines during the conflict, Halford was also a budding motorcyclist. And he was speedy. Part of this was because of his skill and bravery, and part was thanks to his tuned-up Triumph.

Most engines of the period used a side-valve layout: the valves that let fuel mixture into the motor and exhaust gases out were mounted vertically alongside the cylinder, controlled by camshafts and other mechanical clutter housed within the engine cases (or 'block'). Having the valves here meant a long intake path and a combustion chamber shape that wasn't very efficient. What today's automotive engineers would tag 'sub-optimal'.

Halford designed an overhead valve layout for his bike. This located the valves above the cylinder, facing downwards and splayed 90 degrees apart. The benefits were many: it gave a shorter and more direct inlet, a far better combustion chamber shape – hence a boost in torque (the force you feel pushing you along; the work done by the engine and size of its punch) – and also power (how frequently the engine delivers this punch, and the headline-grabbing number used to entice customers). Overhead valves also safely allowed higher revs, which generated even more power. They also allow a natty acronym: OHV.

With access to Ricardo's workshop facilities, Halford made a cylinder head out of bronze, shoved in four valves – two letting the fuel in, two letting the spent gases out, when most bikes just had one of each – and put the spark plug in the centre. Halford bolted the assembly, perched on a cylinder machined from solid steel and using a lightweight aluminium piston, onto his new chain-drive Model SD in 1921. He immediately started winning races. This success obviously caught Triumph's attention and they commissioned Ricardo's company to build them a four-valve, OHV engine with a view to putting it into production.

The unit they created made a headline-grabbing 20hp. Mounted in the existing SD and ridden enthusiastically by Halford, it shone during tests at Brooklands, the vast banked 2.8-mile racing circuit in Surrey frequently used for speed records. Suitably enthused, Triumph sent three examples over to the Isle of Man to be ridden in the Senior TT by Stanley Gill, George Shemans and Charles Sgonina.

Triumph also sent a gaggle of their 500cc side-valve bikes. And it was a good job they did. A side-valve bike set a new lap record and finished in a respectable fifth place (average speed 52.49mph, beaten by a Sunbeam, two American-made Indians and an unexpectedly swift 350cc AJS, which won), but only one of the Ricardo trio finished. And that was in a lowly sixteenth position. It could have been worse: rivals BSA entered six hot-shot OHV bikes with inclined engines and other radical features, developed in secret at a cost of £10,000 – and they all retired after melting their exotic lightweight pistons.

Anyway, the problem wasn't that Triumph's bikes weren't fast enough. The issue was that the engine was too powerful for the SD's chassis, which was basically as it had been when Triumph's engines wheezed out 3.5hp. Here was a bike that could nudge 80mph given a modest slope and a favourable breeze, at a time when the national speed limit was still 20mph. One works rider later declared that the 20hp bike could go faster than he was willing to ride it.

Triumph stuffed their fingers in their ears, went 'la-la-la' and got on with readying the bike for production. The cylinder was swapped for a cast iron design and engine geometry was revised with a shorter stroke and wider bore. With both Triumph and Ricardo desperate to save face, Halford was bundled back to Brooklands just before the 1921 Olympia Motor Show, where the covers were due to slip off the racy new four-valve Model R. The Major established a world record for average speed over an hour (76.74mph), the record for 50 miles from a standing start (77.27mph) and the British record for a flying mile (87.80mph). The standard-setting Model R – known affectionately as the 'Riccy', after Ricardo's input – would become almost as famous as the Trusty Model H, and the Coventry factory had little trouble selling the new-for-1922 sports model, despite it costing £120. Three times what the budget Model P would sell for three years later …

Despite everything – despite Schulte clearing off, the utter failure of the Model LS, the quality issues with the Model P, skint buyers, a market in decline and high-profile TT failure – Triumph continued to soar. With their unbreakable reputation, record-breaking performances and the 'everyman' Model P, they were one of Britain's largest automotive manufacturers. Export was huge, with catalogues printed in ten different languages. The works on Priory Street in Coventry continued to expand, and with other additional facilities and the original Gloria Works on Much Street they had a total factory area of almost 615,000 square feet by 1927. That's over 57,000 square metres or, put another way, an area greater than 14 football pitches. With 3,000 staff beavering away, annual production numbers strode beyond 30,000 units.

Triumph was, quite literally, massive.

HANG ON, YOU SAID . . .

All this success with motorbikes was even more exceptional given that Triumph had been distracted by something else. Automobiles. Yes, after all the fuss and hoo-ha in 1919 that resulted in Schulte bickering with Bettmann and leaving the company, they decided that cars looked quite lucrative after all. In 1921, just two years after Schulte's creative-differences departure, Triumph purchased a car company.

It was Claude Holbrook's fault. The general manager shared the belief that four-wheelers were where the company's future lay. He used his friendship with and influence over Bettmann to convince the German to buy the assets and premises of the Dawson Car Company, based on Clay Lane, Stoke, Coventry.

Alfred John Dawson had previously been the works manager for car manufacturer Hillman and had designed one of their models before setting up his own company in 1918. The Dawson 11-12 was a 'light car' that went on sale in 1919. It was available in four styles, ranging from two-seat coupé to four-seat carriage. Bodywork was formed by Charlesworth, a coachbuilder based on Much Street, just up the road from Triumph's Gloria Works. Propulsion came from a water-cooled 1795cc four-cylinder engine, with a thoroughly modern overhead camshaft that glamorously replicated the design of the celebrated Hispano-Suiza aeroplane engine. Power was dished out through a three-speed gearbox. With most components made in house, just like at Triumph, the Dawson was a luxury, high-quality car featuring a mahogany dashboard and lots of brass fittings for you to polish at the weekend. Adverts trumpeted about 'distinction and grace', and how 'ideal carriage comfort is realized to a remarkable degree in the Dawson'.

All very lovely but, unfortunately, firms including Austin and Morris were firing out proven rivals for considerably less outlay. The cheapest two-perch Dawson was £750. Around £32,500 in today's cash and three times more than a Morris Oxford two-seater. Come to think of it, this was more than the average house cost – and nobody could afford a house, which was why around 80 per cent of the UK population rented their property from a rosy-cheeked, round-bellied landlord with a swollen wallet. Only 65 examples of the Dawson were built.

After mopping up the remains of Dawson's failed enterprise, Triumph took the basic underpinnings of their car and re-engineered it. Or rather, some engineers at Lea-Francis did, to whom Triumph then had to pay a royalty for every example sold ...

Harry Ricardo designed a new side-valve 1393cc inline-four engine and the chassis featured hydraulic brakes on the rear wheels – these were made by Lockheed and were the first on a British-made car. Called the 10/20, Triumph's first four-wheeler copied the naming convention of many British cars and got its uncatchy title from the misleading RAC taxation system. Introduced in 1910, the tax slapped on top of your car's price was based on its engine's power rating, which the RAC calculated with a daft and inaccurate equation using the bore measurement. Savvy car manufacturers would therefore design long-stroke engines with miniscule bore dimensions to ensure an artificially low 'official' power rating and qualify for cheaper tax. The Triumph 10/20 was 'officially' rated at 10hp but produced 20, giving a top speed of just over 50mph. More than fast enough when ricocheting down corrugated roads and bouncing around on cart springs.

Initially available as a steel-bodied, two-seat convertible tourer with a 'dickey' seat that opened out the back for a third occupant (who you presumably didn't want to speak to), it was followed by a sporty version with the body fabricated from lightweight aluminium. Next came a four-seater saloon in 1924, with fabric bodywork and two rows of seats.

Costing just over £400, Triumph's first car wasn't cheap. It wasn't a huge seller either. Larger, more powerful versions came along: the 1872cc 13/35 in 1924, the first car with hydraulic brakes on every wheel, and the 2169cc 15/50 in 1926. Neither had much of an impact on the UK car market, although the 15/50 did alright in export with many of the 2,000 produced in its four-year run making it all the way to Australia.

However, this was all part of the plan. These cars were high quality and very well built, echoing the standards that had built an enviable reputation for Triumph's motorcycles. Having proven they could also build decent cars and established themselves, Triumph could release what they'd been busily working away on in the background: the Super Seven.

SIMILAR ... BUT BETTER

Herbert Austin was an inquisitive man who ran the UK arm of the Wolseley Sheep Shearing Machine Company. This was an Australian firm that made ... well, yes, those. Apparatus for giving sheep a haircut generally brought seasonal sales, so Mr Austin had built a few cars in his free time while at Wolseley to investigate possible alternative business. As you do. His bosses failed to see a future in these automobiles, so Herbert left and, with permission to use the Wolseley name and backing from the Vickers steel and engineering enterprise in Sheffield, set up on his own in 1901. Within four years, he'd turned Wolseley into Britain's largest car company.

Falling out with the brothers behind bankrolling Vickers over engine layout, he again moved on, sourced fresh investors and bought some disused buildings in Longbridge, just south of Birmingham. The new Austin Motor Company Limited showed off its first four-cylinder, chain-driven car at the site in April 1906; by the start of the First World War, they employed 2,300 people and were producing 150 cars a year. Like Triumph, they had a reputation for sturdiness and reliability – and, also like Triumph, they secured a lucrative military contract. The Longbridge works supplied three-ton trucks, generator sets, shells and hefty guns. And cars and chassis. New buildings sprung up and the workforce soared to over 20,000 people. A truly vast enterprise.

Herbert put all the company's eggs in one 3620cc, 20hp basket after the war. This single platform was used as the centrepiece for various vehicles, but in the post-war dip, Austin failed to muster enough sales to make proper use of the giant factory they'd built while supplying the military. The receivers were called in during 1921 – the same year that Siegfried Bettmann decided to buy floundering Dawson.

Any of us who marvelled at the fancy talking dashboard in a 1983 Maestro will know that this wasn't the end of Austin. With a new finance director and a freshly recruited works director, Herbert was back on track by 1922 – and introduced one of the first small, inexpensive, modest cars aimed squarely at Mr and Mrs Average and the mass market: the Austin 7. There had been an open two-seater using the same name for a few years before the war, designed by Austin but manufactured by the Swift Motor Company – another firm who'd made the progression from sewing machines to bicycles, then to motorcycles and cars. It failed miserably. But the new Austin 7 couldn't have been more of a success. Playing to the stupid taxation rules and initially powered by a four-cylinder 696cc engine with an RAC rating of just 7.2hp, the simple, super-light-weight car only tipped the scales at 360kg (794lb) and was tiny: its track was miniscule, the wheels only being a metre apart, and the whole car was only about two-thirds of the size of the revolutionary Ford Model T. And just how the Model T had transformed car ownership in the USA, so the 'Baby Austin' revolutionized the automotive world in Britain. Assorted body styles were produced, with saloons, soft-tops, tourers, sports cars and even vans. It unexpectedly became a race sensation, capturing numerous 750cc class records with the 747cc engine introduced in 1923 and prompting a swarm of home-built 'specials' using the 7's mechanicals.

More than 290,000 were made before production finally ended in 1939. And this doesn't include all the versions made under licence by American Austin, Rosengart in France, Dixi in Germany (who'd turn into BMW), Datsun in Japan and more. Fair to say, the Austin 7 did quite well.

Triumph's new Super Seven took the principle of this über-successful 'people's car' and enhanced it. Rather than build a direct rival and steal some of Austin's buyers, they looked to generate new customers with what was effectively a more luxurious and upmarket version of the Baby Austin. They could snare a few owners looking to upgrade too.

It was designed by Stanley Edge and Arthur Sykes, both of whom had worked on the original Austin. The Super Seven was 150mm (6in) longer and 50mm (2in) wider, and its engine was larger and gave more grunt. The 832cc side-valve inline four yet again had Ricardo input, and its crank span in three main bearings, rather than two like the Austin unit, was sturdier, more reliable and smoother. Unlike Herbert's car, the Triumph also had a 'monobloc' engine, with the cylinders and crankcases formed from one casting. There was a three-speed gearbox initially, and a rear axle promoted for its robustness. With 21hp, the 400kg (880lb) car could cruise comfortably at 40mph and skip along at 50mph when required. The Super Seven also featured fancy hydraulic drum brakes on all wheels – a real selling point next to hugely inferior mechanical rivals – and, true to form, Triumph did as much in house as they could, including fabricating the bodywork.

The swanky new motor was revealed in September 1927. The Super Seven Popular Tourer, a full-bodied, two-door version, and the entry point to the range, cost £149; pricier than the Austin, but a better car – yet not straying anywhere near 'luxury motoring' territory. Triumph didn't hold back with their marketing.

> *The hall mark of the motor industry is the name Triumph. Smooth, turbine-like running, vibrationless and silent; powerful beyond expectation; brakes, velvety smooth, Lockheed hydraulic, perfectly compensated, positive – ensure safety at all speeds. See this small car, try it, compare its performance and comfort. It is the finest small car in the world.*

During the Super Seven model's run, there would be plenty of body styles offered, including a four-seat tourer, a two-seat, fixed-roof coupé, fabric-bodied and coach-built saloons and a four-door, pillarless model – the doors swung out like barn doors, with nothing between. Surely the one to go for would be the delightfully named Tickford Sunshine Saloon with a fully retracting roof. Inspired by a bit of success in trials and competition, there would also be a Sports Special, with open-top, pointed-tail aluminium bodywork and a 747cc engine (to allow entry into the popular 750cc classes). This was equipped with a supercharger, which forced more air into the cylinders, allowing the engine to burn more fuel and create extra power. With favourable conditions (a mighty gale and a steep descent), it could rattle along at 80mph.

Though not matching the Austin 7 on overall sales figures, the new Super Seven rapidly became Triumph's bestselling car. Around 17,000 were produced during its model run from 1928 to 1932. Triumph was no longer just Britain's leading and most trusted motorcycle manufacturer. They were now a true automotive colossus.

CHAPTER 4

THE CAPTAIN OF INDUSTRY

RIGHT MAN FOR THE JOB

Queen Victoria died on Tuesday 22 January 1901. Two days later, her eldest son, Albert 'Bertie' Edward, was proclaimed King Edward VII, and so started the Edwardian era with all its social upheaval, political change, and rapid advances in engineering and science. And on the same day as the new king was announced, there started what would lead to an Edwardian period within motorcycling, with the birth of a certain Edward William Turner.

Even while he was still a teenager, it was obvious that Turner was a grafter. Keen to enlist and help with the effort during the First World War, he figured out how he could sign up at 16 years old, rather than twiddling his thumbs until reaching the usual age requirement of 18. There was a scheme run by the Marconi International Marine Communication Co. Ltd that allowed him to train as a telegraphy engineer and serve on an armed vessel in the merchant navy; learning plenty of colourful language and enjoying a delicious diet of tinned beef and stale biscuits, he was a senior officer by the time he was 17. Post-war, Edward took engineering evening classes at college, found employment as the works manager for a company making assorted parts for ships' engine rooms and spent a period at his father's engineering outfit.

Turner felt restricted by toiling for the family business, though. So he branched out on his own, buying a motorcycle sales and repair business: Chepstow Motors. Despite the name, his premises weren't based on the Welsh border in Monmouthshire, but on Peckham Road in south-east London.

Having had his first encounter with a motorcycle when he was just 15 (on a 293cc, two-speed New Imperial – Jeff Clew's official biography states Turner later recalled as 'a most formidable machine of uncontrollable power'), Edward owned an ABC with a 496cc flat-twin engine. This was a model made for just a few years in the early 1920s by Sopwith, the factory famous for its gun-shod Camel biplanes. The ABC was a brisk conveyance and capable of quite a lot more than the national speed limit of just 20mph. The young Turner clearly enjoyed the thrill of speed. He was regularly collared by police speed traps, and on one occasion had to be bailed out by his father after ending up in the slammer.

He sold high-performance machinery, too. As well as selling and repairing second-hand motorbikes and light cars, Chepstow Motors was a Velocette dealer. Well known for their respected zinging 250cc two-stroke, Velocette had also introduced a 348cc four-stroke single that didn't just make a step forward in engine design but took a lengthy leg-stretching stride. Rather than just having the valves located in the cylinder head like Ricardo's pioneering OHV layout, the Velocette stuck the camshafts up there too. The overhead cam (OHC) configuration gave far more precise control over when the valves opened, meaning not just improved engine performance but also superior reliability. Other brands had tried OHC, generally on race machines before the war, but the pathetic metals of the day weren't up to the job. Velocette also had more than a few niggles with their bike when it was thrust upon the wide-eyed public in 1925. However, they'd got the materials and processes pretty much sorted out by 1926, and the high-tech new Velo won the Junior TT by a whacking great margin of ten minutes. Customer demand went through the roof – Velocette had to shift to larger premises and dealers had to beat rowdy customers away with a stick.

Turner spotted that this new OHC was clearly rather good. So, suitably inspired, he thought he'd try coming up with his own OHC engine. Let's take a moment to think about that. Yes, he'd been to engineering classes, and yes, he'd done a stint at his dad's engineering firm. But learning about Whitworth screw threads in stuffy night-school classrooms and being able to competently operate a lathe isn't quite the same as inventing a brand new spark-ignition internal combustion engine. Turner's ambitions weren't quite like setting off a few fireworks on bonfire night and then deciding to build a spaceship, but you see where I'm coming from.

Based around the bore and stroke dimensions of the Velocette, Edward's design used an unconventional arrangement to stop the cylinders from flying off the crankcases. A series of gears drove the camshaft from the crank, giving super-accurate timing. There was a spur gear driving the magneto too. It was all cutting-edge stuff.

A description of Turner's engine appeared in the 16 April 1925 issue of *The Motor Cycle*, with enquiries invited to his home address (87 Rye Hill Park, London), and 'Turner Engineering Company' was daubed on the windows above Chepstow Motors. The enquiries didn't appear, however, so he was back in the pages of the biking publication in January 1927 with a redesigned engine. Edward's patented new motor featured an unusual vertical camshaft running up the side of the engine, operating the valves by horizontal tappets. The camshaft also drove the magneto and the oil pump, reducing parts and weight, and the 348cc unit thudded out its power through the tried-and-trusted Sturmey-Archer three-speed gearbox. And it was now much more than a sketch: an engine was fitted in a complete bike with the latest expanding-shoe drum brakes (not feeble bicycle-style nonsense) and proprietary front suspension, and the 'Turner Special' prototype was registered for road use, carrying the number YP 9286. He'd built his spaceship. Intended as a production bike for the following year, Edward raced it on the 'path' track at Crystal Palace and in a 60-rider field for the 350cc Kempton Cup Race, and his good mate Alf Russell rode it in the 1927 London-to-Exeter trial.

No bikes were shifted off the back of all this endeavour, for two key reasons: first, the £75 price for the hand-built Special was quite a chunk more than the £58 you'd pay for the proven TT-winning Velocette; and second, when Turner competed on a Velocette himself he won the club race that he'd entered, highlighting that his own machine needed, er ... let's say a little more work.

The revised Turner Special was made in 1928 with a more refined engine, better brakes, wheels and tyres, and far more pleasing aesthetics. The first prototype had been function over form, but this second bike displayed a clear eye for styling, along with some fine finishing too. Registered as UX 3750, it didn't make it to the pages of the motorcycling press and nobody came forward to invest in its production. However, Turner proudly took his design to Birmingham to wave under the noses of the established manufacturers. He went to BSA, who made some ambivalent murmurs. And then Turner visited Ariel, who were rather more intrigued. They collected Turner from London and drove him to their works for a proper interview, offering him a job as a designer and engineer with their development department. Goodbye, Chepstow Motors.

Ariel's interviewers, sales manager Vic Mole and chief designer Val Page, were impressed with the clever OHC single. But they were far more smitten with Edward's back-up designs for a 500cc four-cylinder engine.

Rather than sticking the four pistons in a row or arranging them in a V, as several manufacturers had, Turner's bold concept was for a square arrangement: two cylinders at the front, two cylinders at the back, like a pair of parallel twins having a cuddle. With the cranks geared together and a unit construction, the square four would be compact and light, making it easy to package in a motorcycle and allowing for a nimble chassis. Each 'twin' would balance the other and remove vibrations (the single- and twin-cylinder bikes of the era still tried to shake themselves from your grip and buzzed your glasses down your nose). With a chain-driven overhead camshaft and single-piece 'monobloc' cylinders and head, the square engine could be cheap to manufacture too.

The prototype 498cc engine was so trim that Turner squeezed it into one of Ariel's 250cc single-cylinder models (with some gentle persuasion of the frame tubes). He carried out much of the road-testing himself, the design giving strong acceleration and smooth running – Ariel draughtsman Bert Hopwood commented that it emitted 'a sewing machine noise' …

Keen to keep an eye on costs, managing director Jack Sangster ruled that the new four-pot unit would need to use the frame and cycle parts of an existing Ariel and not a bespoke chassis as Turner hoped. The engine also had to be redesigned to allow use of a separate Burman gearbox, making it heavier and losing performance. The Ariel Square Four made its first public appearance at the 1930 Motor Cycle Show as a 1931 model. Yours for a slightly salty £70 (plus another fiver if you fancied the extravagance of lights).

As well as being pricey, the Ariel Square Four had a tendency for its rear cylinders to overheat (the engine was air cooled, and the back pair were screened from the breeze by the front pair) and for head gaskets to fail. And yet Turner's bold design still proved itself. Growing to 601cc for improved sidecar-hauling ability in 1932, the 'Squariel' (a widely used nickname first coined by Dennis May in *The Motor Cycle*) won the Maudes Trophy – a celebrated award for endurance achievement – for covering 700 miles in 700 minutes. Later redesigned again as a 997cc OHV unit to cure the overheating and give extra low-rev wallop, the model would stay in production until Ariel canned all their four-stroke models in 1959.

However, despite the attention-grabbing Squariel and their other acclaimed (and, crucially, far more affordable) models, Ariel was struggling. They went bankrupt in September 1932. Managing director Jack Sangster bought the company's assets; this allowed bike production to continue, and he registered Ariel Motors (JS) Ltd as a new private company. Shortly after, Val Page went to work for Triumph, meaning Turner was promoted to technical director. With Edward now involved in almost every aspect of Ariel's activities, the brand was rejuvenated. And at the start of 1936, his career would leap up another rung or three when he became director and general manager ... but not for Ariel.

The man who designed sewing machine-like engines was off to work for the firm that knew all about machines that deployed thread. Turner would be in charge at Triumph.

MORE. AND MORE. AND . . .

Triumph's clever, desirable-yet-affordable Model P had continued to fly out of dealers through the 1920s, along with the N, Q and QA variants that followed. With 30,000 bikes bursting from the factories every year, the rest of the range was still pleasingly buoyant too, including the Model SD.

Though it had (eventually) proved itself in racing and served the job of flagship model, the Model R 'Riccy' was superseded in 1927 by the Model TT. A speed-loving chap called Vic Horsman had been winning races on the intimidating Brooklands race circuit with its banked corners, riding home-brewed bikes. These long, low racers were based around Triumph engines but used Horsman's own two-valve OHV configuration. Gulping down alcohol rather than normal petrol, there were versions of the bikes in assorted sizes from 498 to 607cc, and between 1923 and 1926, they were so fast that they set various British and world speed records. Not just solo records, but ones for dragging a sidecar too.

Vic's antics didn't go unnoticed by Triumph, who ran one of his bikes wearing their name at the TT in 1925. Not a full-on 'works' entry, it was ridden by a man called C. H. Young and finished in eighteenth – but it proved the engine had durability, as well as its well-documented speed. In summer the next year, Triumph announced they'd be putting the Horsman engine into production, and the new Model TT arrived for 1927. The engine would provide the basis for Triumph's motorcycles until the mid-1930s. (Triumph paid £1,500 for Horsman's design, more than £75,000 in today's money, though Vic reportedly said he'd have let the factory have it for free if only they'd asked.)

For 1928, there were rakish new looks for Triumph's models. Previously the petrol tanks had been 'flat', mounted inside the frame and hanging from the top tube above the engine, but the factory followed the hot new trend for 'saddle tanks'. These mounted over the top of the frame tube and got their name from the saddle bags often carried draped over the rear rack. They would become the standard placement for the fuel – bikes still have saddle tanks today, though the 'saddle' bit of the name was dropped a long time ago. The same year, Siegfried Bettmann was appointed president of the somewhat pompous-sounding British Cycle and Motorcycle Manufacturers and Traders Union Association.

More new, spangly, fresh designs followed the Model TT. The standout was a 350cc model introduced in 1929, which was Triumph's first smaller bike to use the OHV arrangement. Not only that, the 349cc single also had Triumph's first recirculating oil system. Previously, engines had been 'total loss', with the components all hopeful that they might get splashed with the lubricant that was randomly slopped in. The new system supplied oil from a tank using a gear-driven pump, squirting oil to where it might actually be needed. Imagine how much easier playing 'pin the tail on the donkey' would be if you could take the blindfold off – for getting the oil where it was required, it was pretty much this large an improvement. And then the oil returned to the tank and was redeployed. There was a brand-new Triumph three-speed gearbox too, with luxurious needle-roller bearings throughout and a gearshift action that didn't sound like dropping an anvil into a skip.

The hip new craze of 'dirt track racing' was making an impact at this time too. Later known as speedway, all the major manufacturers started offering suitable competition bikes by 1930, Triumph included. And speedway would become huge, going on to be the UK's most popular spectator sport after football. These days, speedway meets are watched by a handful of hardcore fans; at the height of its popularity, even 'local' meetings attracted tens of thousands of fans, and more than 86,000 crammed into Wembley to watch the world championships in 1978.

There was even more coming out of Triumph. With members of the car design squad turning their hand to a bit of bike sketching, Coventry's designers followed the trend of inclining the engine for some models in their eight-bike range (there was no specific advantage at the time, but boy, they looked racy). They also introduced the Model X Junior, an advanced 175cc unit-construction two-stroke that cost £23 17s 6d including leg shields and lights, which is a little over £1,000 today. Keenly priced and then some.

TURBULENT TIMES

All good, then? Er … not quite. Triumph desperately needed more bikes to suit those on a budget because in the autumn of 1929, the American stock market crashed. The world plunged into an economic nosedive.

All the optimism, spending and easy credit of the partying Roaring Twenties started to cause cracks in the foundations of the US economy from early 1929. Construction dawdled. Car manufacture slumped. Steel production slowed drastically. Grey hairs appeared in the slickly oiled barnets of financiers. The National City Bank invested $25 million in credit to try to stop everything collapsing, but still the market started to crumble. Men in expensive suits from all the major banks held panic meetings to try and find a solution.

It was no use. Stock trading is a befuddling affair, with points, bonds, underwriters and something called the 'Dow Jones'. It's impenetrable to most of us. All we need to know is that on Tuesday 29 October 1929, after a bewildering 16 million shares were traded on a single day, the whole American economic system came crashing down. Stock worth $14 billion was lost in a single day and the aftermath and continued decline wiped out investors, companies and banks. It caused a decade of economic woe known as the Great Depression, with widespread unemployment across the USA, and the effects were felt around the world. Rising unemployment in Britain lead to protests in 1930 and 1931, with lots of disgruntlement over the 'means test' that dictated whether you qualified for government benefits.

Triumph felt the blow.

The Wall Street crash caused the Coventry outfit to promptly sell the German arm of the business, by then called Triumph Werke Nurnberg (or TWN – it would continue to churn out bikes until 1957, along with typewriters carrying the Triumph logo). Cash flow became patchy and the company finances started to look the opposite of peachy. Triumph's creditors and investors started to complain and the firm's founder and managing director – the inspirational and inspired Siegfried Bettmann – was shuffled across to the role of vice chairman. Lloyds bank waded in and appointed their own man to manage the factory, with Claude Holbrook taking the position of assistant managing director. In 1932, the bicycle side – the part of the business that caused the whole motorcycling thing and which was always precious to Bettmann – was flogged to a Mr Downes.

Val Page (the ex-Ariel chief designer) hadn't had the impact that Triumph had hoped for either. Page was an acclaimed designer; before his previous high-ranking role at Ariel, he'd worked for JAP and designed the engine used in the Brough Superior SS100. This legendary 998cc V-twin is famed for its power, speed, high quality and exclusivity – it was punted as 'the Rolls-Royce of motorcycles'. The SS100 dominated race events and set speed records at over 130mph, and was the favoured steed of T. E. Lawrence. You might have heard of him.

But Page's top-of-the-range 500 and 550cc creations for Triumph were a bit of a flop. Promoted as delivering the lucky owner 'quality, comfort, speed with safety', the inclined single-cylinder engines featured a valve system that was outstandingly quiet (or at least didn't emit the same clattering hubbub as the exposed valve gear on older bikes) and brought the name Silent Scouts. There was a 549cc side-valve Model A and the 493cc OHV twin-port Model B. Plus, there was a Model BS (which stood for sport, not what you might be thinking), which had a raised compression ratio and fancy high-rise exhausts for more clout. All were available with quick-detach leg shields and a tank-mounted instrument cluster. But in 1932, nobody could afford, or wanted, a blingy new Triumph. They shifted 600-odd Model As, about 1,000 of the Model B and a couple of hundred examples of the BS. Desperately small quantities for a company that had been annually producing 30,000 bikes just a couple of years previously.

Keen to stabilize their desperately rickety bike business, Triumph had 11 new Page-designed models for 1934. These used a modular approach. There were six different engine displacements with a mix of side-valve and OHV configuration, and an assortment of styling and type of bike. Plenty of machines for the customer to choose from, but that all shared parts to simplify design, production and manufacture, and reduce the variety of spare parts needed.

What wasn't simple was getting your head around the line-up, thanks to model names that managed to pull off the impressive feat of being both simple and confusing at the same time.

Lots of brands used the established naming convention, offering a 'Model D' or a 'Model 18'. Triumph's new idea was that each name would be made up of two numbers. The first gave a vague indication of the engine size, while the second told you which model within that capacity band it was. So, for example, 3/1 would be the entry-level 343cc bike, and 3/5 would be the swankiest version with that displacement. You can sort of see the logic.

The problem was that the 3/1 was a side-valve engine, but the 3/2 and 3/5 boasted a superior OHV unit. And there weren't 3/3 or 3/4 models. It was just as befuddling with the 500cc-ish bikes: 5/1 was a 549cc side-valve whereas 5/2 all the way to 5/5 were 493cc and OHV. Some bikes in the bewildering fleet had three-speed gearboxes, some had four ratios. Some came with an attachment for the trendy new foot-operated gear change, rather than the old-fashioned tank shift, but on others it was an extra you had to pay for. With 11 bikes going from a 249cc single (2/1) to the flagship 649cc parallel twin (6/1), walking into a Triumph dealer must have been like walking into an electrical store today and trying to work out the difference between the 200 different-but-all-the-same laptop computers. (Have you tried to buy one recently? Mind blowing.)

Page's engines were good. But everything else made riders say 'oh' rather than 'ooh'. These days, buzzword-obsessed marketing types would be asking where the all-important 'USP' was. Triumph's 1934 range didn't really have one; the designs were a tad lacklustre. And who'd want to go for a pint of mild after work and say they rode a bike called a '5/3' when they could instead be boasting about owning a Norton International, Ariel Red Hunter or Enfield Bullet? Bikes with names that were compelling and dashing.

Triumph's 6/1 had a particularly tough time. The 649cc OHV twin was supposed to be the desirable machine at the head of the range and the go-to choice for anyone attaching a sidecar, but it looked dated next to the V-twins offered by competitors and sales were poor. Adding two more models to the range in 1935 only made things worse: the entry-point L2/1 (L for lightweight) was well received but only because it was so cheap that the factory can't have been making any money; and the 5/10 racers at the opposite end of the scale had to withdraw from the TT due to what today's race teams would brush under the nearest carpet as 'technical issues'.

Factory boss Claude Holbrook's solution was to follow his belief in four wheels – ignore bikes and focus on the cars. The launch of the Super Seven was followed by many four-wheelers of increasing ambition, including the 1.2-litre Scorpion (great name) and the Southern Cross sportscar, which did well in the famous Alpine and Monte Carlo rallies. There were six-cylinder family cars and the bestselling Super Seven was then superseded by the Super Eight. And bigger is always better, right? There was a wide range of Gloria-branded vehicles too.

Yet despite leaping in with both feet, Triumph's automobile business struggled too. *Really* struggled, in fact. With the company disappearing into a financial black hole, motorcycle production was canned completely to focus on building cars at Coventry's Foleshill Road works. Val Page quit and went to BSA. And things continued to deteriorate. Even the supercharged straight-eight Dolomite sportscar – designed by Donald Healey, based on Alfa Romeo's successful 8C-2300 Monza, and potentially the fastest sports-touring car of its era – couldn't revive interest. Only one complete car was made (and got hit by a train in the Monte Carlo rally). Focused on saving their beloved but floundering car business, and having overspent drastically trying to keep it afloat, Triumph made an announcement to the press in late 1935: the motorcycle business was to be terminated. Closed, shut down, wrapped up, no more.

Enter stage left, full of ideas and brimming with personal confidence, a jaunty Mr Edward Turner.

TURNED ON ITS HEAD

Things were going well over at revived Ariel, but Turner wasn't content. He told his boss Jack Sangster that he'd look for work elsewhere unless he got a more secure role and a more generous paycheck. And he had a suggestion. Triumph was in a spot of bother, so Edward recommended that his boss should buy the famous brand and let him run it.

Sangster's first attempt at negotiating a deal fell flat, but when he learnt that the receiver for Lloyds Bank would be making a train journey from the Midlands back to London in the middle of January 1936, he went and loitered at the station. The deal had been done by the time the locomotive chuffed its way into the city. Sangster bought Triumph's assets, plant, machinery and 'goodwill', plus arranged to lease the Coventry factory, for just shy of £50,000 – or almost £3 million in today's money. A jolly nice lunch for suppliers and dealers was held at the Kings Head Hotel in Coventry; Siegfried Bettmann was slotted into the position of chairman and 35-year-old Turner was the director and general manager of the new Triumph Engineering Company Limited. He was a shareholder too (4.9 per cent) and had a generous salary that included 5 per cent of the firm's net profits.

To ensure his cut would pay for a nice house and a decent family holiday, Turner needed to turn things around, sharpish. And cheapish. Edward wasn't someone in a smart suit swanning about the factory to help count all the money. They didn't have any. Employee wages for the first week had to be covered by an overdraft and most of the 850-ish staff took a pay cut with the takeover. Edward's dreams of creating flash engines boasting vertically joined crankcases and elaborate valve systems had to be put on hold – the revived firm was limited by the existing machinery and tools as there was nothing left in Sangster's piggybank, and this meant carrying on with the existing engines.

Partitioning off part of the assembly area for his office, allowing him to literally keep an eye on proceedings, Turner employed Bert

Hopwood, who he'd worked with at Ariel, and implemented changes right across Triumph's purchasing, accounts and sales departments. He standardized the Triumph logo to make it instantly recognizable. And he opened his pencil case too, standardizing more parts across an 11-bike range to reduce costs. These were based on Page's bikes, but the engines were refined, classy new colours (plum red and black with swish gold pinstripes) made the bikes stand out, and chrome plating gave a luxurious feel. And the stodgy 6/1 was discontinued. Turner's real genius came in the model names: the range-topping 250, 350 and 500cc models became the Tiger 70, Tiger 80 and Tiger 90, indicating their top speed and causing much stirring within the loins of excitable young chaps.

Turner's vision, grafting and inspired choice of names – plus the unpaid weekend overtime put in by phenomenally loyal factory staff – immediately paid off. The gleaming brightwork and exciting names of the reinvented bikes made them a hit with attendees at the 1936 Olympia show, especially as asking prices remained attractive. Many wallets were deployed. Triumph's three-rider team won gold medals in the ISDT, the company was in profit by the end of their first year, and in 1937, some Triumph models secured the prestigious Maudes Trophy for ridiculous high-speed antics in dismal weather at Donington Park race circuit.

Turner wasn't content with turning the factory's fortunes around, though. He had plans to flip motorcycling upside down with a striking all-new model. His creation was revealed to the press in July 1937: the Triumph 5T Speed Twin.

When he'd been developing the silky Ariel Square Four, Turner had run some tests with the front crankshaft removed so that the rear bank of cylinders functioned as a parallel twin. Having liked what he'd seen, he had ideas in mind when wading into the new model. He was also skilled at spotting when something worked and employing it in his designs – why put in the hard design work when someone else has already done it for you? Edward's new 498cc parallel twin used the same bore and stroke as Triumph's 250 (for that economically important commonality of parts) and used features from all over the place: the hemispherical cylinder head echoed Page's 250cc single; the crankshaft design was similar to a Vauxhall car and other mechanical aspects were as Turner had spotted on the Riley Nine car he owned. With the pushrod tubes for the valve train secreted away behind the cooling fins, his motor had handsome visual simplicity; astonishingly, the twin was also narrower than the firm's single-piston 493cc Tiger 90 engine and only a couple of kilograms heavier – which meant it could borrow the Tiger's frame and keep grasp of costs.

The finished Speed Twin made 26hp at 6000rpm, weighed 161kg (355lb), used girder-fork front suspension, and was lavished with chrome and polished niceties and finished in amaranth red. It had lights as well, and an electric horn. And the Smith illuminated 'chronometric trip speedometer' indicated all the way to a giddying 120mph.

Seen by the public for the first time at the Earls Court Motorcycle Show in August 1937, the new bike was a revelation. Turner's engine was as slender and light as 500cc single-cylinder rivals, but far smoother, quieter, easier to prod into action and had superior acceleration. The Speed Twin was also light, making it easy to manage and bringing nimbleness. It was a showstopper and at £75 – only a fiver more than the instantly outdated Tiger 90 – an immediate showroom success. Demand was increased further when *The Motor Cycle* went speed testing and achieved 107mph on one run. It was with a howling tailwind but nobody cared: it was truly phenomenal velocity for a 500cc road bike.

Speed freaks around the globe clamoured to get hold of a Speed Twin. A supercharged bike ridden by Ivan Wicksteed established a record flying-lap speed at Brooklands of 118.02mph (and it still stands, as the circuit closed shortly afterwards). A lunatic called Les Fredericks did 805 miles in 12 hours at the Coorong Circuit in Australia, riding through the night and in drenching sea spray to set a new distance record (he wanted to set a 24-hour one, but the conditions were so bad he literally couldn't see where he was going). In 1938, the Metropolitan police chose the Triumph Speed Twin over rival machines presented by seven other manufacturers, and the bikes achieved massive mileages: by the mid-1940s, the Met's average plod bike had done almost 100,000 miles, with one machine still going strong after 161,000 miles.

Already a man of solid reputation, Edward Turner confirmed himself as a captain of the motorcycle industry. He had not only put Triumph back in place at the top of the two-wheel tree but set the blueprint for the future of motorcycling – the Speed Twin would become generally considered as the definitive British motorcycle and its engine would define Triumph for the next 50 years.

CHAPTER 5

TRIUMPH OVER ADVERSITY

HERE WE GO AGAIN . . .

Brass monkeys. That's the best way to describe the latter half of 1940 and the first half of 1941. It was the longest series of consecutive colder-than-average months of the twentieth century – 11 on the bounce – with penetrating frosts and chilly fingers. Snow covered the ground of northern Britain for more than 50 days, with depths of 900mm (3 feet) in the Scottish Highlands. For good measure, there was torrential rain thrown in too, with February claiming the miserable record of being the soggiest second month of the century – it was four-and-a-half times wetter than average. Oh, and there were some particularly soup-like night fogs as well. Just to keep things interesting.

In Portsmouth on the evening of Tuesday 22 April 1941, nobody was too concerned about what was falling out of the clouds, however. They were more bothered by the relentless barrage of bombs tumbling out of Nazi aircraft.

The British naval base at Devonport, formally known as Plymouth Dock, was under attack from the Luftwaffe. This was an important port for the Allies due to its proximity to the French coast at Normandy, and so a target for the advancing German forces. Most people had retreated to the air-raid shelters, but Pamela Betty McGeorge was threading her way through the blacked-out streets riding her 342cc Triumph. A third officer with the Women's Royal Naval Service (affectionately known as the Wrens), McGeorge was a despatch rider and had a memo for

Devonport's commanders tucked in the messenger bag hanging at her side. A bomb exploded close by, hurling her from the bike, and with the machine destroyed by the blast, she covered the final half mile to her destination on foot. And then, obviously, went straight back to her base and continued her despatch duties on another bike. McGeorge was awarded the British Empire Medal for her heroic actions during the Plymouth Blitz.

The Wrens had been established during the First World War. The navy was the first of Britain's armed services to recruit women, who filled roles as telegraph operators and code experts. When the world started blowing itself up again in September 1939, they went back into action. 'Join the Wrens – free a man for the fleet' begged recruiting posters. Initially, they took on tasks that were still traditionally seen as suitable for women – administration, radio operators, meteorologists – but soon they'd take over a vital role during the conflict: motorcycle despatch.

With lines of communication in tatters, two-wheelers were essential for delivering messages and orders. The first women riders were those who had already proved themselves on a bike. There had been a surge in high-profile female racers before the war, with the likes of Beatrice Shilling, Florence Blenkiron and Theresa Wallach achieving 100mph laps at Brooklands and inspiring countless female club racers with their derring-do. Capable of hurling a bike around at silly speed and also understanding how they worked, these experienced club racers were recruited by their local Wrens – but as the war slogged on, non-riding volunteers were also trained up on motorcycles. At the height of the conflict, there were 74,000 women involved, carrying out more than 200 different jobs, but it was the role of despatch rider – and many other heroic exploits like McGeorge's – that got them world-wide recognition.

'I was only just old enough to ride a bike and my mother was terrified, but I thought it was heaven,' recalled perhaps the most famous Wren, actress Honor Blackman, as quoted by *Motorcycle News* – yes, Pussy Galore from the James Bond movie was a Triumph-mounted despatch rider. 'It was pretty dangerous because we were in the midst of war and had to mask the headlights during the blackout. Bombs were falling, but the roar of the motorbike engine used to drown out the sound of the doodlebugs [Germany's flying bombs] so we never heard them coming. It seemed terribly exciting to me.'

The exploits of the Wrens and the contribution of the motorcycle can't be overplayed. The orders for D-Day were sent out in the Wrens' messenger bags ... and they were probably riding Triumphs.

DEVASTATION

Motorcycle manufacturers were instructed to forget about making bikes to put into showrooms and to prioritize churning out machines for the armed forces. All the major brands thrust bikes into the fray: BSA had their crudely suspended 250cc models, with the side-valve C10 and overhead-valve C11, and Enfield had a 350cc side-valve model that evolved into an OHV design later in the war. But it was Triumph machinery that again came to the fore, most notably the Triumph 3HW: a 342cc OHV machine built specifically for the military and based on the successful Tiger 80.

And under Edward Turner's guidance, the Coventry firm had become successful again. The car side of the business had started to be wound down in 1936, with a decision not to faff about with sports cars and to use their own engines rather than buying in fancy ones. The firm's original Coventry premises on Much Park Street were sold, and the car division would go into receivership in 1939, getting swallowed up by the Standard Motor Company. (Cars badged as Triumph, including the famous line of TR sports cars, would continue to be made by Standard and then Leyland, British Leyland and Austin Rover, until the brand name was dropped in 1984; the last Triumph car was the Acclaim, which was essentially just a rebadged Honda. The trademark is currently owned by BMW, the German automotive behemoth acquiring it when they bought the Rover Group in the early 1990s. They retained the name when they sold everything else, so maybe one day ...)

Focusing on motorcycles, Triumph progressed at speed back up the road to glory. The fanfare and trumpeting caused by Turner's game-changing 5T Speed Twin hadn't died down, with orders from around the world from more police forces wanting to have the performance upper hand on the bad guys. The model had been selected for a two-wheeled guard of honour during King George V's sightseeing holiday in Canada too, and there'd been an unsolicited celebrity endorsement from multiple world land-speed record holder Sir Malcolm Campbell. 'In my opinion the Triumph Speed Twin has no equal,' gushed the man who'd three times been the fastest human on the face of the planet in Turner's official biography. 'It is a machine eminently suitable to all purposes, is an extremely sound engineering job, and the workmanship is superb.' I think he quite liked it.

Campbell wasn't just bluster. He'd put his money where his mouth was and bought not only a Speed Twin but also a new Tiger 100. Released in 1939 to replace the single-cylinder Tiger 90 and selling for £80, the Tiger 100 was the hopped-up, go-faster version of the Speed Twin. The parallel twin featured stronger cylinders held in place by more studs, lighter pistons, and polished and strengthened internals. With a greedier carburettor pouring more fuel into the chirpier motor, power output increased to a heady 33 horses. The brochure stated that every bike's engine 'was individually tested ...

then stripped and reassembled by skilled mechanics. A Test Card, signed by the Chief tester was supplied with each machine.' The chassis was altered for more stability and had new front suspension, there were more chrome finishes, and the Tiger 100 also used narrower, rubber-mounted handlebars plus a larger fuel tank, wearing a diecast Triumph badge and finished in racy chrome and silver.

Top speed was 96mph. However, the endcaps of the 'cocktail shaker' exhaust were removable, letting owners whip out the baffles to release the perkier engine's full potential – and giving the benchmark top speed boasted about in the model's name. Obviously, this feature was for racing and you'd never do it for riding on the road ... Triumph's development rider Freddie Clarke headed to the famous banked sweeps of Brooklands with a bored-out 503cc Tiger 100 and blasted to a new class lap record at 118.02mph. He also set a new 350cc record by hitting 105.97mph on a Tiger 80.

Then it all came slamming down. First, Edward Turner suffered a huge personal trauma in July 1939 when his wife Marion was tragically killed in a car crash.

Two months later, Britain was at war again.

Petrol rationing was almost immediately introduced, with the smelly fluid from brand-name pumps all replaced with a low-octane 'pool' fuel. This was far from ideal for sporty engines, as in the Tiger 100. It made the engine detonate (or 'knock' or 'pink'), which is where the air/fuel mix doesn't combust properly, and it can ruin engine internals. Aluminium couldn't be used for motorcycles as it would be needed for making Spitfires and Lancasters, so had to be replaced with heavier steel and iron.

Turner had grand plans for a new 3T model, a 350cc twin-cylinder little brother to the 5T Speed Twin, which would be the glittering highlight in a nine-model line-up for 1940. Civilian bikes could initially still be built in limited quantities, so Triumph raised the gearing and adjusted carburettor settings across the board to give better economy on the used washing-up water that passed as petrol and confidently booked advertising space on the cover of motorcycling pamphlets. And then ... the 1939 Motor Cycle Show was cancelled. Military bikes would be the only thing allowed to roll out of the factory, so the new 3T was canned as well, along with new SE models designed specifically for export. All the gushing adverts were pulled at the last minute, meaning front covers had to be reprinted.

Securing a contract to supply the military was the number one focus. Men with interesting moustaches and highly polished footwear had devised a set of requirements for their army bikes: they must be over 250cc and capable of 60–70mph, but also return 80mpg at 30mph and be inaudible from half a mile away. Maximum weight was a delicate 113kg (250lb) and any machine had to haul itself up in less than 11m (35 feet) from 30mph. At least 150mm (6in) of ground clearance too.

War had been bubbling away on the horizon for a while and so most major motorcycle manufacturers had suitable bikes under development, including Triumph, but when the conflict erupted none of them were ready. Civilian bikes were thrust into action, their dashing chrome and luxurious paint swapped for dull finishes and hide-in-a-field olive drab. Within six weeks of all the conflict kicking off, 1,400 roadsters – a mixture of 350 and 500cc singles with a smattering of Speed Twins – were whisked away from Triumph's works.

Triumph cracked on with their military-specific bike, which was called the 3TW. It took some of its concept from the cancelled 3T civilian model and performed well in tests conducted by burly army types, even after its weight had crept above the maximum due to all the cast iron that had to replace the aluminium. Triumph got a contract for the bike in July 1940.

And then the Luftwaffe bombed the Triumph factory to smithereens.

PUSHING ON

Coventry was the target for a blitz on the night of 14 November 1940. Triumph's works and the adjacent cathedral were destroyed. Hundreds of lives were lost, two-thirds of the city was affected and thousands of homes were wrecked. So was the first batch of 50 3TW models, which had been waiting patiently to be despatched to the military. Amazingly, the factory's petrol tank had survived and still contained 2,000 gallons of fuel.

Tooling and machinery were lost in the bombing, along with most of the firm's records and drawings. Most, but not all. One switched-on employee had run to the factory when he'd heard the air-raid sirens and grabbed as many drawings and blueprints as he could. Just imagine, you're a 25-year-old draughtsman for Triumph, spending your evening reclining in a nice velour seat at the cinema in Leamington Spa. On hearing the ominous wail of the siren, your first thought isn't to scamper immediately to the nearest shelter but instead to travel ten miles to your place of work and fill your arms with rolled-up drawings. The chap who did it was called Jack Wickes. They were a different breed back then.

Despite initial objection from the local council – and, in typical headstrong form, going against the opinion of his boss Jack Sangster – the ever-confident Turner bought a site at the village of Meriden where a fresh new factory would be built. In the meantime, any salvageable machinery and equipment was extracted from the rubble to relocate at temporary premises, including items that were damaged but deemed repairable. They may have been able to get more but someone stumbled across a massive unexploded bomb in the debris. Triumph set up in a place known as The Cape, next to the canal in nearby Warwick; it was the ex-works of a cement company and included an old chapel clad in corrugated iron that would house the commercial staff. They called it 'the Tin Tabernacle'.

With the designs and tooling for the 3TW all destroyed, along with existing bikes, Triumph pushed on by basing their military machines on the older 342cc single-cylinder models. The military ordered the 12hp side-valve 3SW in its thousands, with the last ones built on 31 October 1941. Four months earlier, after sourcing copies of drawings and details from various suppliers and recreating everything that had been destroyed, the makeshift Warwick factory had started on its replacement, the 17hp overhead-valve 3HW.

Triumph supplied 10,000 motorcycles to the military over the course of the Second World War. Eighty per cent of these were the later 3HW, which was used across Europe and in India, North Africa and Greece. The Greek army kept hold of a load when the fighting eventually stopped and carried on using them for the next decade; Triumph might have thrown the bikes together in a period of much adversity but they weren't lacking in the firm's trademark quality.

SPIRITUAL HOME

Most of the 3HW army machines were made at the glinting new factory at Meriden. This was the site that would become forever associated with Britain's legendary motorcycle brand. Even today, you can't say Triumph to riders of a certain vintage without the name Meriden cropping up in the conversation. It remains Triumph's spiritual home (and the location of much attention, but more of that later).

The most advanced and modern motorcycle factory in the country started firing out motorcycles in 1942. This wasn't a place where bought-in components were bolted together, as can often be the case with modern manufacturing. Triumph still understood how keeping things in house allowed them control of quality and the finer details, and the new factory did … well, pretty much everything. Triumph produced their own pistons, shafts, gears, clutches and wheel hubs.

They fabricated their own frames. There were machine shops, paint shops and plating shops, with all the polishing and chrome plating of handlebars, wheels, exhausts and all the other shiny bits done on site. As the country was still at war, Triumph also manufactured aircraft parts, bits for the tracks on tanks and stretcher carriers. They also built generators for the RAF using a version of the Speed Twin engine, featuring an aluminium alloy cylinder head and barrel, known as the AAPP – airborne auxiliary power plant. It would be unexpectedly repurposed into something far more exotic after the war ...

Turner must have been rubbing his hands together at the prospect of what he could achieve with his amazing new facility. But he got sacked instead.

There had always been a bit of beef between Edward and Jack Sangster. It started at Ariel and carried on at Triumph, and centred around rank, pay and ownership of patents. Essentially, Turner thought he should be paid a heftier salary, have a larger chunk of the company's shares and a greater income from net profits, and keep the rights to his designs should he decide to go and work somewhere else. Sangster thought the opposite. With the move to the Meriden site, the pair tried to thrash out an agreement to become equal partners, but the patent issue wouldn't go away. Solicitors got involved. On 23 July 1942, Turner was dismissed.

The chief executive of rival firm BSA immediately recruited Edward the moment that word of his departure got out. In his new position as technical director, he redesigned some of BSA's cylinder heads, did quite a bit of problem solving and even delved into issues with the springs on some of the firearms they made. Importantly, Turner also cracked on with a new military bike. The news filtered back to Triumph and flustered Sangster, who ordered Bert Hopwood (now filling Turner's shoes) to come up with a new Triumph military machine as well – and it must be completed for evaluation ahead of the BSA presentation. That was just three short months away.

Hopwood used a combination of bits from the never-made 3TW and the Tiger 100 with a few of his own ideas, and he came up with a 500cc side-valve twin with a four-speed gearbox. It also used telescopic front forks, rather than the established girder set-up – it was the first Triumph to feature what would become the go-to solution for motorcycle front suspension. Just up the road at BSA in Birmingham, Turner also employed telescopic forks on his prototype 490cc side-valve twin.

Triumph's 5TW was rolled out in front of the press in February 1943, after just seven weeks of concentrated graft, and well ahead of BSA's machine. Neither bike did more than inspire the army to revise the spec for military machines and neither was produced; however, when he saw BSA's prototype, Sangster regretted having dismissed Turner. He got in touch soon after, offering more acceptable terms to try to entice him back.

Edward returned to Meriden on 1 September 1943 as managing director, with an eight-year contract, a fat salary and plenty of perks. It was the start of a golden period in Triumph's story.

CHAPTER 6

TAKING ON
THE WORLD

SNEAKY SPEED

It's late. Most of the factory is in darkness. The majority of the workforce have headed home for a nice evening by the wireless, listening to excited folk trying to win assorted local produce and a bit of cash on the hit show *Have a Go*, hosted by Wilfred Pickles. But you aren't worried about answering a few questions on a stage in the village hall to try to secure Mrs Fotheringhay's excellent chutney and slip £1 18s 6d into your pocket. You're working after hours because you've got something a little more exciting going on. It's certainly a lot more daring. And it's top secret.

Your boss is the undoubtedly talented but also slightly domineering Edward Turner, a man who has made it clear that Triumph shouldn't have any involvement with road racing. Turner believes that all racing does is swallow up time, money and resources in the pursuit of short-lived publicity. While high-profile events like the Isle of Man TT had started out as challenges for road-going touring machinery (hence the Tourist Trophy name), manufacturers quickly started building bespoke racing bikes. These days, victory requires something special; the machines are fast, loud and intoxicating, but also nothing like the bikes available in Triumph showrooms. Or so Turner thinks. So, well, what's the point?

But Turner's away overseas a lot, working on growing exports from the Meriden factory. He's been to America so much he should have developed a drawl. And as the head of experimental development, you're taking advantage of being unsupervised to do what you're paid to and develop something experimental.

Working at night, you've taken the proven Tiger 100 engine and, in an inspired moment, fitted the lightweight aluminium cylinder and head from the AAPP generator engine made for the RAF. It still has the bosses on the cylinder for fitting the AAPP's cooling fan cowling. The 498cc motor has jumped from 30hp at 6500rpm to a thoroughly impressive 47hp at 7000rpm. Suitably pleased with your activities, you're going to slot this rabid twin-cylinder engine into a frame fitted with racily mounted footpegs and Turner's new and not-yet-in-production sprung-hub rear suspension. It'll carry an experimental 200mm (8in) front brake as well. And, with complete disregard for the boss's views, it's going to be entered into the 1946 Manx Grand Prix ...

Can you imagine doing that today? Not only going against the wishes of your boss (who happens to oversee everything the factory does), but doing it sneakily and on the sly? The jobsworths in the HR department would have an absolute field day. But it's exactly what ambitious Freddie Clarke did.

A well-known racer himself, Clarke had become Triumph's head of development in 1936. He'd helped get the Tiger 100 – the firm's flagship model – up to scratch and set some speed records at Brooklands on factory-prepped bikes before the Second World War. He gave his hush-hush hybrid racer to an Irish farmer by the name of Ernie Lyons for the Manx GP in September 1946. It was the first time the famous Isle of Man mountain course had been used for seven years and it enjoyed some particularly terrible weather conditions. The island was abused by howling winds and battered by torrential rain. Rider Ernie swiped the longer front mudguard from his own road-going Tiger 100 and bolted it to the racer.

Starting from twelfth, Lyons came through the field. The prototype bike's unproven suspension provided handling best described as entertaining, and the frame's front downtube snapped on the last lap, but he won – the first Triumph victory on the island since 1908.

He finished 43 seconds ahead of the second-placed Norton, with an average speed of almost 77mph.

Edward Turner returned from his overseas jolly to discover that an unsanctioned Triumph, screwed together using war-surplus engine bits from the auxiliary generator made for Lancaster bombers, had won the Manx Grand Prix. To show his appreciation for what Lyons had achieved, Turner authorized a slap-up dinner and invited the press. This was a month after the Manx, on the same day as the Shelsley Walsh hill climb, which Lyons had entered on the same bike. He won again, setting the fastest time of the day, and turned up for his celebratory meal still wearing his leather riding gear after the meeting had run on.

Turner was rather less impressed with what Freddie Clarke had done behind his back, and so had him officially denounced by the works' manager. Clarke quit and went to work for Associated Motor Cycles (AMC), the parent company of Matchless, AJS, Francis-Barnett and others. (He was killed testing a prototype twin the following year.)

Some half-hearted development of the Triumph race bikes carried on through 1947, with established rider David Whitworth achieving a bit of success in races across Europe. This was probably permitted due to demand from dealers for a replica of the Manx-winning machine for amateur racers – Lyons' victory was big news in the club racing world. True to his beliefs, Turner didn't allow development of a specialist race bike. But while he was off skipping around the globe again, including visiting Columbia Pictures in the USA and hobnobbing with movie star Rita Hayworth, the boss did permit a lightened, tuned-up version of the Tiger 100 to be created. The engine's internal workings were polished and lightened, two gulping great carburettors were attached, and the chassis featured beefed-up forks, the bouncy sprung rear wheel, lower handlebars and a larger fuel tank. Engine and frame numbers featured an 'R' in them, so you knew you were getting something a bit racy. Yet despite these amendments, most of the bike's parts were shared with the road-going Tiger 100, meaning that, as far as hard-nosed businessman Turner was concerned, it could actually be a solid commercial venture.

Although not a thoroughbred racing machine, the Grand Prix T100R claimed 'to enable the non-professional rider to compete on level terms in all types of long and short circuit racing'. The R model went on sale in February 1948 and Turner had his arm twisted into allowing a semi-factory racing effort to enter the TT later in the year. Some famous racing bums were perched on the machines, including multiple TT-winner and former European 350cc champion Freddie Frith. All the bikes conked out with expired engines. You can imagine Turner's reaction ...

And yet the T100R *was* a commercial success. They say there's no such thing as bad PR and maybe it's true. Despite flopping in a high-profile event, the T100R quickly developed a reputation as being fast. Quite a welcome attribute for a racing motorcycle. And successes followed: later in the year, the tuned-up twin won the Manx Grand Prix again, and in 1950, one set a record race-speed on its way to winning a 100-mile amateur race at Daytona in the United States. Bikes were snapped up in dealerships, especially in the USA, and the over-the-counter racer made money.

MUCKING ABOUT

Customer demand for a speedy Triumph shouldn't have been a surprise. Punters weren't buying the bikes because of their good looks. Actually, perhaps some of them were. Edward Turner's abilities when it came to styling a motorcycle and his choice of colours and glimmering brightwork meant that Triumph's models were definitely good-looking devices.

However, for most bike-obsessed folk, the attraction was surely the performance of the twin-cylinder engines. Post-war production of bikes for civilians had been permitted from July 1945 and models started rolling out through Triumph's gates again in November 1945 – and there were no more cranky, wheezy singles. Triumph's focus was twin-cylinder models, and the first two bikes that returned to showrooms were the flagship Tiger 100 and extremely popular 5T Speed Twin. These had become closer in specification (Turner's fondness for uniformity) and both had improvements over their pre-war forerunners, including the use of modern-style telescopic front forks. The people's favourite, the Speed Twin, now cost £110, plus £30 purchase tax, and the speedometer added another £3 10s (plus tax) to the total, despite being a legal requirement. Eager buyers also had to get a Licence to Acquire from the Ministry of War Transport and select bikes from brochures, rather than being able to excitedly bounce up and down on one at a dealer. It was a magnificently pointless arrangement (thankfully soon dropped).

These two 500s were swiftly followed by the new 3T model. Turner had planned a 350 sibling for his admired 500 before the war and now it saw the light of day. Costing about a tenner less than the 5T, the 349cc OHV machine was essentially a mash-up of the Speed Twin and the military models. Wearing the excellent moniker 3T DeLuxe, the 19hp device could beetle along at 74mph and returned 80mpg even on the watery nonsense still being passed off as petrol.

Before the war, Triumph had been successful in a couple of off-road disciplines: trials, where riders negotiate ridiculously bothersome terrain, and scrambles, with competitors in a mass-start race over a rough track, known these days as motocross. Today, both events feature highly specialist machinery ridden by athletes of worrying focus, but back in the forties, the entrants were largely normal folk riding lightly spruced road models. Perhaps while enjoying puffing on a roll-up cigarette.

Edward Turner could clearly see that all this was a fine demonstration of a bike's robustness and therefore had sales potential. After attending a few events to watch riders who were tipped by his sales office manager, he signed up a trio for an official team. He tasked his greenhorn advertising, publicity and competition manager with announcing it to the world in January 1946.

The riders were: Allen Jefferies, who'd competed for Triumph before the war, Bert Gaymer and Jim Alves, who Turner had seen racing on a home-prepped ex-military Triumph 3HW. The low-rev power of a single-cylinder engine suited dirt-flinging antics – it still does – but as Triumph didn't make them anymore, they decided their jockeys would ride the new 3T. There wasn't a workshop for building race bikes, so a machine was modified for the rigours of banging over boulders and ricocheting through ruts in the factory's repair shop. All unnecessary clutter was stripped off, more suitable tyres were bolted (literally) to the wheels and a two-into-one exhaust swooped up the left-side flank to improve ground clearance. Jim Alves, suitably dressed in cap and long trench coat, easily won first time out against the cream of British trials riders in March 1946. And he won the next time out too.

Alves wouldn't have known it then, but he had started what would become Triumph's total domination in off-road sport.

(The 3T in question was registered in October 1945 as ENX 674 and it featured in gushing advertising hurriedly issued after both events; it still shows up on the DVLA database as a black Triumph 3T, with the last V5C logbook issued in May 2007. If that reg plate sounds familiar, nip out to the shed – you might own a rather significant machine.)

INTERNATIONAL FORCE

Few competitive motorcycle skirmishes were tougher than the ISDT. Having started out at the turn of the twentieth century as the Great

1,000 Miles Test, it became the ACU Six Days Reliability Trial under the guidance of the Auto Cycle Union, the governing body for rapidly growing British motorcycle sport, before being taken over by the FIM – the important-sounding Fédération Internationale de Motorclisme – in 1913. Riders had to maintain a predetermined average speed over a heavy-going route of thousands of miles, with tests of flexibility and speed chucked in for good measure. Points were lost for things like stopping in an area where stopping wasn't permitted, straying from the schedule or having a defective bike. In the early days, you'd be penalized for a dirty bike too, despite all the unpaved sections of the course. Just to keep the riders busy.

Countries entered teams in the ISDT to try and win the International Trophy and Vase awards. All riders had to be on bikes made in their country, but they didn't all need to be the same brand. There was also a Silver Vase for a junior team (each country had to enter riders in more than one capacity class), a manufacturers' team award, plus gold, silver and bronze medals were dished out for individual riders … With the variety of demanding riding involved, the abuse inflicted on the machinery and all this complication, the event was known as the 'Olympics of Motorcycling'.

British riders and machines had enjoyed a lot of success in the trial since the home-grown team had won the very first running at Carlisle in 1913. They'd taken most of the trophies and medals during the 1920s – one of the riders was TT-winner Graham Walker, father of legendary sports commentator Murray – and had wrapped things up for the final three ISDTs before war stopped play.

Triumph's successful new trials and scrambles team was thrust into the 1948 event held in San Remo, Italy. Three bikes based on the 5T Speed Twin were prepared for Gaymer, Alves and Jefferies. The latter was the team's captain, and he got a special prototype featuring the ex-generator alloy head and cylinders used on the Grand Prix. Despite the competition being flooded with single-cylinder bikes, the 5T proved both pleasingly fast and steadfastly reliable over a 1,272-mile challenge that saw more than half the field retire. The British team containing Jefferies on his Triumph (with other riders on Royal Enfield, AJS and Norton) lost no marks and was victorious. The Silver Vase team, which included Alves, didn't lose any marks either. There were gold medals flung all over the riders and Triumph strutted away with what in their eyes was the biggie: the Manufacturers' Team Award.

There couldn't have been a better demonstration of the Speed Twin's capabilities than all this glory. Things were less rosy behind the factory doors, though. It seems that the riders had been forced to rely on their extensive abilities to make up for a few shortcomings with their 5T-based machinery, which had been somewhat unwieldy and not the easiest to handle. Something better was needed if the factory was to defend its ISDT reputation and keep the exceedingly patriotic Turner in fine spirit.

Triumph's new TR5 Trophy was rolled out under the spotlights at the Earl's Court Motorcycle Show in November 1948 and was something a bit special. Breaking with Triumph's modular approach, it featured a bespoke frame that was much lighter and shorter than a regular 5T. It had increased ground clearance, larger wheels that made it easier to roll over obstacles and a headlight that could quickly be taken off for competition use. It was the 498cc motor with the alloy goodies, but with a single carburettor rather than the Grand Prix's twin slurpers, and the bike could be specified with different pistons: high compression for more power in scrambles and ISDT-like duties, or low compression for a softer delivery suitable to fiddly low-speed trials riding. Finished with a chrome tank (the last regular production Triumph to feature one), the bike's Trophy tag was an obvious link to the firm's successes the previous year. Yours for the rather considerable outlay of £200 13s 3d, including good ol' purchase tax.

Triumph had invented something new: the world's first dual-purpose motorcycle, one that was as adept on tarmac as it was handy in the muck. The team was joined by Bob Manns (a Triumph test rider), and the Triumph entries on swish new TR5s again bought home major ISDT trophies, with success continuing into the early 1950s. In America, Bud Ekins won the Catalina Grand Prix in 1955 on an updated TR5 Trophy. We'll be hearing plenty more about him …

You've probably detected something of a trend here. The model and its later iterations would remain the trials iron of choice for budding clubman riders right into and through the 1960s.

Clearly a fine tool, the TR5 Trophy was a significant sales success. It was particularly well received in the USA. Following Edward Turner's efforts to grow overseas markets, less than a third of the Meriden plant's output was for British buyers by the end of the 1950s – 70 per cent of machines got boxed up for export. Firing out well over 250 bikes a week, the factory had to start a nightshift to keep up with orders. Triumphs were definitely in demand and the company was on the up.

And things were going to get busier still. Edward Turner had been back doodling at his drawing board.

TIME TO GROW

These days, the launch of a new motorcycle is elaborate and involved. It's also drawn out. The bike will have been in development for typically four or five years, its computer-analysed design being subject to endless poking, prodding, simulations and testing. Young marketeers with a degree in social media will drip-feed teasers about the new product for months. There'll then be an embargoed press announcement disclosing the headline news, followed by a full disclosure of all the information and the release of many achingly arty images taken by a photographer who's charged an extortionate amount.

All this fluff and bluster will be followed by the press riding launch. A fleet of shiny new bikes will be transported to Spain or Corsica or somewhere else nice in a couple of big trucks to be fussed over by a team of technicians. Staff from the factory, PR company and photo/video agency will spend a couple of weeks in a very comfortable hotel by the coast, doing reconnaissance of the roads and taking on-location press images. Key factory personnel with job titles like 'head of brand' and 'executive collaboration liaison' will then be flown in ready for the arrival of journalists and 'influencers' from around the globe. These attendees will sit through glitzy presentations stuffed full of words like 'premium', 'signature' and 'brand defining', eat and drink very well indeed, and do lots of important networking. Representatives from different countries arrive in alternating groups over anything up to a couple of weeks, often taking over the hotel. Oh, and the new bike will be ridden. Probably not very far – just enough to get a feel, take a few riding photos and do a handful of look-at-me posts on 'the socials', while hopping between very pleasant coffee and lunch stops.

Triumph used to do things rather differently.

In September 1949, four spanking-new Triumphs were laden with spares, including tyres, and ridden from the factory to the Autodrome de Linas-Montlhéry near Paris, France. The various circuit layouts at Montlhéry included a 1.6-mile oval with banked corners, allowing sustained high speeds. Setting off at 9 a.m. on 20 September, under the supervision of an ACU (Auto-Cycle Union – the governing body of motorcycle sport in Britain) official and the watchful eye of Edward Turner, three of the bikes started haring around and completed 500 non-stop miles at an average of over 90mph. The riders included Jefferies and works riders Alves and Manns, who had headed to Montlhéry directly from the rigours of that year's ISDT. Yes, they definitely earned their wages. Looking desperately dashing in white Triumph-branded overalls, they then nipped back out to do a lap averaging over 100mph for the benefit of the assembled press. Running on weak 'pool' petrol that necessitated a restricted compression ratio and so limited the power output, it was a staggering achievement.

A swift phone call confirming the achievement was made to the factory and pre-prepared adverts were thrust into the two weekly motorcycling titles to go alongside the excited stories about this rapid new machine. The BBC got wind and interviewed Turner. The new Triumph 6T Thunderbird had arrived – and, modest as ever, Triumph's adverts declared it the Best Motorcycle in the World.

Since then, there has been an iconic Ford car with the same name. There have been wobbly-headed puppets, who lived on an island in the South Pacific and carried out rescue missions with a variety of wondrous craft. It's been the name of a Marvel Comics superhero and a particularly lovely Gibson bass guitar. And there's the rocket-fuel fortified wine that introduced a generation of underage teenagers to the joys of a hangover during the 1980s and 1990s. But the first Thunderbird was a Triumph. Well, kind of …

The main driver behind the new model's creation was that Triumph's boss was convinced the brand's prosperity lay in the US market – and this meant they needed a larger machine. Silver-tongued Turner had already convinced an American lawyer called Bill Johnson, who he'd befriended while at Ariel when Johnson had bought a Square Four, to make a complete career U-turn and become the British firm's West Coast distributor. But Triumph needed larger machines to pour into the $100,000, glitzy showrooms that Johnson Motors had set up. American motorcycles were vast compared to the tiddlers putt-putting around the UK: Harley-Davidson made huge V-twins of over 1200cc, and the 1950 Indian Chief had a twin-cylinder motor displacing 80 cubic inches – a whopping 1311cc. They weren't much faster than Triumph's existing Speed Twin and T100. The Harley and Indian had power outputs nudging 60hp but both were hefty machines, typically weighing the best bit of 100kg (220lb) more than the delicate British 500s, so the all-important power-to-weight wasn't impressive. But these huge motors produced loads of torque, romping effortlessly on a whiff of fuel, and their sizeable internal engine parts could shrug off all manner of abuse. Perfect for lazy progress down America's long, straight highways.

In early 1949, Edward Turner had been droning along such typically corner-free routes in South Carolina when he'd passed the Thunderbird Motel. He knew immediately that it was the name to use on his upcoming new 650 twin. The name originates from the indigenous people of North America, for whom the Thunderbird is a bird-like spirit that causes thunder by flapping its wings and shoots lightning out of its eyes. Not only something of a fire hazard, but a symbol of power and strength. The Thunderbird name and the symbol of the bird were both perfect for the largest Triumph yet produced.

These days, motorcycle engineers and designers use a bewilderingly in-depth computing tool called finite element analysis (FEA). When they design a new engine, it allows them to look at all manner of complicated stuff, including structural analysis, fluid dynamics, electromagnetic potential and heat transfer. They can run full simulations to tell them what torque and power the engine will produce, what revs are safe and whether (and how) it vibrates, what it will feel like and how many miles it'll manage before exploding, all without making a single component. Turner didn't have access to FEA. He had a drawing board and a nice selection of sharp pencils. Having redesigned the 5T Speed Twin engine for his new larger bike with fatter pistons (from 63mm diameter to 71mm) and a longer crank throw (2mm increase) to take capacity to 649cc, the only way to really see if the motor worked was to make it and test it.

Two of Triumph's sales reps were told to hand their Speed Twins – and they were their own, not company machines – to the experimental department. When they got them back the bikes looked unchanged ... but performed very differently. With a lot more power and a sharper response, they readily thundered to 100mph, shrugged off carrying pillions with unprecedented ease and left many other Speed Twin owners wondering why they couldn't keep up. The engine numbers might have still been stamped with '5T' at the beginning in order to divert suspicion, but the two reps were proving the capabilities of the 6T.

Two more people from within the experimental department also racked up testing miles in races, and it was their results that gave Turner the idea for the Thunderbird's grand launch.

RAMPAGING ONWARDS

Despite all the Thunderbird's speed and shouty figures, road racing at the time favoured the 500cc class. The Thunderbird was planned as a pure roadster – and yet would achieve some high-profile victories.

It was the Triumph TR5 model that achieved the string of ISDT wins from the late forties and into the fifties, but the later bikes should really have been called the TR6. They'd got Thunderbird engines. And there was a whole load more glory awaiting away from the world of dirt-flinging competition. Just as the 5T Speed Twin had forced rival manufacturers into using more than one piston in their engines, so the arrival of the 6T Thunderbird in 1950 forced them to explore larger displacement engines. Sales of the 650 were strong; the AA started using 6T sidecar outfits for their patrols; police forces across the globe switched to the larger Triumph to ensure those on the run couldn't escape; and the big new Brit was well received in the vast US market it was aimed at. After American motorcycling pamphlet *Cycle* declared that 'the riding characteristics leave nothing to be desired', the 649cc twin made a massive impact by setting a new AMA (American Motorcycle Association) speed record. Johnson Motors took the first Thunderbird in the USA and fitted open megaphone exhausts, camshaft parts from the Grand Prix model and special super-high-compression (13:1) pistons, plus a tiny headlight fairing. They gave it to a brave fellow by the name Bobby Turner, who stripped down to just his limb-hugging trousers, lay flat on the bike with his legs sticking out the back, and scorched to 135.84mph on Rosamond Dry Lake in the Mojave Desert. It was the fastest-ever run in the unstreamlined class.

The following year, 1951, brought more wreaths, champagne and back-slapping. Bobby Turner continued to set records on his hot-rodded Thunderbird, and the bike also won the first-ever Catalina Grand Prix as well as the Peoria TT. Desperate to expand their already-swollen US order book, Triumph also set up a new factory-owned distribution business – Johnson Motors would continue to serve 19 West Coast states, and the new TriCor distribution thrust motorcycles into the rest of the country. It was a wise decision: Triumph's imports almost tripled through the course of the year.

Back in Britain, the slow-selling 3T was dropped from the line-up, as was the speed-junkie Grand Prix model; however, those craving speed were served up something rather un-Turner. Though Triumph's leader retained his fixed dislike for bespoke race machinery, he'd started to see the commercial potential from success in production-based racing. In the 1950 Clubman TT, there were four Triumphs in the top eight finishers, and 29 in the entry list in total – the most bikes from any manufacturer. So, to serve these racers and fill the competition gap left by the Grand Prix, the factory released a race kit for the Tiger 100. Costing a princely £35, the package contained racing carburettors, pistons, valves, camshafts, exhausts and other bits to wedge into the engine, plus lower handlebars, a different oil tank and other paraphernalia. Fitted at home or by your favourite local mechanic, it boosted the 498cc twin's power by a third, from a decent 32hp to a race-ready 43hp. It was well received by horsepower-hunting amateur racers in the UK, and Johnson Motors shifted plenty in America. In

1952, the Clubmans Senior TT on the infamous Isle of Man was won by Bryan Hargreaves on a Triumph fitted with the over-the-counter race kit.

And race kits weren't the only thing being flogged. Jack Sangster sold the whole Triumph business to rivals BSA.

Though the Meriden factory was doing well, BSA were doing better in the UK and were in a stronger financial position. They were a force in British racing too, thanks to their legendary Gold Star models. The expansive Birmingham firm agreed to buy Triumph in March 1951 for £2,450,000 – over £65 million in today's money; it would continue to be run as a separate business with Sangster as chairman and Turner as managing director. The sale also included ET Developments, the firm Edward had set up to protect his patents, for £250,000. That'd be £6.5 million today.

Perhaps inspired to prove that his beloved Triumph was the superior brand, Edward Turner went into overdrive. New models came thick and fast through the 1950s, and the factory had to be extended to allow for the increase in production. To take on the modest two-strokes dominating the sub-200cc commuter market (including BSA's perennial Bantam), there came a new 149cc OHV single called the T15 Terrier. Proclaimed as 'A Real Triumph in Miniature' in the catalogue, it boasted unit construction and was followed by the Tiger Cub, essentially a larger 199cc version of the Terrier but cunningly painted like the larger Tiger models. At the other end of the range came the Tiger T110, which featured the improved 649cc engine tested in Alves' ISDT bike in 1953 along with its swingarm rear suspension and twin shock absorbers. Easily capable of the 110mph promised by its name, the 'Ton-ten' was the first production Triumph with modern rear suspension and also the first with a centre stand, rather than just a side stand (or prop stand, or kick stand, depending on where you're from). It was a new datum for affordable, sporty two-wheelers. All Triumph's twins sprouted swingarm rear suspension from 1955.

Speed and sportiness were selling bikes. But enticing customers into showrooms and getting them to empty the contents of their wallets all over the counter had been made much easier due to outside assistance. Thanks to Triumph's glamorous new links to the movies, the power of celebrity was at work.

FAME AND FORTUNE

Every Fourth of July through the 1930s, there'd been a motorcycle rally held in Hollister, California, run by the AMA and involving a spot of racing and some good-mannered socializing. It was a cheery gathering that brought welcome trade to the small town. Cancelled during the Second World War, it kicked off again in 1947 – and I mean *really* kicked off.

Bikes were booming in popularity in the USA. Many more riders than anyone had expected descended on the town – with 4,000 motorcyclists, including several clubs and gangs with the sorts of names you wouldn't use in polite company, the population of Hollister was doubled. Much drunkenness, brawling, chaos and choice language ensued, with the overpowered police arresting as many perpetrators as they could. They even threatened to use tear gas. Mass media coverage of what became known as the Hollister Riots gave the occurrence national prominence – and the bad-ass biker image was born.

A writer by the name of Frank Rooney created an acclaimed short story called *The Cyclists' Raid*, based very loosely on the events at Hollister and published in 1951. Two years later, Stanley Kramer used it as a basis for his film *The Wild One* starring Marlon Brando – and put Triumph onto the silver screen. Brando had a knack for picking stage and screen roles that would become popular icons. In *The Wild One*, he plays the character Johnny Strabler, leader of the ominously

Above: The first all-Triumph motorcycle, the 1905 3hp Motor Bicycle, modelled here by Mr A. W. Ayton.

Below: Triumph's bargain-priced Model P undercut all other 'big' 500cc models. It was staggeringly popular.

Right: After starting on Much Park Street, Triumph relocated to Priory Street, Coventry, before moving to the famous Meriden site.

Below: Sharp-suited Edward Turner congratulates the riders of his new 650cc Thunderbird in 1949. They had just ridden 500 miles at over 90mph at Autodrome de Linas-Montlhéry, France.

ON THIS SITE
SIEGFRIED BETTMANN
FOUNDER OF
THE TRIUMPH COMPANY
SET UP HIS
PRIORY STREET WORKS
1896

COVENTRY HERITAGE PLAQUES

JAC770

JAC771

JAC769

TRIUMPH CYCLES

PATRONISED BY ROYALTY

£ 15 · 15 · 0   EASY PAYMENTS

£ 10 · 10 · 0

WORKS, COVENTRY.

DEPÔT
96 Newgate St, LONDON EC

Left: Triumph's bicycles established the brand's reputation, as seen here in this early twentieth-century advert.

Right: Bob Leppan in the wild Gyronaut X-1, which was powered by two 650cc TR6 engines and reached over 245mph.

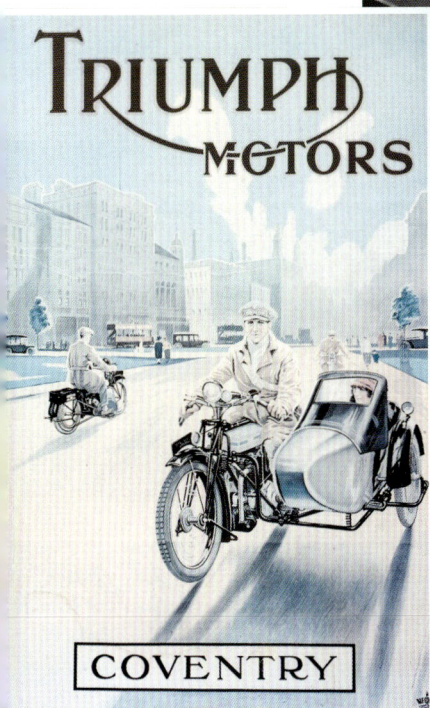

Left: Sidecars – or 'outfits' – were hugely popular in the first half of the 1900s. Triumph's reliable power made them a go-to brand.

Right: Despatch riders for the Women's Royal Naval Service (Wrens), attached to the Royal Navy Admiralty, sit astride their Triumph 350cc 3SW motorcycles on 1 June 1942, London.

Above: Johnny Allen poses with the 'Texas Ceegar' at the Cycle and Motor Cycle Show, Earl's Court, 1955. The streamliner would hit over 214mph.

Right: Triumphs were used by police around the globe, as shown here in France, 1955.

Opposite: Huge movie star Steve McQueen in Erfurt, East Germany. He rode for the first all-American team in the ISDT – International Six Days Trial, or the 'Olympics of motorcycling' – in the 1964 event.

Opposite: Marlon Brando and the iconic 1950 Triumph Thunderbird on the film set of *The Wild One*, 1953.

Above: The most famous movie bike scene ever – Bud Ekins doubles for his friend Steve McQueen in *The Great Escape*.

Below: Launched in 1915, Triumph's Model H was loved by soldiers in the First World War and is the bike most associated with the 'Trusty Triumph' nickname.

Above and below: Triumph's famous – and infamous – Meriden factory. These photos were taken in 1975, during the Norton Villiers Triumph period of disruption.

titled Black Rebels Motorcycle Club. He rides into a town and wades into a plot involving theft, fighting, drinking, crashes and, of course, romance. Hey, it's the movies.

When the film was being made, Triumph's US distributor Bill Johnson tried to get it stopped. Brando's character was riding a 1950 Thunderbird and the film's portrayal of bikers as drunken louts and general hoodlums went against Johnson's desire to promote motorcycling as a wholesome activity. He failed. The next angle was to try and get the Triumph's tank badges removed. That failed too. The Thunderbird was used as planned and was as high-flying in the film as Brando himself.

Despite Johnson's fears, it had a positive effect. *The Wild One* caused a bit of controversy, being uncertificated by the British Board of Film Censors and effectively banned for 14 years – which obviously inspired a generation of easily influenced young men to model themselves on Brando's character. Black leather jacket, turned-up jeans, questionable cap, roll-up cigarette – the lot. And that of course meant riding a Meriden-made bike. Triumph had stumbled into what today would be called 'product placement'.

One fellow who was inspired by the film was another young actor going by James Dean. Riding since his mid-teens, Dean had owned a Czech-made CZ, a British Enfield and an American-built Indian. When he moved to Los Angeles after landing his first starring role in the film *East of Eden*, he added to his fleet by buying himself a T110 Tiger. A couple of days after filming concluded, Dean popped back to Ted Evans Motorcycles, Culver City, California, and swapped his T110 for a TR5 Trophy, which he modified with a boisterous open exhaust, knobbly tyres and higher handlebars. He also attached the pillion seat backwards, to replicate the look of the one on the Thunderbird in *The Wild One* – he was a bit of a Brando fan.

Dean stored his Indian at a garage in Greenwich Village, where he met a young bike racer who was using his winnings plus the bit of cash he earned as a part-time mechanic to pay for acting classes. The two hit it off. The man's name was Terence Stephen McQueen ...

James Dean was killed in September 1955 when he crashed his Porsche Spyder car. The second film he'd starred in, *Rebel Without a Cause*, was released just four weeks later. Dean became an icon overnight, not just in the USA but around the world, and remains so to this day. With his known love of Triumphs, the British factory basked in the reflected celebrity glory.

Dean's TR5 was sold back to the original dealer after his death; it got altered and raced, but in the 1980s, his cousin bought it and restored it to how it had been when the international superstar had owned it. The bike went on display in a museum in Indiana, where Dean was from.

PRICELESS

Those Thunderbird-powered TR5s from the ISDT finally made production in 1956. The new TR6 Trophy was aimed at the cross-country events that were becoming hugely popular in America, and to launch the bike, Triumph entered three standard showroom examples in the Californian Big Bear Motorcycle Run. This was a wondrously chaotic desert race where hundreds of riders lined up handlebar-to-handlebar and streaked off across the open scrub. It was such a popular event that 1,000 riders turned up for the 1960 running, causing the flustered Highway Patrol all sorts of traffic headaches and resulting in the amazing spectacle being banned.

At the 1956 encounter, the new TR6s were ridden by Bill Postel, Arvin Cox and Bud Ekins (there's that name again) and they ended the wild event in first, second and third, having led the entire race. It laid the foundation for Triumph and the TR6 Trophy dominating off-road racing in the USA for the following decade. The TR6 and the T110 had quickly become the Triumphs in demand, pushing the brand to the fore in racing around the world, whether on hard surfaces or loose stuff. Triumphs didn't just have model names promising speed, they had proven performance.

As well as being a top-class off-road racer, Ekins ran the largest Triumph dealership in the USA at Sherman Oaks, California, helped by his brother Dave – another celebrated dirt rider. The popularity of America's large-scale desert racing and high-profile off-road events had caused a boom in what were known as 'desert sleds'. These were bikes that were stripped back, lightened, tweaked and enhanced for fooling around in the dust, rocks and sand, just like the racers, but that were road registered. Triumph's T100, T110 and TR6 were the bikes to have. Owners would head into the desert simply for the joy of riding around on motorcycles with their buddies and the Ekins brothers were at the centre of the movement.

In around 1960, Bud had a lightly used, year-old Triumph on his sales floor. It had been bought by Norman Powell, son of actor Dick Powell, but his wife wouldn't allow him to keep the bike, so it ended up back in the dealership. Ekins sold it on – to Steve McQueen.

McQueen had a tough upbringing. Coming from a broken home, he left school early, spent a period in the Boys Republic Reform School and joined the US Marine Corps when he was 17. But he'd always been attracted to things with engines and wheels. He helped an older friend build a Ford V8-powered hot-rod when he was just 12, and in the Marines, he and some colleagues took it upon themselves to tune the engine in their old tank. After the Marines, Steve put himself through acting classes, funded by that job at the bike garage and also by his racing – starting out riding a dilapidated Indian, McQueen went from winning a few bucks in illegal street races to getting proper winnings at official events. He could definitely ride; in fact, McQueen was so skilled that a career as a professional racer was a serious consideration. (In the early 1960s, he was offered a job as a works racing driver for British factory Cooper, too.)

But Steve was quite handy at acting as well. Moving from stage to screen, McQueen relocated to California in 1956 and was on the path to becoming a major Hollywood star – and the life that came with it afforded easy access to whatever two-wheel delights (and four-wheelers too) that he fancied.

'There were always interesting Hollywood people hanging around the shop', recalled Dave Ekins in *McQueen's Motorcycles* by Matt Stone. 'Steve McQueen and Robert Wagner were just two of the big names who would just come through the alleyway of the shop, give us a nod, and make their way unnoticed to the local hot dog stand.' His brother Bud wasn't bothered by any don't-you-know-who-I-am nonsense, and McQueen's cool, laidback, anti-hero persona was miles away from the showbiz glitz. With an obvious shared interest in bikes, the pair hit it off. 'Steve started hanging around my motorcycle dealership shop', remembered Bud Ekins in *McQueen's Motorcycles*. 'He saw all these bikes there that didn't have lights on them and they had number plates and skid plates, and all that kinda crap. He wanted to know what that was all about, so I told him about desert racing. I asked him to come out with us. He came out one time, and that was it. He was positively hooked.'

In 1962, McQueen casually asked Ekins if he wanted to head with him to Germany to help with a new movie. There was some motorcycle riding in it and, with his similar physical build and hair colour, Bud could be the Hollywood star's double for the serious action.

The film was *The Great Escape*. The movie McQueen is most famous for, and the one that cemented his reputation and helped him become the world's highest-paid actor by 1970, contains the most famous movie motorcycle action of all time. Based loosely on the true story of allied officers escaping from a Nazi prisoner of war camp in the Second World War, the leading actor and his director rewrote the script to include 'a hairy motorcycle chase', as McQueen put it in Matt Stone's book. His character, Captain Virgil Hilts, breaks out of the camp and steals a German soldier's bike, uniform and gun, before being chased by a swarm of disgruntled guards. The Germans should have been riding period BMWs, but the producers were concerned the aging machinery wouldn't cope with what they had in store – and so the film crew used 649cc Triumph TR6s with the badges removed, weathered military colours, blacked-out brightwork and headlamps, and old seats and luggage racks to make them look … well, nice and old.

There was a gaggle of German stunt riders ready and waiting, but McQueen did much of the riding himself. In fact, he was so much speedier over the rough terrain that in much of the film the footage is of the Hollywood star chasing himself – he played both roles. Bud Ekins also played a pursuing German, as well as doing any of the action that the producers considered too risky for their highly paid leading actor.

One such risk was the scene for which the movie will forever be famous. Trapped on all sides, the only way out for McQueen's character is to ride a grassy incline at speed and jump a large barbed-wire fence to freedom. CGI and other modern-day trickery didn't exist, and so the only way to make the huge leap look right was to do it, for real, at speed. McQueen tried a few practice jumps, but he was still new to off-road riding and so his friend Ekins stepped in. The iconic jump was done, helmetless and wearing casual clothes, in one take.

Released in summer 1963, and with a cast that also included famous names like Charles Bronson, James Coburn, Donald Pleasence and James Garner, *The Great Escape* had one of the highest box-office takings of the year – $11.7 million, or $120,500,000 today. It was nominated for Golden Globes and Oscars, and McQueen won the Best Actor award at the Moscow Film Festival. The friendship between Ekins and McQueen blossomed, and the pair would work together on many other movies.

You couldn't put a price on the positive publicity for Triumph. Association with McQueen and the smash-hit movie did wonders for the brand during the 1960s and 1970s. And the 1980s … in fact, even today it's something advertisers and eager marketing executives can rely on to stir interest and provoke buyers. There were Steve McQueen limited editions of the modern-day T100 in 2012 and the Scrambler 1200 in 2021. And in 2019, famous British road-racer Guy Martin reenacted the legendary leap for his TV show *Guy Martin's Great Escape* on a modern-day Triumph.

CATCH US IF YOU CAN

Circuit and off-road success with the T100, T110 and TR6 had done Triumph's reputation and sales figures, and Turner's ego, the world of good. But at the same time as all the movies were being made and the celebrity endorsement was happening, Triumph motorcycles started going really, *really* quickly.

Bludgeoning along preposterously fast in a straight line became a bit of a global fascination through the 1950s. Ever-growing engine capacities and climbing power outputs were allowing ever-more unlikely speeds to be achieved. German manufacturer NSU were particularly obsessed, due in no small part to the pestering of Wilhelm Herz, who raced their machines on round-and-round circuits. He convinced NSU to support a record-breaking venture using a radical bodywork shell made by pioneering aerodynamicist Reinhard Freiherr von Koenig-Fachsenfeld. Powered by a supercharged 500cc engine, Herz rode the distinctive, pointy-shaped creation to 180mph on the autobahn between Munich and Ingolstadt – yes, a public road – in April 1951. It was a new world record speed for a motorcycle (and NSU set seven other various class records the same year too).

Four years later, the goalposts moved again. This time the bike was a Vincent V-twin, ridden by a New Zealander called Russell Wright. He'd already set an NZ record on a British-built Vincent he imported using cash saved working as a builder, hitting 140mph on a road just outside Christchurch, but in July 1955, he set a new all-out record too. The model of bike was the Black Lightning, a competition version of Vincent's legendary 998cc V-twin Black Shadow road bike, of which only 34 were made. Already making 70hp and good for 150mph straight from the factory, Wright had the engine tweaked and wrapped the bike in an aerodynamic shell, and then proceeded to scurry along in front of FIM officials to record a two-way average (speeds recorded in both directions to avoid using weather or surface conditions for an advantage) of 185mph. Not on a runway or an expansive motorway. Not even on a wide-open beach. No, it was down a narrow country lane lined with bushes, barbed-wire fencing and nosey spectators who were standing literally on the edge of the road as Wright bellowed past. Eek.

Everyone now recognized that 200mph was no longer hiding over the horizon but, if they stretched hard enough, within reach. Herz was the first to get there. In 1956, NSU shipped themselves out to the Bonneville Salt Flats, Tooele County, Utah, USA, a truly vast open expanse of hard-packed salt. Used for setting speed records since the early 1900s, there was a 'speed week' every August and a 'world of speed' a few weeks later, where the Southern California Timing Association and the Utah Salt Flats Racing Association ran officially governed gatherings. Officials from the FIM would turn up for special runs too, as they did in July to witness Herz becoming the first person to ride a motorcycle at over 200mph, with a two-way average of 211mph on his supercharged NSU.

Passing the magical 'double ton' inspired a new generation of record breakers and a stream of bigger, more powerful and increasingly advanced machinery. Triumph would be front and centre. And it all started with a couple of US hot-rodders: an airline pilot named J. H. Mangham (known as 'Stormy') and his engine-tuning mate Jack Wilson, with their cigar-shaped streamliner known as the Texas Ceegar.

Imagine a round-nosed tube that's over 4.5m (14 feet) long and only 600mm (24in) wide, with a wheel just about visible protruding underneath at each end and the rider's helmet sticking out halfway along the top. That was the Ceegar. Using a chromoly steel stube chassis, it was built to accept twin-cylinder Triumph engines, using either a 498cc T100 engine for attempting records in the 500cc class or a 649cc Thunderbird motor for the larger classes. It was the Thunderbird making its mark again.

During 1954, the Texas Ceegar had scythed along the salt at 155mph on regular from-the-pump petrol, so the duo returned in 1955 with a man called Johnny Allen at the controls. The owner of a chrome plating business and a sponsored and successful AMA racer, Allen's flat-track career had ended due to a leg injury and so he fancied going outrageously fast instead. He'd already set a record for standard machines, and his involvement persuaded distributor Bill Johnson to get involved. With Meriden sending special Dunlop tyres, Allen covered the measured flying kilometre at a two-way average of 193.7mph. Quite obviously faster than Wright, the record holder at the time, it was only recognized by the AMA and not the FIM, though, as the former wasn't affiliated with the latter. So it was fast – but it wasn't official.

When NSU and intrepid Herz battered their way to 211mph the following year, Allen was ready to retaliate. Although Triumph had offered to supply a fancy aluminium cylinder head, Mangham and Wilson modified their existing Thunderbird engine's iron head to accept some enormous GP carburettors and fuelled the bike up with nitromethane, the highly explosive stuff that they used to pour in rockets and that makes your eyes stream. Fitted with new and improved aerodynamic bodywork, in September 1956 – just two months after

Herz's new record – the bike recorded a two-way speed of 214.17mph. This time overseen by pernickety types from both the AMA and the FIM, it was the fastest motorcycle ever.

Briefly, at least. The FIM decided shortly after to disregard it as a world record over some pedantic timing technicality. The AMA upheld it, however – and so, crucially, did Edward Turner, who decided that every Triumph would leave the factory wearing a sticker that proudly proclaimed 'World Motorcycle Speed Record Holder'. This showiness resulted in a legal bunfight between Meriden and the FIM, with Triumph suspended from FIM activities for a while, but it didn't stop the British brand dominating speed records for the next 15 years. And the aggro was all worth it as the benefit to the brand was huge.

Which was helpful, as away from the thrills of the salt flats, things had become somewhat shaky. The US market continued to swell, but home-market bike sales were declining. Britain, France and Israel invaded Egypt in 1956 to try to get control of the Suez Canal, which didn't do Britain's international relations any favours and caused shortages of petrol and oil. Scooters were prospering, being cheaper to both buy and run. But Turner's response with the BSA-built Tigress scooter, plus enclosed 'bathtub' styling on a new swarm of affordable 348cc twin-cylinder Twenty-one models, was about as popular as jelly trousers.

The innovative new 'Slickshift' system introduced on 500s and 650s, where you could change gear without the clutch, was equally shunned. Triumph's boss was also distracted by designing V8 engines for the Daimler car range (Jack Sangster had become chairman of BSA in 1956 and made Edward the chief executive for all their automotive work, which included Triumph, BSA, Ariel, the firm that made London's black cabs, and Daimler).

Triumph turned things around and made the most of their record attempts with a brand-new model for 1959. Returning to the brand's famed attributes of performance, style and quality, they based the design on the existing 649cc parallel-twin engine. The new bike had a 'splayed port' cylinder head carrying two carburettors, rather than the usual one. The often-fragile, three-piece crankshaft used in the T110 was swapped for a forged, stronger, one-piece item. With an increased compression ratio and larger-diameter exhausts, the power output soared by 10 per cent, from 42 to 46hp. Tested at over 120mph at the Motor Industry Research Association (MIRA) test ground at Nuneaton, it was christened the T120 Bonneville – named in recognition of Allen's achievements and, no doubt, to supply a poke in the eye to a few FIM stuffed shirts.

Edward Turner hadn't been convinced that a high-performance, twin-carb 650 was the right thing to do. Neale Shilton, the police fleet sales manager, is often credited with the idea for the model, while Turner is quoted in his biography as thinking it would 'lead us to Carey Street' (where the bankruptcy court was located). He didn't pass the 1959 model for production until August 1958. And the T120's press debut was almost a disaster. A selection of Triumph big bosses took the 1959 model line-up to a swanky hotel in Shropshire, stuffed the assembled media with fine dining on the Friday night, and then let them ride the new bikes on Saturday morning. Edward Turner was supposed to start off on the Bonneville … but the headline new machine wouldn't start, and so was left behind.

It mattered not a bit. The bike's initial look-at-me tangerine, grey and black paint might not have been to everyone's taste, but the new T120 Bonneville was the runaway star of the Earl's Court Motorcycle Show in November 1958. Its power and speed were unprecedented. Its name was inspired. Costing £294 8s 3d, it was the new benchmark for sporting motorcycles. 'The Triumph Bonneville 120 offers the highest performance available today from a standard production motorcycle,' gushed advertising. 'It is intended primarily for the really knowledgeable enthusiast who can appreciate and use the power provided. Although its performance is quite exceptional it is tractable and quiet in the best Triumph tradition.'

The Meriden factory had nailed it. The new 'Bonnie' would become the bestselling British twin-cylinder bike ever, arguably the most significant model of all time and a style icon around the world. That first Triumph bought by the king of cool, Steve McQueen? It was a Bonneville.

There's not been a more famous motorcycle. When you say the word 'Bonneville', everyone knows you're talking about a Triumph – whether they're motorcyclists or not.

CHAPTER 7

THE BIKE TO BE ON

ENDORSED BY THE KING OF COOL

It's Wednesday 11 September 1963 in bustling London. The 1st Earl of Stockton, Harold Macmillan, is the UK's prime minister, local football club Tottenham Hotspur recently became the first English team to win the European Cup, and it's gloriously warm for early autumn. The 28°C heat and subtle breeze make it feel like it's the height of summer.

You're strolling through the city doing a spot of shopping, looking in the new 'boutique' shops that are springing up everywhere selling striking, vibrant, modern fashion aimed specifically at younger buyers. You no longer need to dress like your parents. Income is at its highest since the Second World War and you fancy splashing some newfound disposable income on something by of-the-moment designer John Stephen. Or perhaps by Mary Quant. Just like you've seen people wearing on that new *Ready Steady Go!* live music programme that's recently started on ITV every Friday evening, featuring excited teens, wall-to-wall pop stars and the catchphrase 'The weekend starts here!'

Traffic flows past steadily – the constant stream of FX4 black cabs and towering red Routemaster buses dotted with Austin 1100s, the decade's bestselling car (and the model that would find stardom in later years for being royally thrashed with a branch by a livid Basil Fawlty in iconic sitcom *Fawlty Towers*). The fabulously uplifting 'She Loves You' by new hit band The Beatles carries on the air from someone's wireless and you stop at a shop window to gaze at one of those new-fangled push-button telephones.

And then it happens.

A distinct burble of twin-cylinder motorcycle, the flash from glinting brightwork – and Hollywood actor Steve McQueen rumbles past. Helmetless, no gloves, oozing his casual style in a Triumph T-shirt, he slices between traffic down the centreline … and is gone.

Just think about that for a moment. It's a normal midweek day, folk going about their business, and the superstar lead from *The Great Escape* film that's currently showing and drawing huge crowds into cinemas has just ridden past. No chaperone or bodyguards, no big fanfare – just a bloke out riding his motorbike. Imagine strolling through a city today and seeing Tom Holland thrumming past, or Chris Hemsworth, or any other modern-day movie super-celebrity. It simply wouldn't happen.

As this was Steve McQueen, it wasn't just *any* bike. The machine he was threading through London was a racer. One of four bought by Triumph America's West Coast distributor Johnson Motors, it was a 650cc TR6SC model – registration number BNX822B – that McQueen would be racing in the following year's ISDT, in what was then East Germany. He was running in the new engine himself by swanning around London.

First held in Carlisle, just south of the English–Scottish border, way back in 1913, we already know the ISDT was – and still is, under its current International Six Days Enduro (ISDE) moniker – a punishing test for both rider and machine. Teams representing their country compete for trophies in a variety of categories: junior, national, women and manufacturer teams of three or four riders, with individual gold, silver or bronze medals for the individuals. More than 1,200 miles can be covered over the six days of competition, on every manner of surface and in increasingly arduous conditions. Strict rules inflicted on competitors cover time allowances for each stage. Spares and tools must be carried. Only the riders can do maintenance work or replace motorcycle parts. It's a team sport, but one that requires huge individual strength and resourcefulness.

A serious challenge for even the most hardened off-road rider, Bud Ekins would sum up the 1964 ISDT perfectly in *McQueen's Motorcycles*: 'Olympic cross-country skiing, but on motorcycles, running through a forest behind the Iron Curtain, on a course that was changed every day, on the worst surfaces you can imagine, and with ever-changing weather.'

This doesn't sound like the sort of place you expect to find an A-list celebrity. However, with his friendship with McQueen strengthened after working together during filming of *The Great Escape*, Ekins was well aware of the superstar's desire to compete in the legendary mud-plugging event. Ekins knew what the ISDT entailed: after competing in scrambles and European motocross during the previous decade, he'd done his first ISDT in 1961 and won a silver medal (for finishing within 25 per cent of the winner's time), then secured gold gongs (for getting within 10 per cent of the winning time) in 1962 and 1963. And he knew that McQueen was capable of not only surviving the event but of getting a medal.

The four-rider team Ekins pulled together for the 1964 event was the first ever all-American squad. Actually, make that the first all-Californian team. Bud selected teammates who he was either related to, good friends with or connected to through racing – his brother Dave, a seasoned off-road competitor; Cliff Coleman, an imposing figure who pioneered off-road racing in the US and who also happened to direct the odd movie; and McQueen. Reserve rider was John Steen, a well-known off-road parts specialist. Rules required the team to have bikes across different capacity classes, so McQueen and Coleman had 650cc bikes while their three colleagues piloted the 500cc T100SC Sports Tiger model.

As we know, Triumph had form in the ISDT and knew what to expect. Their bikes had frequently been deployed in the rigorous trial and they had been used by the British team to secure five major wins between 1948 and 1953. Supplying machines for a world-famous movie star and his mates to race in this notoriously testing event was still significant for the brand, however. There could be no better endorsement than an A-lister choosing Triumphs for his high-profile, headline-grabbing antics.

Further commendation was provided by the team's T100SCs and TR6SCs being standard machines. Nowadays, the ISDE is populated by specialist enduro bikes designed to survive being flung at rock faces and hurled down unlikely mountainsides, but back in the 1960s, the machinery used was just like that which you or I could wander into a showroom and buy ourselves. Standard road bikes. Proof if ever there was of the capabilities of the British motorcycles and the faith placed in them by loyal riders.

Turning up at the ISDT with unprepared bikes would be like going to dig the allotment wearing slippers, however, and so the Triumphs did receive some tweaks. Sizeable mudguards, low-slung dual exhausts, road tyres and lots of gleaming chrome are not the sort of things that'd be at the top of the 'must haves' list. So McQueen, Ekins and the team got hands-on in preparing the Triumphs in the workshops of Comerfords Ltd in Thames Ditton, Surrey, a large and respected dealer who'd found much success with their Comerford Wallis speedway machines during the 1930s and who were well known for their focus on dirt bikes. The Americans helped fit the bikes with longer-travel suspension to deal with the rough surfaces and knobbly tyres to bite into loose, sloppy terrain, and they modified the air filter housings to allow the engines to breathe better. Map holders were added to the fuel tanks, and tools and spares were hidden under the seats and attached to various parts of the bikes, including a large pair of grips strapped to the handlebars on McQueen's bike. Numberboards were bolted on too, Steve's bike wearing a number that would become famous: 278.

The riders practised not only their skills at the controls but also how to maintain and repair the motorcycles – and of course, McQueen ran in his bike's air-cooled twin-cylinder engine on London's streets.

LONG-REACHING INFLUENCE

In the run up to the ISDT, things very nearly went rather wrong. McQueen stood in some oil and lost his footing while unloading bikes at Ekin's shop, resulting in a cast over his left wrist. Less than ideal in the run-up to such a high-profile competition, it was also somewhat inconvenient given McQueen's upcoming appearance as a presenter at the Academy Awards. Fortunately, it healed quickly enough for the cast to come off before the team headed into Europe.

Things started well in East Germany for the quartet of Americans. Despite a broken fuel tank bracket on McQueen's bike, the team finished the first day with a strong time and no penalty points – in fact, they earned bonus marks for their performance. McQueen had once said that he didn't know if he was a bike racer who acted or an actor who raced bikes – but his ISDT shenanigans seemed to be confirming it was the former, with the squad putting in an even stronger performance on day two. They were on gold medal pace.

Things got a little less cheery from day three. Ekins collided with a bridge and broke his ankle, taking himself out of the event. After earlier bumping into teammate Coleman and damaging his bike's exhaust, McQueen had to take avoiding action when charging down a road supposedly closed to traffic and meeting a lad on a scooter coming the other way. His swerving bike careered into a ditch where the movie star was tossed over the handlebars, smashing his goggles and cutting his face, and leaving him visibly in shock. With his TR6SC damaged beyond repair, his ISDT was over. The American all-stars were one rider short of the required four, but Dave Ekins, Coleman and reserve jockey Steen were permitted to continue as individuals (Ekins achieved a gold medal; Coleman would have too, but he was disqualified for leaving a tool behind in a service area.)

Despite failing to finish, the exploits of McQueen and his Triumph captured public imagination, especially in the USA where the team's adventures were the cover story for *Modern Cycle*'s October 1964 edition. And the number 278 Triumph arguably became as famous as its celebrated rider.

Movie production schedules prevented McQueen from fulfilling his craving to have another bash at the ISDT in 1965, but a straightened-out BNX822B took part, ridden by Ed Kretz Jr (the son of Ed 'Iron Man' Kretz, the winner of the first-ever running of the famous Daytona 200). It changed hands in 1967 and became the property of another off-road racer, Frank Danielson.

Dirt and desert racing was booming on the Baja Peninsula in Mexico, and the Triumph was entered into the Baja 1000 – a gruelling 1,000-mile route devised with help of a certain Bud Ekins and first ridden by Dave Ekins. The bike raced it three times, winning its class fitted with a sidecar. Yes, the already famous ex-McQueen Triumph was turned into an outfit with a 'chair' bolted to the side.

Years later, a chap by the name of Sean Kelly acquired the rights to the Johnson Motors name. Kelly tried to unearth the whereabouts of the five bikes used by the US squad, and though the locations of four remained unknown he tracked down Danielson, owner of McQueen's bike. Kelly bought not only Steve's TR6SC but also his Barbour wax cotton jacket with the American flag embroidered on the chest and McQueen's original gloves. The bike and clothing went on display at his motorcycle clothing and accessories store in Pasadena, California.

BNX822B has influenced many home-adapted bikes over the years – and also a dead-ringer replica too. Barbour, esteemed makers of wax cotton bike gear, whose clothing was used by almost every British

ISDT team from 1936 to 1977 and who kitted out the USA team in 1964, commissioned Ace Classics to recreate the famous Triumph. Built using new components around an original 1964 Trophy frame, the British twin-cylinder Triumph specialists pored over period photographs to perfectly replicate the ISDT modifications and parts used on the original. The result – complete with Hi-fi Scarlet and Silver Sheen paint, 278 numberboards and even the registration BNX822B – would fool anyone. It was so well received by fans of the actor and the Triumph brand that Ace started taking commissions for further replicas.

Such is the long-standing influence of the King of Cool's racing antics – and of the legendary Triumph name.

CELEBRITY ASSOCIATION

There's no doubt that McQueen's connections with Triumph are the strongest and best known. But in the same decade that brought us the American's smash-hit *The Great Escape* film and his celebrated ISDT exploits, a long list of other people in the spotlight selected Triumphs for their silver-screen appearances, as their mode of transport or for carrying out improbable, crowd-pleasing stunts.

Often claimed to be one of the greatest songwriters of all time, American musician Robert Allen Zimmerman – better known across the world as Bob Dylan – got into bikes at an early age. In his *Chronicles* autobiography, he makes many references to Harley-Davidson bikes and talks about how he was something of a 'rough, tough' character at a time when riding bikes could be seen as a little maverick. His first motorcycle, bought while he was still a teenager, was a Harley-Davidson 45 (a 746cc 'flathead' air-cooled V-twin with around 21hp and the basis for the bikes used by the US military). But after moving from Greenwich Village to Woodstock, New York, in 1964, Dylan bought himself a new Triumph T100SR. The 498cc parallel-twin machine became his main form of transport and the music superstar was often seen with other musicians and artists perched on the bike's pillion seat. Yet another super-cool global star choosing Triumph motorcycles over everything else.

Dylan crashed his T100SR near his manager's house, not far from Woodstock, on 29 July 1966. Though a detailed explanation of what happened has never been disclosed, the star says he was blinded by the sun – and so either lost control or simply ran off the road. He suffered lacerations to his face, concussion and cracked vertebrae in his back. Or at least, that's what he claims. Despite Dylan later saying that he spent a week in hospital following the incident, there's no official record of this – or indeed of the crash itself, to which no ambulance was called. Not sure about you, but if I'd sustained those sorts of injuries, I'd fancy a trip in a nice comfortable white van with blue lights on the roof to be looked after by attentive medical folk. This has given rise to a common theory that the hectic, non-stop lifestyle of a 1960s music star became too much for the still-young Dylan and the bike crash story was fabricated to allow the singer to escape the limelight for a while. Whatever truly happened, an upcoming tour was cancelled and the American singer-songwriter became something of a recluse – for the next eight years, he was rarely seen, and public performances were extremely few and far between. What happened to his often-photographed Triumph has been lost to history, although Dylan filed the bike's 'lost registration plates' with the State of New York Department of Motor Vehicles in 1967.

Perhaps the biggest star to fall head over heels for the legendary British bike brand was The King himself. Singer, film star and hip-waggler Elvis Presley started his two-wheeled antics on a little 165cc

Harley-Davidson two-stroke, before progressing to the firm's far-better-known big V-twins. He bought a couple of 305cc Honda CA77 Dreams so he could go out riding with his wife Priscilla too. But in 1965, while making the *Frankie and Johnny* musical in Hollywood, he got to sample a Triumph T120 Bonneville. It had been bought from Robertson & Sons, Santa Monica Boulevard, by Jerry Schilling, who was part of Elvis's group of friends known as the 'Memphis Mafia'. Presley was so smitten with the bike that he ordered his transport manager to buy nine brand-new Triumphs for him and his mates – immediately, right then, that day. Robertson's supplied seven bikes by that evening, a mixture of T120s and TR6s, with the extra two machines finally being sourced a couple of days later. The Memphis Mafia spent the summer bellowing around on British twins. Elvis would later ride a Triumph desert sled (albeit briefly) in his questionable 1968 flick *Stay Away, Joe*.

In summer 2024, Triumph released an Elvis Presley Limited Edition version of the current Bonneville, with one-off paint, special graphics and a handlebar clamp etched with his signature.

Most people connect stuntman Evel Knievel (born Robert Craig Knievel in 1938) with riding Harley-Davidson 750s. The most famous jumper of motorcycles of all time, he launched very many of the American-made V-twins into the air, tossed them into the side of things and bounced them off the floor between 1970 and 1977 (when the company withdrew sponsorship following Knievel's conviction for assault). Sometimes, he even managed to get them onto the landing ramp. However, it was Triumphs that the world's best-known motorcycle exhibitionist chose to literally launch his career.

After starting out by leaping over a pit of rattlesnakes and a couple of bemused lions (yes, really) on a 250cc Honda, the Montana-born daredevil did a few shows on a Norton before switching to the renowned T120 Bonneville in 1967. It's the Triumph that he rode for perhaps his most famous jump – the Caesars Palace leap in Las Vagas in 1968. Well, make that his most famous *attempted* jump …

Knievel was always looking for bigger, more impressive and more preposterous things to do with his bike. Spotting the fountains outside Caesars Palace casino when visiting the Convention Centre to watch some boxing matches, an idea formed for a true showstopper. After meeting with the casino boss Jay Sarno and convincing him to let it go ahead (which he did by faking TV company ABC's interest in broadcasting the leap live), the stage was set for a spectacular show on New Year's Eve, 1967. It would be Knievel's longest jump to date at 43 metres (141 feet).

These days, we see riders on modern motocross machines doing ludicrous jumps. They use specially prepped machines, and they perform stunts that have been calculated carefully and simulated. The ramps are millimetre perfect; the precise speed and angle and effect of the breeze and every other factor nailed down exactly. Things were very different in Evel's day. Planning and ramp design was more along the lines of 'that'll probably be alright', which is part of the reason why the stars-and-stripes stuntman had so many bone-wrecking spills. Like the one at Caesars on his Bonnie. Later claiming the bike's twin-cylinder engine unexpectedly lost power on the launch ramp, Knievel's flight wasn't long enough, and he landed on the 'safety ramp'. This was a flat section designed for such a situation, but simply propped up by the roof of a van. The impact wrenched the handlebars out of his grip and sent him tumbling across the car park of the adjacent hotel, breaking his femur and pelvis, fracturing both ankles, a hip and a wrist, and giving himself concussion. The Triumph was, understandably, also slightly worse for wear.

He might have failed in (his usual) spectacular fashion but the Caesars Palace carry-on brought Evel fame, especially as he was invited onto the late-night TV chat show of comedian Joey Bishop in March 1968. This gained Knievel national exposure; by the end of the year he was reputedly making $25,000 per stunt show. Quite a wedge of cash in the late sixties. After riding (and falling off) Harley-Davidsons for the rest of his career, Knievel returned to Triumphs after retiring, performing wheelies on a T120 to help start the stunting career of his son Robbie.

At the same time as being piloted by the world's favourite stuntman, Triumph's reputation and public perception was further bolstered by the use of their bikes by another big-name star, Clint Eastwood. Playing the character Walt Coogan, a rural copper who travels to New York in pursuit of a fugitive, the 1968 film *Coogan's Bluff* has Eastwood riding a 1967 Bonneville. It was a new bike, bought for the movie and featuring the paint scheme of bikes produced in the latter half of the year, but with the model's standard tank-mounted rubber knee pads removed. The flick has Eastwood liberating the Bonnie from a passer-by who's been knocked off by the fleeing bad guy, who of course is also on a Triumph – a 1967 T100R Tiger – and engaging in a pursuit that's widely regarded as one of cinema's best motorcycle chases.

Though he had a stunt double for obvious reasons, it's clearly Eastwood riding the bike in much of the footage. And with the film regarded as the one that set up Clint's career, dictated his roles and defined movies of the genre for the next 25 years, the association with Triumph only helped put the British brand in an even brighter light.

IMPROVING THE BREED

It really should be no great shock that the famous and the daring chose Triumphs, especially those from the USA. Throughout the 1960s, the firm's American racing activities and high-profiles success confirmed their status as the bike to be on.

The long, flat, straight expanses of Daytona Beach in Florida had been used for land-speed record attempts since 1902. However, by the mid-1930s, the speed-obsessed drivers and riders had migrated to the smoother, wider and much longer Bonneville Salt Flats in

Utah, and so a local race promoter arranged to relocate a grand motorcycle race from Savannah, Georgia, onto a beach course at Daytona. Approved by the AMA, the race would be over 63 laps of the 3.2-mile course, and the first Daytona 200 ran in 1937. By the latter half of the 1950s it was becoming difficult to run these beach races, however. It was down to Daytona's rapid urban expansion and lots of people wanting to engage in more traditional beach activities, like sunbathing and eating ice-creams, and so funding was found to build a new tarmac oval with banked corners and a twisting infield circuit close to Daytona airport. Daytona International Speedway opened in 1959. The motorcycle race moved there in 1961, riders swapping from the flat track-style bikes used on the sand to Grand Prix-style road-racing machines.

The size, status and importance of the Daytona 200 grew swiftly through the decade. And Triumph was at the head of the action. Home-grown manufacturer Harley-Davidson was the company to beat in flat track, having dominated on the beach course through the 1950s, but going round and round in circles on a hard-paved surface presented a different challenge – and the 1962 event was a battle between Californian Dick Mann on a British made Matchless and Don Burnett from Massachusetts riding a Triumph. Reported on by *Cycle World* as a head-to-head that 'will without doubt go down in history as one of the best road races of all time', the two men duelled it out in a race filled with drama and edge-of-your-seat action. Mann had to take avoiding action and divert onto the grass when a slower rider slipped off in front of him. Harley-Davidson rider Neil Keen caused much commotion when he and his bike both caught fire during a refuelling pit stop. By halfway through the event, the leading duo of Mann and Burnett had lapped the entire rest of the field. The pair were in a class of their own.

After issues with a petrol supply pipe coming detached from his engine, Mann spent the final third of the race chipping away at

Burnett's lead, which had grown beyond 30 seconds. Tension grew and nails were nibbled shorter with each passing lap. The Matchless rider was desperate to make up ground and took to the grass on several more occasions while dealing with the (much slower) lapped riders. Calmer Burnett employed a steadier and more patient approach, controlling his lead without tangling with tired, emotional riders who might accidentally punt him into the greenery or even knock him off completely. The pair exited the final corner on the last lap just a few bike lengths apart but, despite using the slipstream, Mann couldn't coax his bike past Burnett's Triumph.

The British brand won their first ever Daytona 200 race – and with his average speed nudging almost 72mph, Don Burnett had beaten the previous year's record race time by almost seven minutes. Not seven seconds, as would be expected these days, but seven minutes. Staggering.

Harley-Davidson riders ramped up their efforts for the next three years to ensure the winner's trophy wasn't handed to some upstart spoiling their flagship American race on a foreign machine. The course layout changed too. Initially, there were worries that it wouldn't be wise to let motorcycles howl around the 31-degree banked corners of Daytona's outer oval, so they had used the in-field course and only strayed onto the straight bit of the oval to use the start/finish line. But someone must have said, 'Nah, they'll be alright', as from 1964, bikes were permitted to tear around the ominously steep slopes, the lap distance growing from two miles to almost four. And the Daytona spectacle became even greater.

Winning the flag-waving event was becoming increasingly important for manufacturers wishing to shove themselves into the limelight. This was important for Triumph, who had concerns about potential damage to their extremely lucrative American market from the new 450cc model from Honda, the rapidly growing Japanese firm. So, they decided on a big factory effort for 1966 and built something special.

Doug Hele and Bert Hopwood set to work on a new 500cc bike with overhead camshafts, but with concerns that they'd run out of development time the decision was made to upgrade the existing 498cc T100 model – a bike derived from Edward Turner's successful Speed Twin that had been in production since the late 1930s. To extract more power, the engine was fettled to allow larger valves, an increase in compression ratio and twin Amal GP racing carburettors. It now produced just shy of 46hp at 8500rpm – around 30 per cent more than standard. This hopped-up motor was placed into a new frame that was lower and stiffer than the road bike version, and made from Reynolds 531 tubing. Featuring 483mm (19in) wheels and aluminium fuel tanks swiped from BSA, four examples were built ready for Daytona and shipped to the USA. Another two bikes were made by Triumph's distributor Johnson Motors, with slightly less extreme engines.

As this was a full factory venture, it required top-flight riders, and so the squad included Gary Nixon (up-and-coming AMA rider), Dick Hammer (previous winner of Daytona's lightweight class) and Buddy Elmore. Skilled hands. However, practice at Daytona swiftly highlighted the fact that, yes, Hele's tuned engine was fast – but it was also delicate and rather prone to failure. The bikes were plagued with con-rod breakages and troublesome valve train issues. This concerned Nixon, who opted to ride one of the slower but more reliable T100s created by Johnson Motors; Hammer and Elmore stayed on the rapid but fragile works bikes from Meriden and struggled in qualifying – Elmore would start the race from a lowly forty-sixth on the grid.

Things looked like they'd deteriorate further in the race when Hammer's engine went pop. But Elmore's motor stayed together. Picking his way through the field, he caught leader and fellow Triumph rider Nixon, and the pair exchanged the lead repeatedly until Nixon was forced out of the skirmish due to a puncture. Elmore pushed on and brought victory for the Triumph factory, setting a new record average race speed of over 96mph and becoming a Daytona legend for his charge to victory from the back of the field. And on a bike that everyone thought wouldn't make it …

With Daytona happening early in the racing calendar, this success put Triumph on the front foot for the rest of the 1966 season in the USA. The AMA Grand National Championship was a fabulous multi-discipline series, with riders and teams competing in various road and dirt events through the season. Both Elmore and Nixon won other road races, and Nixon put Triumph at the front in flat-track racing, winning the prestigious meeting at the famous mile-long dirt oval in Springfield, Illinois, finishing overall runner-up in the championship. Well-known dirt specialist Bill Baird continued to dominate in National Enduro (think scrambles but over a long course), and with further wins in the 'steeplechase' TT Nationals (a cross between flat track and scrambles) and the Grand National Enduro series, Triumph made a huge impact in the United States. You could see Harley-Davidson's fingers tightening worriedly around their beloved AMA number one plate.

They were right to have concerns. Buoyed by his victory the previous year, Doug Hele further enhanced the T100 engine with cylinder head work and a new exhaust; peak power didn't increase by much, but it was delivered over a wider rev range, making the motor more flexible, easier to use and more reliable – it could also now hit over 130mph. With further changes to the frame, forks, brakes and wheels, it could be argued that it was an all-new machine – and one that dominated the 1967 Daytona 200.

With the previous year's star riders joined by Larry Palmgren and devilishly handsome Gene Romero, the British bikes ruled the race from start to finish. Nixon won, taking the average speed to over 98mph, and then continued his fine form. With further victories through the season on tarmac, flat track and short track (like flat track's dirt ovals but, well, not quite as long), the rider from Anadarko, Oklahoma, wrapped up the 1967 AMA Grand National Championship.

Triumph's first AMA title was a massive boost for the Meriden factory's already solid reputation. With the various disciplines involved, it highlighted the British bike's flexibility and adaptability, not just in the USA but around the world.

To drill the point home, the Triumph factory effort and rider Gary Nixon won the title again in 1968. Though they didn't manage to repeat the Daytona victory, there was success in assorted disciplines all across the States – and Triumph were quick to capitalize with their 'Look who's Number One again!' advertising campaign highlighting everything they'd managed over the year:

> *It takes a great bike and rider to win just one National Championship. Gary Nixon and Triumph just combined to win their second in a row. While Bill Baird was clinching his seventh straight National Enduro Championship on the Triumph. And other Triumph riders were winning National Championships in TT and Cross Country. And nobody managed to top Triumph's AMA Approved World's Speed Record ... So why should you miss out on the World's best and fastest bike? Make your move up to the Triumph.*

And there was even more international success to celebrate, thanks to a pig farmer from the small village of Little Shrewley, not far from Birmingham, England. Percy Tait was also a legendary Triumph test rider, who clocked up in excess of 1,000 miles a week on prototype and development bikes, and raced assorted Triumph machinery at the weekends. One such event happened to be the Belgian GP at the iconic and fearsomely fast 8.76-mile Spa-Francorchamps circuit.

Grands prix were being completely dominated by Italian brand MV Agusta. Their multi-cylinder, overhead cam, high-revving, bespoke race bikes were head and shoulders above the competition, which was largely British-made singles and a few twins. In the skilled hands of stars including British riders John Surtees, Mike Hailwood and Phil Read, not to mention annoyingly good-looking Italian legend Giacomo Agostini, MV won the premier 500cc class every single year from 1956 to 1974.

Though Triumph never officially backed a GP effort, Tait entered in Belgium on a development bike powered by a 498cc, pushrod, OHV twin. With its roots back in the old Speed Twin, there was no way he could live with the mighty MV. Sure enough, Agostini cleared off into the distance for one of his usual runaway victories. But heroic Tait bought his outdated and outclassed Triumph – based on a road model – home in second place, ahead of all the regulars and some specialist metal, with an eye-opening average speed of over 116mph. The only rider not to be caught and lapped by the flying Ago, he delivered Triumph's first-ever Grand Prix podium finish.

It would be Triumph's only GP podium until 2019, when the factory became the official engine supplier for the Moto2 class. There have since been podiums and wins aplenty, but it's a given – no other brand can win because everyone has to use Triumph's motor …

MOVING THE MARKER

You may have noticed Triumph's excited frothing about speed records in the US advertising quoted earlier. Along with pushing themselves on racetracks, they'd yet again been pushing the limits on the legendary salt at Bonneville. At the same time as Burnett was thrusting his machine over the line for Triumph's first Daytona 200 win in 1962, another American rider was using his British twin to go faster than ever before.

The 1960s are usually remembered as an era of peace and love and VW campervans with flowers painted on the side. But it was also a decade of jets and rockets and – literally – reaching for the moon. America and

Russia were going head-to-head in a 'space race'. The month after the Russian cosmonaut Yuri Gagarin became the first person in space on 12 April 1961, American president John F. Kennedy stuck his chest out and announced the eye-opening and hugely ambitious goal of sending a human safely to the moon (and hopefully bringing them back too) before the end of the decade. Talk about grabbing the world's attention.

The United States Airforce and the National Aeronautics and Space Administration (NASA to you and I) had also already started research with an experimental rocket-powered plane called the X-15. Crewed by plucky pilots keen to leave their mark in history, including Neil Armstrong (who'd become the first person to set foot on the surface of the moon) and Joe Engle (who would become commander of the Space Shuttle programme), the unfathomably fast X-15 was capable of nudging the edge of space and of travelling at over 4,500mph – a record for a powered aircraft with a human at the controls, which still stands today.

The futuristic jet age became accessible to normal folk too, with the arrival of jet-powered passenger aircraft completely revolutionizing travel. The first jet airliner, the de Havilland Comet, had suffered some tragic and highly publicized accidents after entering service in the 1950s but by the early 1960s, the rival Boeing 707 was delivering widespread jet propulsion. It could travel from Paris to New York in half the time of a traditional propellor plane, while carrying twice as many passengers. Remarkable. And, perhaps most significantly of all, in 1962, Hanna-Barbera released animated science fiction sitcom *The Jetsons*.

The jet age might have seemed a world away from the traditional and relatively simple air-cooled motorcycles coming off the end of the Triumph production line, but the two merged together to sensational effect. Joe Dudek was working as the chief mechanic for the aerospace division of North American Aviation at Redondo Beach, California. Inspired by the X-15 rocket plane, he built a streamliner – a machine shaped to be as aerodynamic as possible – for a land-speed record

Above: The last bike made at Meriden, the T140W TSS, next to their very first powered two-wheeler: the No. 1.

Below: Launched in 1959, the Bonneville was the defining 'big Brit twin'. This is a 1968 T120R – the best of the breed.

The Fonz (played by Henry Winkler) rode a
Triumph TR5 Trophy in hit US show *Happy Days*.
It was customized by Bud Ekins.

Above: The 1938 5T Speed Twin was Turner's masterpiece and redefined the shape of motorcycling.

Below: Daniel Craig as James Bond in *No Time to Die* (2021), on a Triumph Scrambler.

Above: The Rocket III was the largest series-production motorcycle of all time and achieved instant cult status.

Below: Developed with Indian brand Bajaj and launched in 2024, the Speed 400 was a huge hit and an immediate bestseller.

Above: Intended as the sportsbike in 'new' Triumph's modular line-up in 1991, the Daytona was a short-lived flop …

Below: … but the 1994 Speed Triple was a massive hit. The all-attitude 'streetfighter' model would go on to define Triumph.

Above: Developed with Williams and replicating the performance of the Speed Triple, the TE-1 was Triumph's very serious exploration of battery power.

Below: Guy Martin was chosen to pilot Triumph's most recent land-speed record attempt. The TT racer and TV celebrity achieved 274.2mph – the fastest Triumph of all time. So far …

Above: Triumph started supplying 765cc engines for the Moto2 championship in 2019. Álex Márquez (*front*) won the title.

Below: Simple yet capable, classy but affordable, the 2022 Tiger Sport 660 was Triumph's most popular UK model.

Launched in 1996, the T595 Daytona completely changed buyer perception of Triumph. It was a model that raised the brand towards their current elevated position.

attempt based around a tuned, bored-out (wider cylinder bores and larger pistons, to increase capacity) T120 Bonneville engine. Measuring over 5m (16 feet) in length, the fully enclosed two-wheeled tube featured retractable outriggers to support it while stationary, and an aircraft-style canopy that was fixed in position once the rider was aboard. Dudek didn't ride the bike himself, instead leaving that duty to Bill Johnson – not to be muddled with the Bill Johnson from Triumph's distributor, Johnson Motors.

At the annual Speed Week held at Bonneville in 1962, this intimidating, barking, gleaming mobile tube streaked its way into the record books. Previously, it had already gone faster than the 211.4mph 'official' record that had been set by Wilhelm Herz on a German NSU, but for various reasons the duo's exploits weren't recognized as a new record (hmm, sounds familiar …). There would be no such faff and disappointment this time. On 25 August, with the runs carried out under strict AMA sanction and overseen by Bonneville referee Earl Flanders, gritty Johnson took Dudek's creation to an average speed (taken over runs across the salt flats in both directions) of 230.27mph. It became the AMA-sanctioned 'world's fastest'. This still wasn't an international FIM-approved title, however, and so on 5 September, the team returned to the salt while being scrutinized by serious people with clipboards from the FIM.

First, they ran the bike on regular petrol for a new gasoline-fuelled record of 205mph, before emptying the tanks and refilling with nitromethane. The fuel used by drag racers (and once used in rockets) gave the Triumph that extra oomph required to go faster than Johnny Allen's unofficial Texas Ceegar record and reach a new, definite, underlined and undisputed motorcycle world land-speed record of 224.57mph.

Just imagine that. You're strapped into a long, thin tube with a deafening nitro-burning engine wedged in behind you, perched with your bum cheeks a few inches off the floor, and thundering across the disorientating white expanses of Bonneville at 3.75 miles every minute. Or, put another way, the length of a football pitch every second. Other bikes would go faster over the coming years, but the specification of Dudek and Johnson's bike meant that its class record – 'streamlined, altered frame/fuel' – would stand until 1992. In the ever-changing and constantly evolving environment of land-speed records, having the Triumph-powered device retain its title for 30 years is just remarkable. (The motorcycle itself, unfortunately, didn't last quite as long: it was destroyed in a fire in 1974.)

Triumph's excitable advertising experts obviously seized the opportunity to trumpet loudly about the firm yet again being the fastest manufacturer on the face of the planet – and they cited the AMA record of 230mph because, well, who wouldn't? But as impressive as this was, it was just the warm-up for what would terrorize the salt flats a mere three years later: the radical multiple-engine Gyronaut X-1.

NEW BREED OF RECORD BREAKERS

At the start of the 1950s, Bob Leppan formed a motorcycle club called the Satan Saints. It was made up of youths aged between 15 and 19 years old, and they'd meet in someone's garage in their black leather jackets and head out riding bikes. Triumph was the brand of choice. By 1959, Leppan was running a Triumph dealership in Detroit and building hotted-up bikes to take drag racing (where two riders sprint side by side over a quarter-mile strip). Most notable was a stretched machine powered by two 650cc engines. Knocked up by Leppan and his mechanic Jim Bruflodt and called Cannibal II, this hairy device won races all over America's Midwest as well as trophies at bike shows, thanks to the pair's obvious engineering skill.

By the early sixties, even Leppan's dual-engine creation was being outclassed by a new craze for bikes powered by comically oversize car engines. People like Elon Jack Potter – better known just as EJ Potter, or 'the Michigan Madman' – were somehow squeezing 327 cubic-inch (almost 5400cc) Chevrolet V8 motors into spindly two-wheel chassis, creating racers that were not only preposterously rapid but also hugely entertaining thanks to their wild, slewing, tyre-smoking runs. And so Bob and Jim turned their attentions to Bonneville instead, and in 1963 purchased a streamliner from Bill Martin in Burbank.

Having set a speed record for a Triumph Cub (130mph) with a streamlined bike built with his sons, Martin had made a larger version for an attempt at the outright record but was having issues with instability. He'd decided to sell it – and as it was set up to take two 500cc Triumph units, it would be the perfect base for Leppan's new venture.

Modified to accept the proven powerplants from Cannibal II and featuring hub-centre steering, the finished streamliner would prove its potential at the 1963 speed week at Bonneville. Or that was the plan. Breakdowns with the vehicle towing the bike and a major wrong turn saw the pair arrive late – not just by a few hours, but by several days. They only got the chance for one timed dash across the salt, during which the chain broke and damaged part of the bike's chassis. You need a bit more testing and a bit more luck than this if you're looking to become the fastest thing ever on two wheels.

Yet all of this turned out to be rather fortuitous. Though Leppan might not have achieved what he set out to do, his terrible timekeeping led to a chance meeting with the person who'd become the essential third player in the team. Alex Tremulis had worked on bold and often controversial cars for American manufacturers: he was behind the famous boat-like Auburn Cord Duesenberg from the 1930s; sketched various impactful Chrysler and Tucker models; and had been head of the advanced design studio for the Ford Motor Company, creating radical and futuristic show cars. Tremulis had extravagant plans to build what was essentially a two-wheeled car, powered by a Carroll Shelby-tuned V8 and kept upright by gyroscopes – it would be full-on *Jetsons*. And to try to understand how to design such a radical device, he popped along to the 1963 speed trials, a place populated with wild and out-there concepts.

'A funny thing happened,' says Trumulis on gyronautx1.com. 'I was one of the last to leave the salt flats when on the horizon I saw a car towing what looked like a long tube, a war-surplus fuel tank. Emblazoned on its side were the letters signifying its name: "Triumph Detroit – Piloted by Bob Leppan". Bob had experienced engine problems and was one of the last to reach the flats.'

Tremulis, Leppan and Bruflodt hit it off. They joined forces and embarked on a project that would be a turning point for motorcycle land-speed records and usher in a new level of professionalism. Leppan and Bruflodt designed a new super-rigid chassis with advanced hub-centre steering and had it built by leading race-car fabricators Ron and Gene Logghe. You didn't straddle it like a regular bike; to fit inside the long, low, stretched-out device, Leppan would lie on his back with his head propped up, knees pulled up to his chest (worryingly obscuring his view), with the handlebars under his bum cheeks. Maynard Rupp designed pneumatic 'landing gear' that would keep the device upright. These had skids on the bottom that would skim across the salt as the bike accelerated, being pulled up out the way at 70mph – truly high-tech stuff in 1964. Tremulis came up with space-age styling with an enclosed cockpit and stabilizing rear fin.

Hurling the device down the flats would be two Triumph TR6 engines with fancy cylinder heads and camshafts, and race carburettors pouring in methanol. It was called Gyronaut X-1. And once they'd proved it worked, the trio of forward-thinking speed freaks had plans for Gyronaut X-2, which would use a monstrous Ford V8 car engine (and introduce Tremulis's beloved gyroscopes) to target 400mph, followed by a jet-powered Gyronaut X-3 to charge at the sound barrier.

Posing next to this polished two-wheel missile in his black leathers, flame-painted helmet and sunglasses at Bonneville in 1965, with the salt flats shimmering behind him, Bob Leppan looked like a movie superhero among all the shed-brewed creations making up much of the Bonneville entry list. And he pulled off a movie-style performance too. The X-1 streaked to a new petrol-powered AMA record of 217.624mph. The team then returned the following year with its engines tuned to produce even more power, shattering the motorcycle land-speed record by averaging 245.667mph. With Leppan lying on his back, a few centimetres of the ground, peering between his knees …

The FIM grumbled about not recognizing the record – yes, again – as the combined displacement of the engines was over 1000cc, but nobody cared. As far as the rest of the world was concerned, Leppan was the fastest bloke on two wheels, and for the next four years, Triumph slapped a sticker on all new T120R Bonnevilles leaving the factory that declared 'World's Fastest Motorcycle'.

Gyronaut X-1 set the standard and launched a new generation of record breakers, including the advanced, big-buck, high-profile machines of legendary speedster Don Vesco (Yamaha) and Cal Rayborn (Harley-Davidson). It literally changed the shape of land-speed motorcycles. However, the X-1 itself was destroyed in 1970. The salty surface at Bonneville is graded to ensure that it's flat, smooth and safe for all the record-breaking attempts, but Bob Leppan chose to start his timed run from far before the start line. With new engines using 820cc cylinder kits and producing way more shove than the ones used to secure the record, he wanted the longest possible run-up to push his speed out of everyone else's reach – and so started on the unmanicured surface. Unfortunately, Leppan's rough and bumpy approach caused damage to the intricate hub-centre steering on his ballistic craft, which then failed at around 270mph. Leppan was severely injured in the crash, almost losing an arm; he recovered but it was the end of the X-1 – and the staggeringly ambitious Gyronaut X-2 and X-3 never materialized.

PROOF IN THE PUDDING

Producing the basis for the world's fastest motorcycle was something any manufacturer would want, and it was helping the Triumph Bonneville woo customers in dealerships. However, scorching across the surreal expanses of the salt flats at many hundreds of miles per hour in a preposterous nitro-burning tube is quite clearly very different to riding on the road. Apart from having two wheels, there aren't many similarities between a record breaker and the machines ridden by us, the bike-buying public. You don't see too many streamliners on your commute to the office or out for a sunny ride on a Sunday morning. Or you don't where I live.

Racing was – and still is – different, yet still a way to promote the 'real' benefits of a motorcycle. 'Win on Sunday, sell on Monday' was extremely true in the late 1960s, especially if the victory came from races held on real roads. Like the North West 200 in Northern Ireland, or Oliver's Mount at Scarborough – or the most famous of all, the Isle of Man TT. With bumps, drain covers, occasional iffy surfaces and immoveable objects in close proximity, seeing a bike truly shine at the TT was something road-riding fans could relate to perhaps better than any other racing discipline. And in the 1969 event, the evergreen Triumph Bonneville yet again shone a spotlight on its capabilities.

At its inaugural running in 1907, the TT entry list contained lots of normal bikes. TT stands for 'Tourist Trophy' after all, and the event was originally intended to accelerate the development of touring models in real-world-ish conditions. The Peugeot-powered Norton that won the very first twin-cylinder TT was in the firm's catalogue; anyone could buy one, assuming they had £50. But as the TT's status grew, so did the potential of the machinery – and it quickly evolved, with brave types riding proper race bikes. The fields were full of specialist metal, whether factory-tuned race versions of road models, home-built specials or full-on Grand Prix machinery (the Isle of Man hosted the British round of the FIM Motorcycle Grand Prix World Championship, now known as MotoGP, from 1949 until 1976).

We know racing didn't sit well with Triumph head-man Edward Turner, who was completely disinterested in building specialist race bikes. But his opinion became less influential in 1964 when Triumph's captain of industry retired. He kept hold of a directorship and worked as a freelance designer, but was replaced by ex-aircraft engineer Harry Sturgeon, who had been director for one of BSA's machinery businesses. And Sturgeon truly believed in the benefits of racing, especially with production-based bikes.

The change at Triumph's top table coincided with a mid-1960s TT revolution. Understanding the influence that race wins had on showroom sales, more and more manufacturers started leaning on the TT's organizers to introduce a production-based class, using regular bikes with a bare minimum of alterations. The Production TT was introduced for 1967: there were three classes – 250, 500 and 750cc. A Triumph won first time out, with John Hartle taking victory for headlining larger bikes on a Bonneville.

The capability of the already-famous Triumph was written in bold and underlined several times in the 1969 event, however. And it was thanks to a quiet, unassuming bloke from Caerphilly in Wales.

Malcolm Uphill started his biking career aged 15, when curiosity got the better of him and he borrowed his dad's BSA while his dad was out. When he started work as an apprentice for British Rail, he bought a bike to get to work and started riding to watch a few race meetings with his mates. He decided to have a go himself. A clapped-out Manx Norton wasn't the best starting point, but Uphill's engineering prowess was put to good use. Results improved. A local dealer offered support.

He became a front runner in the British racing scene, and by 1965 was winning TTs. He was ninth in the 1968 250cc world championship too. But it was the big production 'proddie' bikes that best suited Uphill's abilities. After partnering Percy Tait to win the 1969 Thruxton 500 endurance race, Uphill then went to the Isle of Man and won the 750cc Production TT – at an average speed of 100mph.

This was hugely significant. Throughout the history of the TT, each 10mph increase in the average lap speed has been seen as the next 'barrier', and for a road bike to break the 100mph mark was huge. Uphill and his off-the-production-line Triumph Bonneville had matched the speed that legendary racer Mike 'the bike' Hailwood had reached on the howling, full-factory MV Agusta Grand Prix bike just five years earlier. In fact, and even more impressively, Uphill's speed on the proddie Triumph in 1969 would have placed him in second in that year's flagship Senior, beating all the highly tuned racers apart from Giacomo Agostini (which is forgiven, seeing as Ago is the most successful motorcycle racer of all time and was again on blingy works machinery).

In celebration, Dunlop, whose tyres were on Uphill's bike, renamed their K81 rubber as the 'TT100'. And in 2011, Wetherspoons opened a pub in Caerphilly called The Malcolm Uphill in his honour.

CHAPTER 8

NEVER GIVING IN

AMAZING. OR MAYBE NOT

Triumph swung their way out the Sixties. The American market reached an all-time high in 1967, with over 33,000 British bikes exported, and over two-thirds of these proudly wore Triumph badges. Two years later, and Triumph's models accounted for 50 per cent of the American market for bikes over 500cc – which, given the US love of larger bikes, pretty much meant the whole thing. Edward Turner had been right about how the USA would be massive for Meriden. Come 1969, and Triumph churned out a record number of bikes, with a whopping 46,700 streaming out the factory.

The Bonneville had suffered a few issues after its launch in 1959 (nobody mention failing frames), but concentrated evolution and a decade of refinement meant that by 1969, the Bonnie had reached its best-ever guise, with its finest-yet specification. The light, handsome, engaging device wasn't just the sporting machine of choice but the defining big British twin. Through the 1960s, its sales were three times greater than those of rival twins from BSA and Norton.

All of Triumph's engines had moved to unit construction at the start of the 1960s, making them neater, more compact and cheaper to knock out. These handsome, potent, trim engines caused a spike in home-brewed specials, with Triumph engines finding their way into all sort of unplanned places. The most famous mash-up was the Triton café racer, the combination of revered Triumph engine with Norton's sweet-handling Featherbed frame being the tool of choice for slick-haired, ton-up boys terrorizing London's North Circular. But there were various other hybrids, including Grumph off-road bikes (498cc Triumph twin in a Greeves scrambler chassis).

By the end of the decade, the Coventry firm's model range was expansive. It covered everything. Though most of the smaller Triumph (and BSA) models failed to make an impact and quietly disappeared, the 100cc T10 scooter soldiered on (originally called the Tina and promoted by pop crooner Cliff Richard). There were assorted 350 and 500cc twins, including the hot T100R Daytona, which was allegedly capable of 150mph in tuned-up race trim, and a swarm of different 650 variants with the TR6 Tiger, TR6 Trophy, T120 Bonneville and many market-specific iterations of each with various suffix letters tacked onto their names.

There was a headline-grabbing new model for 1969 as well: the T150 Trident. Boasting a three-cylinder engine, developed by famous engineer and tuner Doug Hele, the Trident was essentially a 'Tiger and a half' with an extra cylinder wedged into the existing 498cc T100 twin. It shared the narrow bore and long stroke measurements of the TR25W single to keep the engine as slender as possible. With 740cc and 58hp, and using a Bonneville-derived frame, the T150 Trident had the performance to live up to that bragging number in its name. It was capable of sprinting from standstill to 100mph in just 12 seconds, and at Bonneville speed week, Joseph 'Rusty' Bradley caned his Trident – partially faired but with a standard engine and firing on normal petrol – to a blistering 168.9mph.

All this means it looks like the 1960s was a classic period in Triumph's story. For many, it's the firm's golden era. But behind the headlines, things at the BSA Group were anything but rosy.

There were many reasons, each as incommodious as the next. First up and having a massive impact were annoyingly fast, sweet-handling, affordable and well-made imports coming from Japan.

Triumph was very aware of the threat from Japanese manufacturers. In 1960, Edward Turner had travelled to Japan, visited the factories of Honda, Suzuki and Yamaha, and presented an exhaustive report on his findings, reproduced in his biography by Jeff Clew:

> *The Honda factory was everything that one could desire as an up-to-date manufacturing conception for motorcycles ... the whole was a dynamic experience and a somewhat frightening spectacle ... the speed with which the Japanese motorcycle companies can produce new designs and properly tested and developed models is startling ... They are producing extremely refined and well finished motorcycles ... more comprehensive than our own with regard to equipment ... which reach the public at something like 20 per cent less ... It is essential that our industry in general and the BSA group in particular should know the facts and what we are up against in the retention of our export markets ... Even our home markets for motorcycles will be assailed ...*

The course of action taken at Triumph was to wedge their heads in the sand and blunder onwards regardless. But sticking their fingers in their ears, going 'la la la' and hoping the problem would go away was staggeringly foolish. Anyone could see that the newcomer brands were having an impact, with Suzuki, Yamaha and Kawasaki turning out well-received road models and also upsetting the establishment in racing.

In terms of the latter, Honda was the most vexing. After winning the 125 and 250cc TTs in 1961, they won 14 Grand Prix riders' world titles through the rest of the decade – three in 125s, five in 250s and six in 350s. Their road-going creations were just as glorious: the scooter-like step-through Super Cub, the 124 and 247cc Dream models, and the double overhead-cam CB450 in 1965. The inline four-cylinder CB750 of 1969 in particular made their British-built opposition look dated, badly constructed and outclassed.

The CB750 was a revelation: Honda shifted 30,000 examples in the USA alone in the year it was launched, compared to just 7,000 sales of the new British triple – and that's a combination of the Triumph Trident and the version sold as the BSA Rocket 3.

This cross-pollination of Triumph and BSA models was the second cause of problems. Although Triumph was part of the BSA Group and the two factories were just down the road from each other, they had operated completely separately. Processes and methods were different, and there was minimal sharing of parts or even knowledge. Importantly, most casual observers were oblivious to the fact the names were in any way linked. But in 1962, an external report recommended amalgamation. This started with manufacturing materials and spare parts all being stored at BSA's site and was followed by the US distributors moving to a new group premises. Then came the ruling that all Triumph dealers had to also sell BSA models and vice-versa. British buyers were disgruntled and brand-loyal American customers were horrified. Staff at both plants, proud of the marque they worked for, were also the opposite of pleased.

And the third problem? Quality was down the pan. In Triumph's formative years, the high standards of the Bettmann bicycles and motorcycles had stood them apart and forged the glowing reputation, but the wild ambition of new boss Harry Sturgeon put an end to all that. He doubled production rates, causing problems for supply of material and parts, issues with spares and the rapid erosion of quality. The workforce also had to increase, which not only sent the wage bill through the roof but also started causing friction with the ever-more-powerful workers' union.

For added fun and games, Triumphs were also pricey. In 1969, the Honda CB750 had electric start, fancy new disc brakes, OHC four-cylinder performance, unprecedented reliability and was $1,495 for the all-important American market. Or you could pay 300 bucks more for a kick-start, drum-brake, problematic OHV triple bodged together in an unhappy factory.

ROCKY ROAD

Despite this glum background, Triumph started the next decade with high hopes. In 1970, the Meriden factory was working seven days a week to meet overseas demand for 500 and 650cc twins. The last of Edward Turner's designs, a 350cc twin with chain-driven double overhead cams that would be sold as the Triumph Bandit and BSA Fury, reached the prototype stage and impressed Percy Tait with its 112mph top speed. At which point there was an ear-splitting 'bang' as the bubble well and truly burst.

Triumph was still retaining dignity and putting on their best brave face, but the parent BSA Group staggered into the 1970s like a ten-pint drunk with their trousers round their ankles. In 1971, BSA-badged bikes made losses of £3 million, while the overall business loss was £8.5 million. And there was the small matter of debts totalling a mind-boggling £22 million. Three thousand employees lost their jobs at BSA's Birmingham site.

The misery rapidly spread through the group. Something called 'industrial action' looked like becoming the Trendy New Thing over at Meriden, and Barclays Bank strutted in to force wide-reaching management changes. The effect of the Japanese factories was felt too: the combined Triumph/BSA share of the American market shrivelled seemingly overnight to just 6.9 per cent, dropping them from market leaders to the fifth most popular brand, behind four manufacturers from Japan. You know, those factories with the improved production and better developed bikes that the British suits decided to ignore. Home-market sales continued to dwindle too.

More supply and production woe in 1972 brought new-model delays. Triumph missed much of the new-year sales surge in the USA, and by May, there were more than 10,000 Triumphs and BSAs stockpiled in America. Strikes at the overstaffed Meriden factory messed up production. BSA sold off one of its sites and a sports ground in Birmingham to raise cash, then considered all manner of futureproofing new models, including a showboating 1000cc five-cylinder and a rotary Wankel engine that would be built under licence from German outfit Audi-NSU.

It was all hopeless. The country's Conservative government had to wade in and help. They wouldn't save bankrupt BSA but offered a big bag of money – £20 million – to help save Triumph if they agreed to merge with Norton-Villiers, run by Dennis Poore as part of Manganese Bronze Holdings. The outfit also owned the AJS and Matchless brands.

Norton-Villiers-Triumph (NVT) spluttered into life in July 1973 with another multi-million investment from the government. The legendary marque might have been saved but loyal Triumph riders weren't best pleased – Triumph and Norton had been bitter rivals since, well, forever. Blending the two together just didn't sit right; it was like Gibson making guitars with Fender or McDonald's sharing kitchen space with Burger King. Who'd want a McWhopper?

Triumph's workers were even less pleased, largely because just two months after NVT started, Poore announced that the Meriden workforce would be reduced by a third at the end of November. Another third would be made redundant at the start of January 1974 and the factory would close in February. Workers at Meriden were the best paid across NVT's three major factories and Poore wanted to shift all production to the recently upgraded Birmingham plant and focus on the grand new Trident and Rocket 3 rather than big twins. He'd sell the Triumph factory (hopefully to car firm Jaguar).

Unimpressed, the workforce barricaded themselves in at the factory. The sit-in lasted two years.

It all got rather messy and unpleasant. The new Labour government felt sorry for the workers and issued them loans and grants to allow them to set up the Meriden co-operative, supplying bikes to NVT in Birmingham; at the same time, NVT managed to sneak into the Triumph factory and extract some tooling, so started making their own Bonnevilles. Supply of both bikes was dismal, Triumph's reputation was in the gutter and most US dealers abandoned their franchises. Attaching disc brakes to the Bonnie, upgrading to 12-volt electrics and taking the engine out to 744cc – with the new moniker T140 – didn't even scratch the surface of what was required to stave off rapidly developing Japanese rivals. NVT got into increasingly serious financial problems and so sold the Meriden factory to the co-operative early in 1975.

The disruption and misery went on and on. And on. The receivers arrived at Norton's factory in Wolverhampton in August 1975 and more than 1,500 workers were made redundant. The main plant in Birmingham announced it too was doomed the following month and eventually closed in early 1976, a year in which Meriden made losses to the tune of £1 million. There was more squabbling over finances and costs. Within two years, the whole NVT set-up was liquidated.

The co-op had somehow managed to arrange tooling and get the Bonnie modified to meet new US regulations, however (left-foot gearchange, right-foot brake, the opposite way to British tradition). And miraculously, by the late 1970s, the troubled concern almost started to look like a viable business – or it did once the government wrote off an £8 million debt. They introduced electric start, took large orders from overseas police forces and launched a giant dual-purpose bike – the bright yellow TR7T Tiger Trail – in response to worldwide cooing over the 1980 BMW R80G/S. The factory's bosses discussed partnerships with various other big brands, including a very interested Suzuki, who wanted to invest in a new range of bikes and build 30,000 models a year.

Then the Bonnie grew some more valves. In the 1960s, renowned engineering firm Weslake had started a trend to fit 650s with heads with four valves per cylinder, so Meriden approached them for help with the new eight-valve T140 TSS. More valves meant the engine could breathe better, rev harder and produce more power. At the opposite end of the performance spectrum, Meriden also started building Puch Maxi mopeds to make use of factory space.

And yet it all came to nothing. Exchange rates collapsed and Suzuki kept all their Yen. The blingy new TSS was revvy, fast and smooth, but also expensive, delayed, leaky and the cause of much warranty aggravation. Triumph couldn't get their engines – the design of which could be traced back to Edward Turner's early twins – to pass ever-tighter American emission regulations. Dressing up the existing old Bonnie platform as 'new' models, including a Thunderbird 650 and US-biased cruiser-style TSX Custom, failed to pull the wool over anyone's eyes. Triumph was struggling with production and had no way of developing much-needed new machines. The workforce dwindled – and so did sales of the now hopelessly old-fashioned bikes. By the early 1980s, plans to sell the Meriden site were well advanced.

The co-operative shook the last few coppers out of its piggybank at the end of 1982 and production stopped. They waved around ambitious plans for new bikes during the following year, including a 900cc liquid-cooled, eight-valve twin called the Phoenix, the engine of which was known as the Diana. The bike was shown in mock-up form at shows. The co-op also considered buying the struggling Hesketh brand, which had gone into receivership after managing to screw together a handful of their ill-fated V1000 model, and got as far as photographing one wearing Triumph badges outside the Meriden buildings. They also had sights set on shifting into a different nearby factory owned by tyre firm Dunlop. The local council said they'd throw in a cool £1 million to help if a private investor would match it.

Nobody did. The whole thing finally imploded on 26 August 1983.

AND YET THROUGH IT ALL . . .

Despite this period being chock with fuss and bluster and decline, the evergreen Bonneville managed to remain the glinting flagship of the British motorcycle industry. Bizarrely, some UK dealers reported an increase in demand during the messy NVT and co-operative days. And the famous, iconic, legendary Triumph name retained its allure, especially if you were a burly bloke with rolled-up sleeves and a hairy chest. 'A motorcycle for men,' declared Meriden adverts. 'Lusty power, breathtaking performance … carefully planned by men who ride – and ride hard.'

The T150 Trident wasn't hugely popular when launched, thanks to poor build quality, its tendency to attract warranty claims and the boxy styling (by design company Ogle, who also did the Raleigh Chopper bicycle and Luke Skywalker's Landspeeder for the *Star Wars* films). Triumph had to make 124 engineering changes and buy a cringingly expensive new crank-grinding machine for the 1970 model, plus revert to a traditional rounded Tiger fuel tank and classic-shaped exhausts for fussy American buyers. But the three-cylinder machine saved its reputation – and did wonders for Triumph's name – by being an utter weapon on the racetrack.

When the AMA amended the rules for the Daytona 200 to allow overhead-valve 750s, Triumph's US distributors convinced the company bosses to hand over almost half a million dollars to finance a joint Triumph and BSA race effort. Doug Hele tuned the engines, using everything learnt from the earlier 500 twins, and with a specially made rorty three-into-one exhaust they made 84hp at a howling 8250rpm. Transmission experts Quaife supplied a five-speed gearbox, chassis genius Rob North was tapped up to supply half-a-dozen bespoke frames and a new fairing was developed using an RAF wind tunnel.

They also splashed cash on big-name riders for the 1970 Daytona 200. The three BSA Rockets were ridden by Mike Hailwood, Jim Rice and Dave Aldana, while the Triumph Tridents were ridden by Don Castro, Gary Nixon and Gene Romero. Factory testing hero Percy Tait was supposed to attend as an advisor but convinced North to build an extra frame and became the seventh rider. Romero qualified fastest lapping at over 157mph – faster than anyone by a bewildering 5mph. He lost the race by just three seconds to Dick Mann on that irksome new four-cylinder Honda CB750; however, the potency of the three-cylinder Triumph had been clearly demonstrated. And it was backed up later in the year: Malcolm Uphill won the Production TT on a Trident, and the duo of Paul Smart and Tom Dickie took victory in the 24-hour Bol d'Or endurance race (held at Montlhéry, where Edward Turner had launched the Thunderbird all those years ago).

It was all guns blazing for the 1971 season. The full-factory racers were further developed, including not just a reworked engine but a chassis with a repositioned engine, lower, wider front forks and Lockheed disc brakes. For Daytona, the joint BSA/Triumph squad of Castro, Nixon, Hailwood, Rice and Aldana was joined by yet more celebrity racers – Tom Rockwood, Don Emde, Paul Smart and 1969-winner Dick Mann. Hailwood and Smart both retired with blown engines, but Mann decided he'd only rev his bike to 7800rpm rather than the 8250 revs the team said were safe. His less-abused BSA machine kept going … and he won. Romero was second on a Triumph-badged bike and Emde was third on another BSA. It was a podium lock-out and whitewash performance by the British entrants.

For the Anglo-American Match Races back in England, where top British and American riders went head to head (renamed the Transatlantic Trophy from 1972), the home team were all mounted on works triples built to full-fat, all-singing, win-or-explode AMA/F750 specification. They dominated the races at Mallory Park, Brands Hatch and Oulton Park, with Paul Smart and Ray Pickrell the joint highest scorers. Over at the TT, the main-event F750 race was won by

Tony Jefferies on a Trident. Pickrell won the Production TT skirmish on another Trident, famously known as Slippery Sam after it had smothered riders Percy Tait and Dick Jolly with its engine oil during the previous year's Bol d'Or – the first of five back-to-back TT class wins for Slippery Sam on the Isle of Man. On short circuits, the British 750 Championship was ruled by Triumph and BSA triples, and they won the famous Bol d'Or again as well.

A remarkable standout season, 1971 would be Triumph's best-ever year of tarmac racing.

POWERFUL PROMOTIONS

In 1974, US President Nixon resigned, as a result of the Watergate scandal, which had been exposed by the *Washington Post*. However, some might argue that something else far more important and significant happened this year. On 15 January 1974, the first episode of *Happy Days* was broadcast on US network ABC.

Set in the 1950s, the sitcom revolves around teenager Ritchie Cunningham, his traditional apple-pie American family and his group of hapless friends who congregate at Arnold's diner. A high school drop-out and bike mechanic called Arthur Fonzarelli befriends Ritchie and ends up living above the Cunningham's garage. Originally a B-list character in the plot, the black leather jacket-wearing, slick haired, promiscuous and super-cool Fonzarelli – played by actor Henry Winkler and known just as Fonzie or, better still, The Fonz – quickly became the viewers' favourite. It would become America's most-watched TV show of 1976 and 1977, and, through the 11 series and 255 episodes, Winkler would become the lead character of *Happy Days*, getting top billing on the show's credits and finding himself an international star. There was a mind-boggling array of series-related merchandizing sold and Fonz-related items – posters, lunch boxes, toys, etc. – were the biggest sellers. The Fonz's leather jacket ended up in the National Museum of American History.

And the machine this iconic character rode? It was a Triumph.

The series was set in Milkaukee, Wisconsin, home of Harley-Davidson. Initially the plot had Fonzie on a Harley, but Winkler wasn't a motorcyclist. He struggled with the girth and kilos of the American metal – and kept dropping it. The crew sourced a machine that was lighter and cooler, and Fonzarelli's bike became a Triumph TR5 Trophy. Winkler also tipped off that and careered into things on the set. But it didn't matter: the Triumph was as large a star as the lead actor, and the association for the brand was more than a little welcome. The show's TR5 Trophy became a pop cultural icon, spawning home-made replicas and wannabe Fonzies. The most famous TV motorcycle of all time? Surely it has to be.

Actually, that should be most famous *motorcycles*. There was more than one. Our off-road racer and movie stuntman pal Bud Ekins customized a trio of bikes for the production team, removing the front mudguards, painting the fuel tanks silver and fitting high-rise handlebars and different seats. There were a couple of 1949 models that were used a handful of times, but most of the time, the bike used for filming, appearing in the opening credits and on 90 per cent of the merchandizing, is a 1952 model.

When filming ended in 1984, one of the earlier examples ended up with Mean Marshall's Motorcycles in California, where it was mothballed, before being sold in a 'Hollywood cool' auction in 2021 for – wait for it – over $230,000. The other two disappeared, but the 1952 model – the genuine star – was discovered in as-last-used condition at a classic car auction in the late 1990s. A memorabilia buff bought it for an enormous and undisclosed fortune. It ended up in a museum in Michigan.

The third bike? Who knows. If you've got a TR5 in the shed, scruffy and with some Winkler-inflicted knocks and dents, it's probably worth considering listing it on eBay.

And if you have a twin-carb 1966 Triumph T100R carrying the US registration number 356455, with non-standard red and white paint on its fuel tank, you should think about listing that one too. Actor, filmmaker and award-winner Warren Beatty rode the bike in the 1975 comedy *Shampoo*. While it's obviously a stunt operative doing the risky riding in the chase sequence and so on, riding in just a shirt (unbuttoned to the waist in fabulous seventies fashion) and without a helmet, most of the time it's obviously the star himself. A popular theory is that the T100R was Beatty's own machine – hence the custom paint job and his obvious familiarity with it. There's no trace of the bike after filming ended.

While you're looking for motorbikes slumped forlornly in a dirty corner of a shed, see if you can find a 1977 Triumph T140J Bonneville Silver Jubilee Limited Edition 750. In a cunning bit of marketing, the Meriden co-operative used the celebrations around Queen Elizabeth having been perched on the throne for 25 years to generate vast amounts of publicity and shift stockpiled bikes cluttering up their workshops. Based on the T140 Bonneville 750, the limited-edition model looks reserved by today's standards but was considered bold and adventurous, even full-on gaudy, back in the 1970s. The silver bikes featured: blue and red detailing on the fuel tank, chain guard and wheel rims; a blue seat with red striping; chrome-plated engine covers and brackets, plus special Dunlop tyres. Officially approved by Buckingham Palace, each bike also came with a special certificate. Perfect for popping in a silver frame (solid, of course, not plated) and hanging on the wall above your fireplace.

Each Jubilee Bonnie also had a little sticker on the side saying 'one of a thousand'. Nice touch. But demand was greater than expected. Queenie-spec Bonnies made up a quarter of the year's production, so the initial limited run of 1,000 was followed by another 1,000. And then another 400. Rather than being changed to read 'one of two thousand and something', the sticker now simply said, 'limited edition'.

American buyers didn't really get the whole flag-waving exercise and some bikes sat unloved in dealers until into the 1980s. But buyers in Britain saw the model not just as something special but as a potential investment – about half the bikes were put into storage and never even started up, while some were even left in the crate that they'd left the factory in. Which had the unexpected bonus for the limping-along factory of minimal warranty claims …

Today, decent, used examples of Jubilee Bonnevilles aren't worth any more than good regular Bonnies. But those hidden-away, shed-dwelling examples still crop up and fetch proper money; at the time of writing, there's one for sale at a dealer in north-west England. Unregistered, never started, nestled away safely all its life. Yours for £15,000.

There was another royal-spec Triumph just five years later. Made to commemorate the wedding of Prince Charles to Lady Diana Spencer, the electric-start Bonneville T140 Royal Wedding Edition was built in two versions: one in American specification with a small fuel tank, traditional spoked wheels, a deep two-tone seat and royal blue paint; and one for the UK, featuring an 18-litre (4-gallon) tank, cast aluminium 'mag' wheels, and classier black paint and seat. Both had chrome fuel tanks, making the model the first to use a super-shiny tank since the 1949 TR5 Trophy (yes, the Fonzmobile). Going on sale in October 1982 for a princely £1,900 (see what I did there?), 250 were made.

WORLD-WIDE PRESENCE

Someone who missed the first few series of *Happy Days* and didn't get to eat jelly and ice cream at the jubilee street parties was Ted Simon. A journalist who'd worked on Fleet Street, edited a magazine and written a book, Simon found sponsorship from the *Sunday Times* to fund a round-the-world motorcycle trip. In late 1973, he clambered into his ex-Second World War pilot's jacket, bundled some belongings onto his Triumph and set off.

The bike was a T100 Tiger. It was picked for its simplicity and the ease with which it could be fixed in remote locations, for the fact that it was light and manageable with decent ground clearance for rough terrain, and for its sit-up riding position. Ted collected the bike from Meriden, fitted with low-compression pistons to allow it to run safely on the low-octane slop that would impersonate petrol in some of the countries he planned to ride across. This meant the bike had a bit less power, but also reduced some of the vibration. He wrote on jupitalia.com:

> *We had planned all sorts of interesting modifications at the factory, a list as long as a sheet of legal paper, but when the time came to fetch it, I was lucky to get a machine at all. The workers had just decided to lock the management out, it was the end of the road for the old-style Triumph company and I think my bike was the last one to leave the factory for a very long time. It was totally unmodified, and so hastily prepared that a pint of oil fell out of the chain case on my way down the motorway from Coventry.*

Passing through 45 countries and travelling over 64,000 miles in his four years on the road, Simon experienced some amazing things. He also had quite an engaging time keeping his 498cc twin-cylinder Triumph moving, through a string of breakages and failures. The entire journey was covered in his book *Jupiter's Travels*, first published in 1979 and a gloriously written tale, which would become the go-to book for budding adventure motorcycle travel. The hassle caused by the bike is well documented ... and yet somehow the modest Triumph comes out the other end shining. You read the book, and it makes you want an unreliable and needy bike built to dubious standards in Coventry.

It'd be easy to wheel out that phrase again: no such thing as bad publicity. But motorcycles aren't like white household goods. You don't choose one as you would a dishwasher or oven. They're machines that are all about sensations and connection; the way they feel and, importantly, how they make you feel. The bond you develop when riding them. During the 1970s, the Japanese factories ushered in exceptional reliability, smoothness and ease of use which highlighted how basic, crude and demanding a classic British twin genuinely was – but this, bizarrely, is what gave them enduring appeal.

After his epic trip, Simon summed up the British bike experience with typical ease and insight: 'That was what British bikes liked, a bit of trouble. They thrived on attention, like certain people, and repaid you for it. Not a bad relationship to have.'

Along with a starring role in *Jupiter's Travels*, Triumphs were still appearing on the silver screen. Born in Pennsylvania in 1949, Richard Gere came to the UK in the early 1970s to play slick-haired Danny Zuko in the stage production of *Grease* – and found two wheels the best way to get around London. 'I was a 23-year-old kid and I was starring in a big hit in the West End,' recalled Gere in a BBC interview in 2013. 'I remember I borrowed a motorcycle from the Triumph factory and I tootled around London on it. It was a great, wide-open time, when everything was possible.'

Starting to appear in movies during the 1970s and discovering fame in 1980 for his leading role in *American Gigolo*, Gere properly hit the big time thanks to being the lead in the romantic drama *An Officer and a Gentleman* – and Gere again rode a Triumph. The production company had two late-1970s T140E Bonnevilles for filming: one had lowered gearing and a few other changes for use in stunts, and both featured slightly longer raked-out forks for more of a chopper-like bad-boy stance. By the time the film was released in 1982, the Bonnie looked desperately old fashioned – because it was. But the association did wonders for helping the limping Meriden co-operative shift a few more bikes.

UNEXPECTED SAVIOUR

On a nondescript grey day in January 1984, Charmian Turner squeezed through some gates and had her photograph taken outside a deserted building. The youngest daughter of Edward Turner, she wanted a last picture of her dad's famous Meriden factory. The very next day, the demolition crew turned up with wrecking balls swinging from cranes and flattened the lot. Triumph's site had been sold at auction and some developers were going to put up a load of houses. All that remains of the famous site today is a commemorative plaque, placed in 2005, and a selection of motorcycle-related street names: Bonneville Close, Daytona Drive, Pushrod Place and Oil Leak Lane. I might have made up a couple of these.

Attending the auction was John Bloor. Releasing himself from school to start as an apprentice plasterer when he was just 15, he'd quickly found a footing in the building world – the inspired teen had established J.S. Bloor Holdings within two years and built his first house by the time he was 20. Owner of what had become one of Britain's largest house-building outfits, Bloor was looking at the Meriden site for his next development. He didn't buy it. Instead, he slapped down £150,000 to buy the Triumph brand name, rights, designs and tooling (outbidding Enfield India, among several others).

Bloor had ridden motorcycles in his earlier years, but the quiet, camera-shy chap wasn't exactly a hardened biker. However, his building empire also included a machinery rental company, and this had stirred 'a little hankering to build some kind of product'. Stumbling into the Triumph sale was his opportunity. From the outside, it may have looked like the decision of someone no longer in full possession of their senses – what was someone with no manufacturing experience doing buying the clutter to build motorbikes? It's not as if the British bike industry was flourishing. It was non-existent.

Bloor was clearly no fool, however. He not only understood managing big businesses but also recognized what was needed to resurrect the legendary brand. 'In the early 1980s, I was watching the Japanese set up automobile plants in the UK to take advantage of currency exchange rates,' he said in a story by Stuart Brown for CNN, 'and I thought the playing field might be getting more even for manufacturing things again in Britain.'

With his exciting new motorcycle company initially using the unexciting name Bonneville Coventry Limited, one of the first things Bloor did was lease the rights to keep knocking out old-school T140 models to Les Harris Racing Spares. Founded in 1973 by Les and Shirley Harris, the Devon-based wholesaler supplied the trade with parts for traditional British machines and had been part of the auction bidding themselves. Their licence stipulated that the bikes had to be the same specification as those trundling out of Meriden prior to closure, and so the bikes used the crankshaft from the last-of-the-line TSX Custom model but with a slightly earlier design of carburettor for easier starting. They'd all need to be fired up by the kickstart – there'd be no electric starts. Frames would be made in Britain, but as the country's motorcycle industry had all but dissolved, most of the components had to be sourced from across Europe. Switches and brake master cylinders were from German company Magura, and the Radaelli wheels, Brembo brakes, Paioli suspension, Veglia dials and Lafranconi exhausts were all from Italy.

The first Harris Triumph prototype was ready for testing in July 1984 and the first bike was sold in February 1985. They produced a twin-carb Bonneville and single-carb Tiger, but the wincingly high cost of product liability insurance prevented them being sold in the potentially lucrative American market. The bikes were expensive to make which also made them hard to shift in the UK, with a small profit margin. The tooling used for the crankcases, cylinder heads and other important bits was all becoming worn out – and renewing the equipment would cost a fortune.

In 1987, Harris also started making a bike badged as the Matchless G80 around an Austrian-made Rotax engine, and so in 1988, they chose not to renew the licence. The last T140 left their site in March 1988, meaning that Edward Turner's pre-war parallel-twin engine design had been the bedrock of Triumph motorcycles for half a century. Remarkable.

While all these traditional Triumph twins were being created down in Devon, John Bloor had ambitious plans. He was busying himself trying to work out how to make his bike brand viable for the modern world. He re-employed three people who'd been responsible for developing new models at Meriden, and they all hopped on a plane and flew to Japan.

While the British motorcycle industry had scraped its way through the bottom of the barrel and was deep into the earth, the Japanese industry had continued scorching onwards at a breathtaking pace. The rate of development, variety of machines and market dominance was genuinely incredible. While Meriden was still plugging away with leaky OHV twins with old-fashioned chassis, firms like Honda, Kawasaki and Yamaha were making six-cylinder DOHC engines and trying fuel injection and variable timing. They were building lightweight aluminium frames with race-style monoshock rear suspension and fitting wind-cheating fairings. The bikes were powerful, fast, light, agile, flexible, exciting, affordable. They made a T140 Bonneville look like a dinosaur. And they didn't leak oil.

Bloor and his three colleagues wangled invitations to peek behind closed doors at Yamaha, Suzuki and Kawasaki. These companies were probably not too worried about revealing what they did to a man from the UK who owned the scraps of a failed old-fashioned brand. The visitors had their eyes opened wide.

Old British factories had been full of ramshackle machine tools operated by men in brown smocks with roll-ups glued to their bottom lips; the Japanese plants were crisp, new, bright and stuffed with state-of-the-art equipment operated by efficient (and happy) staff. The products were lightyears ahead of what Triumph had been making – and also far more advanced than the development projects and prototypes like the Diana engine that Bloor had acquired when he bought the business. His reaction? 'We decided to scrap the lot and start again.'

Setting up a fresh research and development unit, the boss approved the design and development of new-from-the-ground-up motorcycles. Bloor understood that Triumph's rich heritage would be a strong marketing tool, but he wasn't taking a soft-focus wander down into nostalgia – he saw Triumph as a viable modern business. Rather than the quick-profit management tactics that had helped ensure old Triumph had fizzled out to nothing, Bloor poured millions of pounds into new Triumph with the belief that he could build a business that would – eventually – challenge the omnipresent Japanese. The rest of the world, in fact. This would be a high-quality manufacturer of modern motorcycles with its focus set firmly on long-term prosperity, not one trying to scrape together enough cash to pay for the works' Christmas party.

Triumph had been saved.

CHAPTER 9

BRAVE NEW BEGINNING

OOH, DIDN'T EXPECT THAT

In August 1991, Tim Berners-Lee, a research fellow at Oxford University, did something that would have quite an impact. Hang on, we should use his full title: Sir Timothy John Berners-Lee OM KBE FRS RDI FRSA DFBCS FREng. On 6 August, he posted a public invite on Usenet – an early computer network system that let you read and post messages – enticing everyone to join in with his clever invention: an information management system known as the 'world wide web'.

All the systems and assorted tech equipment had already been invented. The internet itself and other complicated-but-essential things nobody really understands, such as 'hypertext transfer protocol' (Tim's work) and 'multifont text objects' existed. What Berners-Lee did was spot how to bring everything together to create the web. He made the first web server, the first website and the first web browser. All your relentless googling is thanks to Tim.

It was a year stuffed with other standout events, new products and creations that would stand the test of time. It also saw the end of the Soviet Union and various Russian republics declared independence. A much slimmer and greyer Terry Waite, the Anglican Church ambassador who'd been held by Shiite Muslim kidnappers, was released after more than four years in confinement. Grunge rock musicians Nirvana released their benchmark recording 'Smells

Like Teen Spirit'. The famous Bugatti car name was resurrected, attached to a ridiculous hypercar powered by a V12 engine with four turbochargers and 550hp, and set a new production-car speed record, averaging 212.9mph around the Nardò Ring, a banked eight-mile circular test track in Italy. Over in America, they were treated to the Super Nintendo Entertainment System, causing widespread obsession among teenagers (and adults) with a character known as Super Mario.

And in February 1991, someone pressed the big green 'go' button on the assembly line in a pristine factory in Hinckley, Leicestershire. Shiny new Triumph motorcycles started plopping off the end.

After establishing that the prototypes and assorted development material he'd bought along with the Triumph name were, well, a bit useless, John Bloor had given his new (but largely ex-Meriden) design team lots of large sheets of clean paper and permission to start from scratch. Edward Turner would have appreciated their approach. The ideas involved many shared parts and allowed efficient manufacture – and so kept a lid on costs.

In 1985, the team had settled on a modular design centred around a steel 'spine' frame. This was a huge steel tube that curved around over the top of the engine to tie the steering head, engine and swingarm pivot together. About as high-tech as brick, but simple and effective – and it could also be shared across a range of models. Differences in suspension parts and set-up would allow the geometry, ergonomics and feel of each bike to be tweaked this way or that to suit the different styles. There would be various engines of different configuration and capacity, but all sharing the same size pistons. The engines really were embracing Turner-like methods: the 76mm bore diameter would be used with a short stroke (55mm) for a new 749cc, 89hp inline three-cylinder motor, which would have an extra cylinder glued on the end to create a 998cc, 120hp four. There would also be a long-stroke (65mm) version of each, making an 885cc, 97hp triple and an 1180cc, 140hp four. They'd all use the same cylinder head design, valve sizes, everything. From just one design and one piston, the various combinations of crank throw and cylinders gave Triumph four different engines.

As well as rationalizing production and being economically pragmatic, there would be benefits for owners as servicing would be affordable. There were only 11 different service parts across the entire range. Doing things as economically as possible also went as far as the new range of sharing wheels, swingarms, control levers ... even the wiring loom.

Having common components was the only way in which the new range of engines were in any way vaguely like Triumphs of yore, however. These were of-the-moment motors, heavily influenced by what Bloor and his engineers had gawped at while touring factories in Japan. The new engines had horizontally split crankcases, liquid cooling, chain-driven double overhead camshafts and four valves per cylinder. The three-cylinder units had a balance shaft – triples with a cylinder firing every 120 degrees of crank rotation have natural balance and so are double-cream smooth, but they're affected by something known as a 'rocking couple'. Nothing to do with husband and wife enjoying Chuck Berry, this is a force that tries to twist the engine and so the balancer was deployed to keep this in check. All the four-cylinder units got twin balancers to guarantee they were completely, absolutely and resolutely tingle-free. Old-school British bike vibration with its blurred vision and white finger would be relegated to history.

Stuart Wood had been employed designing automatic epicyclic gearboxes for hefty things like tanks. The enormousness of these transmissions was only matched by their wonderful complexity. Wood joined Triumph as an engine designer in 1987, at which point the fresh motors were already advancing nicely. The first new engine running was the four-cylinder 1200, which burst into life late that year. And to celebrate this landmark, Triumph's engineers promptly screwed everything up and started again.

'After the first engines ran, every single component was redesigned,' Stuart told me. The motors worked, but the team knew they could be even better. 'The biggest achievement [of the reformed company] was productionizing our first engines. We were building a whole business, so the manufacturing had to come from nowhere, the purchasing and distribution departments had to come from nowhere … but to go from an idea and an engine that works and runs to one that is manufacturable, durable, reliable, cost effective – that was a real achievement.'

The engine is the key part of any bike, influencing feel and character as much as performance. It really is the heart of the machine. So, Triumph would manufacture the triples and fours to exacting standards. Each crank was subject to plasma nitriding to improve hardness and wear resistance, which involved being popped into a furnace at around 500°C for 30 hours. They were then precision machined to a tolerance of 5 microns. That's just 0.005mm. For context, the average human hair is around twenty times that, at 100 microns thick. With quality and reliability topping the list of important things, once engines were installed in completed bikes they were subjected to a cold test, much prodding and poking, and then given a thorough session on a dynamometer (rolling road) to triple-check their function and performance. (I applied for a job as an industrial engineer at Triumph in the mid-1990s, and seeing the fresh engines being filled with pre-heated oil and thoroughly tested at the end of the production line will forever stick in my memory. I didn't get the job – I can only assume they didn't like my ill-fitting interview suit.)

The new premises in Hinckley – known as T1 – opened in 1990. It was equipped with the latest CNC (computer numerical control) machines from Japan. Robots were used on the production line for the frames and aluminium swingarms; modern welding techniques were employed and about one-third of all the parts were made in house to guarantee standards. Other high-quality components were sourced from Japan including the carburettors, brakes, wheels and suspension. Testing duties were given to a gaggle of professional bike racers. Steve Tonkin (a former Isle of Man TT winner), Mark Phillips (the 1986 British TT F1 champion, not Princess Anne's husband) and Keith Huewen (former Grand Prix rider and a three-time British champion) did thousands of miles. Bikes were thrashed around Bruntingthorpe Proving Ground, an ex-RAF and USAF base in Leicestershire with an engine-stretching two-mile runway, a suspension-testing pockmarked surface and an old-fashioned canteen that did fabulous artery-busting fry-ups.

The factory doors were flung open to the press on 29 June 1990. Though the bike industry and media knew that someone had bought the Triumph name and something was happening, it had all been done behind a veil of mystery. Bloor was quiet, camera shy, almost a recluse, and his limelight-dodging character meant that everything – the development, building the factory, the testing – had all been carried out in secret. It would have been reasonable to assume that whatever was going on with Triumph might involve limping onwards with one foot forever tethered to the bad old days, before the inevitable visit from Mr Liquidator. They'd been soldiering on building Harris Bonnevilles under licence, after all. The bright, modern, state-of-the-art facility and obvious huge investment – sheepish Mr Bloor had slung £80 million into the business – were as astonishing as the thoroughly contemporary products.

After arranging their preproduction examples under the dazzling spotlights at the Cologne show in September 1990, the revitalized Triumph sashayed into the all-important British motorcycle show at the NEC in Birmingham. They presented their six-bike range that December, saying full-on production would start early in 1991.

In complete contrast to the wild optimism and broken promises of ye olde Triumph, it did. Manufacture of four-cylinder 1200s started in February at a rate of five bikes a week, the first batch destined for Germany.

Fitting, really, given that it was where original founder, Siegfried Bettmann, had come from.

CRACKING ON

Triumph's initial new-model line-up had three different bikes, each available in two capacities. All carried nostalgic names to stir something inside those who still remembered how truly great Triumph had been in the past, with all those ground-breaking designs, bestselling models, world records and race wins. The enviable reputation. All that movie-star glamour.

Using the three-cylinder engine, the Trident 750 and 900 were simple, traditional roadsters with perhaps a hint of Meriden style. Maybe, if you squinted, on a misty morning. But handsome either way. The Trophy was essentially the Trident but in sporty-touring form, with a full fairing to shelter you from the windblast, different fuel tank and seat unit, and slightly lower handlebars for a more prone riding position. Triumph's modular approach and interchangeable parts meant they could offer it as both a 900 triple and a 1200 four. And there were the Daytona 750 and 1000. Sportsbikes were booming, with models like the Suzuki GSX-R750, Kawasaki ZXR750 and Yamaha FZR1000 dominating press coverage and showroom sales, and so the Daytona was Hinckley's answer. It would be the firm's sporting tool, using the revvier short-stroke engines along with upgraded brakes and adjustable suspension, and specially designed bodywork featuring racy twin round headlights.

You'll have noticed that there wasn't a new Bonneville in the line-up. This was probably a very conscious decision, to detach the revived company from the final throws of the old Meriden site and the Harris-built machines. Perhaps a wise move.

After production of the four-cylinder Trophy 1200s had started in February 1991, the factory started slinging together triples in the June. The range began appearing in UK dealerships and towards the end of the year, shipments were sent in the direction of France, the Netherlands and all the way to Australia. The factory made just shy of 2,500 machines in the first year. During 1992, the reborn Triumph established a footing in other key export markets including Italy, Spain and Japan, and by October had constructed 5,000 bikes. Solid going.

It wasn't hard to notice how Hinckley's designers and spanner-twirlers had been influenced by what Bloor and his new colleagues had seen on their holiday in Asia. Triumph's new engines had distinct similarities to established and proven machines from Japan, especially those coming out of Kawasaki. Their GPz900R had set a new standard for performance and durability in 1984 and so was the datum when Triumph was settling on their modular format, and Hinckley's motors had a close resemblance to the Kawasaki inline four. Both externally and internally – the short-stroke Triumphs even replicated the 55mm crank throw of the GPz. There were other striking similarities too, including the use of extremely distinct eccentric rear wheel adjusters.

The engines weren't copies, though. Once Triumph had settled on a dual overhead camshaft (DOHC), four-valves-per-cylinder layout and set the internal geometry, there was bound to be visual similarity with other engines of the same specification, given the materials, technology and practices of the day. Anyway, what goes around comes around. Kawasaki's first bike, the W1 of 1965, was an evolution of the BSA A7 –

the classic pushrod British twin – which was being built in Japan under licence by Meguro, who Kawasaki bought out.

You could sense that reliability was built into the new motors. Sounds a bit of a daft thing to say, granted, but they felt over-engineered and bomb-proof. Especially the long-stroke examples – you were aware of the weight and inertia of the internals in how the engines responded, could hear it in the gargling, rumbling, chilling exhaust hubbub. Ride one of the 885cc inline threes today and its robust, old-school charm is as far away from the latest quick-revving, instant-response motors as cranky old Meriden twins were from the Hinckley creations. You get the impression you could replace the oil with extra-gritty Swarfega and feed it the grottiest of petrol and it'd still relentlessly burble onwards with utter indifference.

The press's reception of the three new models varied quite dramatically. Patriotic journalists in bowler hats and Union Flag undercrackers did much exuberant trumpeting; the more analytical and sceptical scribes pondered over the girth and conservativeness of certain models. Running over the top of the engine, Triumph's spine frame was economical to produce and allowed easy swap-and-change model creation, but also meant the bikes were quite tall and top-heavy. For the touring-ready Trophy models, these traits were almost desirable; the bikes had spacious accommodation, steadfast handling and confident roadholding, which complemented the lazy thrust of the larger long-stroke engines. And the Trident worked as a flexible if slightly reserved Sunday morning thrummer. But the Daytona was too heavy and carried its weight in the wrong place to be a true sportsbike. Both the 750 and 1000 versions were unwieldy and a tad ponderous next to the rapidly developing and race-honed Japanese opposition.

Triumph's claimed figures were rather optimistic too. When *Performance Bikes* magazine strapped the flagship Daytona 1000 sportsbike to a dynamometer for their September 1992 issue, it squeezed out 102hp – not just a smidge less than it should, but 18 whole horses fewer than the factory reckoned. With a measured top speed of 155mph with the rider screwed into a tight little ball behind the fairing, its performance was closer to that of a Japanese 750 than a rival 1000.

Customer reaction echoed what the magazines and papers said. The quality was evident. The aspiration was commendable. The Trophy was a fine machine, the Trident was decent and the Daytona was quite a way wide of the mark. And everyone preferred the performance, feel and character (and haunting exhaust tone) of the gurgling, droning, distinct three-cylinder engines.

Heavily influenced by the 'win on Sunday, sell on Monday' approach, the market-leading Japanese factories were making bikes that were increasingly powerful and high revving. That's what worked on the racetrack. It was working in showrooms too, with the sporty bikes being lapped up by speed-loving folk encased in jazzy leathers. But the torquey nature of Triumph's new inline threes felt nicer on the road because, well … it *was* nicer.

Torque is the size of an engine's punch, the force you feel pushing you down the road; power is the rate at which that punch can be delivered. Power is handy in racing and gives you a nice big number to stick in the brochure and slap across adverts, but it's torque that makes a road engine feel strong, luxurious and flexible. Triumph's triples delivered their clout at lower revs than ever more shrieking Japanese fours, which made them feel even gruntier than they were and meant the wallop was easy to access. Not having to try to wrench the twistgrip off the handlebar or wait for the motor to get into its stride made them a breeze to ride. This was especially true of the long-stroke 900. Sharing its geometry but with an extra cylinder and 33 per cent more capacity, the 1200 four wasn't shy with its feel-good thrust either.

Triumph very quickly made the three-cylinder motor their signature. Their original triple, the Trident from the late 1960s, might have only really found success on track, but the new triples were going to propel the rejuvenated firm to greatness.

John Bloor didn't have the same fixed, dogged, stubborn, I'm-right-and-you're-wrong attitude that had often gone against legendary Triumph boss Edward Turner. The new man in charge listened to customer feedback. He reacted to what was happening in the market. For the 1993 model range, after just two short years in production, the unpopular 998cc four-cylinder version of the short-stroke engine was dropped. The Daytona was treated to tuned-up versions of the long-stroke 900 three and 1200 four, along with new bodywork and paint schemes. These couldn't hide the fact it was still a bit chubby, but with a dyno-proven 120hp and a 160mph top speed from the 1200, the big Brit now stood nose-to-nose with the best Japanese bikes when bragging about your bike in the pub. Which, as everyone knows, is of utmost importance. The Trophy and Trident both got improved ergonomics, details and finishes too.

Something that would become a defining attribute of 'new' Triumph and ensure their future success also came into play. Bloor understood that sitting still and having a 'that'll do' approach were major factors in the demise of the old British bike industry and that, just as today, evolution and 'newness' were essential – and so Triumph waded in with fresh three-cylinder models.

In response to customer requests for weather protection, the Trident 900 was adorned with a half-fairing to create the new Sprint. There was a special Daytona Super III, with its crankcases and cylinder head designed by Cosworth, the renowned tuners and Formula 1 car racing outfit, plus racy engine internals and exhausts; power was up by 15 per cent, and so it was given massive brake callipers made by a specialist American firm. There was more. Large-capacity, dual-purpose bikes, designed to be as happy whirring along a motorway as lunging down a rocky farm track, were hugely popular in Europe, so Triumph introduced the Tiger 900. It featured a strengthened frame, long-ravel suspension and other rugged-looking, puddle-jumping features (and instantly became the factory's bestseller in the vast German market).

But best of all was 1994's new Speed Triple. Cleverly playing on the name of Turner's benchmark 1937 model and inspired by a modified bike built by the Italian importer, this was effectively the sporty Daytona – complete with adjustable suspension, Cossie crankcases, low clip-on handlebars and rearset footpegs – but with simple, stripped-back looks echoing the café racers that bellowed around London in the early 1960s. Triumph had gone beyond using old-school model names and pulled the heritage card from up their sleeve. It was an instant hit, especially in the moody all-black paint option.

To promote their new stripped-back racer, Triumph ran a Speed Triple Challenge support race at the 1994 British Grand Prix at Donington Park, using a sack overflowing with prize money to attract top-of-the-bill riders. Regulations were tight to ensure close action, with the race modifications developed by multiple British champion and ex-Grand Prix rider Ron Haslam. A hit with both spectators and racers, it became a televised, one-make series for the following two years.

By the end of 1996, the ambitious British manufacturer had properly realized the power of its heritage and enormous back catalogue of machinery. So, they dusted off the iconic Thunderbird name, dressed up their modular platform in old-fashioned clothing and attached a distinctive grill-style badge – the 'mouth organ' design originally introduced in 1957 – to the fuel tank. It was intended to make those still holding a torch for Meriden models go 'ooh' and form a queue outside their nearest dealer. There was a chrome-splattered, high-barred version called the Adventurer, too. Triumph also waded back into the American market that they once dominated and established themselves in Sweden, Thailand and Malaysia. In just six years, more than 40,000 motorcycles had left Hinckley, where the T1 factory had been joined by a second building – yes, the imaginatively titled T2 – to meet worldwide demand.

Now it was time to get serious.

GOING HEAD TO HEAD

Triumph's modular models had been fine quality with reserved style and a robust reputation, but also rather sensible and, well, perceived as a tad humdrum. Their new models for 1997 were like pumped-up sneakers with space-age materials and super-springy soles. Those things with holes in the sides and curious gel bits.

Sales of sportsbikes were in overdrive, with major markets completely dominated by powerful, light, corner-carving machinery that looked like it had been lifted straight from a race circuit. Honda had turned motorcycling upside down in 1992 with their CBR900RR FireBlade. The normal capacity classes had become set at 600, 750 and 1000cc, but Honda paid no attention; instead, they squeezed an 893cc, 120hp four-cylinder engine into a chassis with the physical size and delicate weight of a 600. It was a revelation, especially in sportsbike-obsessed Europe. (Incidentally, its curious and famous name came about by accident. Part of the development team wanted a name that meant hot, such as fire, while the Japanese representatives preferred the idea of a name that meant sharp, like blade – and during a planning meeting somebody casually said, 'What, like a fire-blade?')

Triumph's response to the anarchist Honda was the bold, all-new 1997 Daytona T595. Over three years in the making, the bike wasn't just a step forward for Triumph but a pole-vault into the next county. Mr Bloor had given the go-ahead for a ground-up new machine in July 1993 and within a couple of months, the factory had been built a development chassis by Harris Performance. The renowned British firm were famous for their frames, components and race success, including racing in Grand Prix, and would run World Superbike teams for major manufacturers.

Triumph's own version was up and running in prototype form by autumn 1995. The old-fashioned steel spine had been junked, replaced with a lightweight structure using oval-section aluminium tubes that curled around the engine. The swingarm for the rear suspension was single sided, with the wheel only held from one side (a design pioneered by Honda), and the front forks ignored the fashion for 'upside down' as the conventional structure was lighter. Nestling in the centre was a completely overhauled three-cylinder motor. Cylinder bores were opened out to accept fatter pistons (up 3mm in diameter to 79mm) to increase capacity from 885cc to a meatier 955cc. A swanky, low-friction, wear-resistant coating was plastered inside the bores. Lotus Engineering redesigned the cylinder heads, camshafts and valve whatnots, and fuel injection was used – still very much a rarity on motorcycles at the time. With engine covers crafted in exotic magnesium, the new engine was more than 11kg (24lb) lighter than the previous 885cc version and bunged out a claimed 128hp.

Keen to make sure their new Daytona wasn't a hopeless clunker, Triumph used the FireBlade and the slim, elegant, striking Ducati 916 that had been launched in 1994 as their datum during development. While it wasn't the first single-sided swingarm, it's a safe bet that the one used on the 916 pushed Triumph's into production. Bodywork was shaped by British designer John Mockett, who'd previously worked with Yamaha, various race teams and designed a car for Suzuki – and there was a hint of the Ducati in the new bike's lines as well.

The finished bike rolled up at the Cologne show in October 1996. With aluminium frame tubes polished and bodywork finished in dazzling Strontium Yellow, the new Daytona T595 sportsbike made a gargantuan impact. Bye bye sensible loafers, hello glitzy trainers. No more safely-safely, no more conservative approach. This was Triumph ripping its shirt open, banging its chest and bellowing 'Come on!' at the established Japanese and Italian brands.

There was a bit less chest-thumping when the bike was pitched directly against of-the-moment sportsbikes. The factory's dynamometer was either still desperately in need of calibration or had been left in its 'wildly optimistic' setting, as the 128hp promised by the spec sheet turned out to be around 110 in independent tests. Though this was on a par with the 916 and Blade, both these key rivals were considerably lighter and so had greater power-to-weight. All the bikes in the 750cc class – the one that was the basis for the prominent World Superbike championship and World Endurance racing – were nimbler than the T595 and easier to usher around a track at speed. The Triumph's suspension was a tad soft, especially at the rear, and there was a small hiccup in the fuel injection's delivery in the middle of the rev range. It was also a little what you might politely call 'big boned'.

Being called the T595 didn't help either. Customers were used to simple names with numbers that made sense: the size of the engines in the Suzuki GSX-R750, Yamaha YZF750 and Kawasaki ZZ-R1100 were obvious. Triumph's factory used internal model codes for each range: the first modular bikes were the T300 range; the Tiger giant trail bikes were the T400. The T595 tag used for the new bike signified it was in the new T500 line, with the '95' referring to the 955cc engine – but slapping this on the side of the seat unit confused a few buyers.

However, the reborn Triumph had built their reputation with grunty and charismatic machines, and everything that had made them popular had been carried over into the sexy, high-tech, desirable new Daytona. While still capable of scorching to 160mph, the emphasis was on usable torque rather than headline-grabbing horsepower. It was geared for exciting acceleration that anyone could enjoy, instead of a bewildering and irrelevant top speed that meant nothing away from circuits. The suspension and chassis set-up were looking towards sporty road riding rather than racetracks, too – a supple ride and stability took priority at a time when Japanese bikes were chasing light-switch handling and steering so sharp you could shave with it. Fastest and raciest in track-based magazine tests? No. Built to thrill and inspire road riders, make them feel gooey inside? Most definitely. With more than enough true sports capability for regular road-riding folk, the T595 had a touchy-feely character that most four-cylinder rivals couldn't muster. Some personality.

Triumph had shifted up a gear and orders for the Daytona flooded in. One T595 for a UK customer would be the 50,000th machine built at the flourishing Hinckley site. Despite a bit of a recall due to issues with frames (what, just like the first Bonnevilles had?), the Daytona almost immediately gathered cult status. And then there was its butch new stablemate …

BRING IT ON

Streetfighters had become 'a thing' in 1990s biking Britain. These were high-performance bikes but created with pub-brawl attitude rather than track-ready refinement. Meaty motors with loud exhausts grabbed attention; stripped-down styling and minimalist bodywork gave an anarchistic appearance. Wide-set handlebars provided a hard-hitting stance for the rider, who'd be kitted out in bomber jacket, jeans and dark-visored helmet (the aggressively shaped Simpson Bandit was the hat of choice) rather than colourful leathers.

Starting as a small movement in the late 1980s, there'd been a few one-off specials built by dedicated owners. They slotted high-power Japanese engines into bespoke chassis built by the likes of

Harris Performance and Spondon Engineering, and they hung twin car spotlights on the front. Going into the 1990s, the movement gathered momentum; regular production sportsbikes were reimagined into modern-day café racers, their owners peeling away plastic and attaching cow-horn handlebars and deafening exhausts to ensure other motorists felt suitably intimidated. These were the bad-ass bikers of the era.

Also, track days were gaining popularity through the 1990s. These let you pay a few quid to zip around a circuit all day on your own bike, exploring its full potential and wearing the edges of the tyres out. Building an on-trend streetfighter was a handy way of doing something with the bike you'd pranged after muddling your intentions and capabilities at Cadwell Park.

Triumph's new 1997 Speed Triple T509 leapt into the streetfighter thing with both feet. And both round headlamps. Based on the new Daytona chassis but with an 885cc, 106hp version of the refreshed engine, the new bike overflowed with pared-down attitude. With its distinct bug-eyed face, flat handlebars, unshielded dials and the indicators hanging off the side of the radiator, it was entirely convincing. It looked like it would drive across your lawn, spill your pint and drop litter. Options included lower clip-on handlebars and a slightly odd dustpan-shaped fly screen, should the buyer wish to have a bit more of the previous Speed Triple's feel – but it was the all-arrogance sat-up version that had the impact, and the high 'bars became standard fit in 1998. You could choose menacing black or Lucifer Orange, joined the following year by a vivid, shimmering and instantly recognizable Roulette Green.

On-the-ball designers at Hinckley did something else with the T509. They invented a new genre of motorcycle. These days, every major manufacturer sells a 'supernaked' – a bike with brain-scrambling power and scythe-like handling, bristling with the latest parts and technology, but with high handlebars, an upright seating position and more than a smattering of usability. Superbike architecture and performance reconfigured in accessible roadster form. Rising to prominence from the turn of the century, there have been many standout supernakeds, including the Aprilia Tuono, BMW S1000R and assorted Ducati Streetfighters. But Triumph's T509 was the first.

Striding confidently forward with their new modern outlook, Triumph started to gradually phase out the modular models. Various retro machines remained valid – by 1997 the Thunderbird had become Triumph's bestselling bike globally, with more than 7,000 bikes finding pride of place in the garages of polish-loving owners – but the Tridents and the large four-cylinder Daytona had run their course. (Although their popularity was highlighted when their demise was announced; there was such demand for the 1200 Daytona that the factory did a limited run of numbered specials with exclusive colours and fancy brakes – they made 250 examples of a 1200SE for Europe in 1998 and another 150 tagged as the 1200SP for America the next year. You never know what you have until it's gone and all that.) Triumph needed to ditch the older bikes to make space in the model range because there was a swarm of brand new machinery waiting to burst from the factory.

A WORLD FORCE AGAIN

Sports-tourer. It promises a motorcycle that mixes the performance and engagement of a sportsbike with the mile-swallowing comfort and distinguished deportment of a tourist. And so therefore it's also suggesting that you're buying a machine that's a compromise, a bike that attempts to be handy in disparate areas but ends up not making a decent fist of either. Something that could be a bit wishy-washy, lacking defined purpose. Too many trades, not enough mastering.

Surely sports-tourer is verging on being an oxymoron. You wouldn't have an aeroplane that was a fighter-airliner, or a whispering loudhailer.

Yet as the twentieth century rushed towards its conclusion, the sports-touring motorbike was very much a thing, very much capable of fulfilling many roles and very much in demand. Extreme advancement was to blame. In nature, evolution occurs over centuries, happening at such a glacial pace that only David Attenborough notices. In motorcycling through the 1980s and 1990s, it zipped along at a bewildering rate, thanks to rampaging Japanese manufacturers. One of them would launch an all-singing new model, crammed with fresh ideas and unprecedented features, only for it to be outclassed by a rival within moments. Edward Turner's landmark 5T Speed Twin was in the Triumph range for almost 30 years, but there were some Japanese bikes that only survived for 12 months before being axed in favour of a completely new design. Blink and you missed it.

If you bought a sportsbike in the late 1980s then yes, it was racy and fast and accurate and made you tingle somewhere personal – but it would also be eminently usable. British riders would buy a Honda CBR600F or Yamaha FZR1000 for its inspiring fruitiness, but would also ride it to work, carry the other half to endure the in-laws, and strap luggage to the back and slog down France to get riotously intoxicated at the Bol d'Or endurance race. But as race results were influencing showroom activity, and because the hugely popular World Supersport and World Superbike championships used machines based on road models, the manufacturers made their offerings more and more extreme. Engines got revvier and more demanding. Chassis became smaller and lighter with ever-stiffer suspension, and riding positions appeared to be tailored to suit people who enjoyed being scrunched into a ball with their bum in the air. Usability? Practicality? No.

Honda had introduced their VFR750F in 1986 as a sportsbike. But by the early 1990s, it looked upright and sensible compared to these ever-more focused creations (Honda had launched a super-racy version called the VFR750R RC30, specifically to race in Word Superbikes). Motorcyclists love a pigeonhole and the road-focused

VFR was slipped into a new one: it became a sports-tourer, and soon the all-round sporty road bike of choice.

Other brands tried hard to get themselves a slice of Honda's tasty pie. BMW, Kawasaki and Ducati created specific sports-touring tools. Triumph had pitched the Trophy models as their device for touring sportily when they'd whipped the sheets off the range back in 1991, but the weighty, sizeable machine had quickly morphed into a fully-fledged, luggage-shod tourer with a vast weather-beating fairing. The half-faired Sprint version of the Trophy had filled the sports-touring role, but with its tall spine frame and considerable heft it looked a bit dinosaur-ish when compared to the opposition. So, Triumph started from scratch.

New for the 1999 model year, the Sprint ST bundled the technology, glamour and ooh-look-at-that of the Daytona into a machine specifically crafted for touring at speed – or riding sportily in comfort with a week's worth of pants strapped to the back. Using a retuned version of the 955cc three-cylinder engine with its peak thrust at even more accessible revs, the Sprint ST had a model-specific aluminium frame with a stout beam running either side of the engine – known as a 'twin spar' design and all the rage – and a single-sided swingarm. Geometry promised precise handling with reassuring manners. Bodywork had clean lines and some family resemblance to the Daytona, while the 21-litre fuel tank allowed you to bluster around Europe with extended spells between shouting 'Do you speak English?' at baffled petrol station attendants. The Triumph also offered something high-profile rivals didn't, with the option of hard-case panniers to stuff with unnecessary travel items. Colour-matched to the solid colour of the bodywork, too. Classy.

Hinckley's designers had reached the turning point. The Daytona T595 didn't quite fulfil the same sportbikes brief as its Japanese counterparts and the Speed Triple T509 was treading new ground. They were both kind of doing their own thing. But the new Sprint ST was the first time that a bike from the revitalized firm could be pushed wheel-to-wheel with the best in its category without excuse or mumbled apology. Fast but effortless, agile yet composed, and with fine comfort and that engineered-in sense of quality, it went straight to the head of the class.

There was little time for celebratory jelly and ice cream at the factory, though. They were busy building the new Tiger, launched alongside the Sprint ST with a new perimeter frame, Lotus-tweaked version of the 885cc T509 engine and a styling makeover. It was a bit less off-roady and more focused on hard surfaces; despite looking like they could compete in the Dakar rally, most big dual-purpose bikes were used for touring on tarmac. Triumph also busied themselves refreshing the T595 and renaming it as the 955i (much easier to understand) and making the muscular Speed Triple even more muscular by crowbarring in the 955cc engine. They had an increasingly swollen retro line-up to assemble as well, now including the Thunderbird, café racer Thunderbird Sport, Adventurer and an affordable new Legend TT. A proper bells-and-whistles model range.

Production topped 20,000 bikes in 1999. The 100,000th bike rolled off the production line. And the once-huge American market started to flower again, growing to more than 200 dealers and making up 20 per cent of sales. Bloor's vast investment was paying off and Triumph were on the front foot. Onwards ...

RACING COMEBACK

Boot still firmly planted on the gas, something significant happened at Triumph as the reborn company romped into the shiny new millenium. At last, in its tenth year of production and after chomping through more than £100 million of investment by John Bloor, the Hinckley outfit started to make a profit. The brand's quiet and more reclusive than ever owner probably celebrated by not having a party.

Triumph leapt into 2000 with an 11-bike model range, divided into new categories: classic, touring and sport. And it was the sport bit where everyone was looking, as the attention-grabbing news for 2000 was the arrival of the TT600.

Having a model range full of three-cylinder machinery had given the British brand its own flavour. Triumph wasn't a niche manufacturer; they'd simply adopted alternative, individual ways of configuring engines and screwing motorcycles together. Put their bikes against those from rival brands in the like-for-like specification comparisons so loved by journalists and the burly triples were clearly following their own groove. Even if those bikes hadn't worn badges, you'd have been able to tell – and hear – that they had come burbling out of Hinckley. Even the Sprint ST, widely regarded as the sports-touring high watermark, was that little bit different to the machines it outclassed.

The new TT600 ignored all that, strutting into the centre of the most hotly contested part of the market and trying to push the big boys around. The supersport class was thriving. It was steered by race regulations which allowed 600cc four-cylinder bikes to race 750cc twins but apart from Italian brand Ducati, every manufacturer went down the four-cylinder path – and they were all 599cc, 16 valve DOHC, with near-as-damn-it identical bore and stroke measurements. And Suzuki, Yamaha, Honda and Kawasaki all made mountains of cash selling light, high-revving, exciting race-replicas: Honda's CBR600F was the face of British motorcycling throughout the 1990s, and in 1999, Yamaha sold more than 4,000 examples of their YZF-R6 in the UK alone. The TT600 was Triumph saying anything you can do, we can do too.

The project had started back in 1996, when the relaunched British brand was still just five years into production. It followed the blueprint for success with a 599cc liquid-cooled, 16-valve inline-four engine tucked inside a twin-spar aluminium beam frame. Running gear came from the go-to Japanese brands and included fully adjustable suspension and brakes that had a similar effect to riding headlong into a wall. Triumph didn't have plans to race their new bike but knew that track capability and searing performance were essential for showroom success, so again deployed tame racers to do the development. Mark Phillips, the ex-British champion and winner of the 1995 Speed Triple Challenge, recalled getting stuck in to *Motorcycle News*: 'I helped out with the start of their first 600, doing all the chassis stuff at the Pau circuit in France, using a Kawasaki 600 donor engine.'

The TT600 didn't emulate its forebears by replicating the Kawasaki, though. Triumph's engine was treading new ground. When the bore and stroke measurements of an engine are the same it's called 'square'; cranky older bikes with a bore smaller than the stroke are 'undersquare' and more modern bikes with a bore greater than the stroke are 'oversquare'. Sporty bikes go for a fat bore and stubby stroke as it means the piston has a shorter distance to travel. For any given engine revs, its average speed is lower (average piston speed is always a limiting factor in performance engines), so you can rev the engine harder before bumping into limits or having parts explode. And more revs mean more horsepower. And more horsepower means more magpie-like customers. With a fat 68mm bore and teeny 41.3mm stroke, the TT600 was radically oversquare – the Suzuki GSX-R600 that was winning in World Supersport measured 65.5 x 44.5mm. Bloor's engineers also ditched carburettors and made the TT600 the first bike in class with fuel injection.

Triumph launched the TT600 at a racetrack (Pau, funnily enough). Its handling was sensational, the steering super-precise, the brakes astounding. Right up there with the very best on offer. But the engine was … how shall I put this politely? It was a letdown.

The significantly oversquare motor had practically no low-rev drive, making it feel gutless and hard work. There was a rush of fuel-injected power at the top of the wailing 14,000rpm rev range, but it clearly wasn't the 108hp that they bragged about. Worse, there were glitches in the fuel delivery. Wrapped in bodywork that looked a bit too much like a five-year-old Honda CBR and seemed a little dated next to ever-edgier opposition, the TT600 bombed. Yes, it handled, but the engine was a huge disappointment – magazine tests found it actually made 91hp, which was a good 10 per cent down on the best Japanese bikes (and 17 whole horses down on the claim; an ex-Triumph employee later told me that they'd waited to see what all the other brands claimed for their bikes, then made sure the number in their brochure was bigger).

I remember my first ride on a TT600. The chassis was sensational, readily darting wherever you looked, but compared to my own three-year-old Suzuki, the engine was breathless. Like it was actually 450cc. Or maybe there was something strangling the motor by stopping it sucking in enough atmosphere, a field mouse nesting in the airbox, perhaps. The throttle response was unpredictable and had curious steps in its delivery too. Triumph would have tested the bike against rivals, so it was baffling quite how they'd decided it was up to scratch.

Triumph turned to Lotus for help in improving the engine's driveability for its second year, with new camshafts, a balance pipe on the exhaust to boost torque at lower revs and reconfigured fuel injection. It was improved, but it still wasn't perfect. The damage was done and the TT600 had a reputation from which it couldn't recover.

Throughout their history, Triumph had managed to dig deep, pull their socks up, make do and mend, and do all the other things that our older relatives told us to do when we struggled as kids. And they did it again. True to their belief in reacting to feedback, the TT600 was completely reworked, thoroughly rejigged and reappeared for 2003 as the new Daytona 600.

This was more like it. As there was nothing amiss with the TT600's chassis, Triumph's engineers adopted the 'if it ain't broke don't fix it' approach and merely shaved a few grams away to make it even lighter. It was the four-cylinder engine that was the focus for an overhaul. The 599cc unit was treated to computer-machined combustion chambers in the cylinder head, a lighter crank (less inertia, quicker response), and had its challenging fuel injection swapped for a system by Japanese fuelling know-it-alls Keihin. A new air intake in the bike's nose force-fed atmosphere into the airbox. And it got a lighter starter motor and covers too.

The change most people noticed was visual – gone were the cuddly curves and old shapes of the TT600, replaced with sharp, angular lines and twin, aggressively shaped headlights. The petrol tank shape had seemingly been modelled on the head of Kryten, the neurotic robot in science-fiction sitcom *Red Dwarf*, but otherwise the bike was of-the-moment.

Better? Absolutely. Under the analytical microscope of a fussy magazine comparison test, the Daytona's 110hp (claimed …) motor still didn't *quite* match the screaming performance of the established Japanese offerings, but it was so close that the difference was a few tenths of a second here, a horsepower or two there. And, crucially, the Daytona 600 was arguably the stand-out road bike among its peers, thanks to oh-so-sweet handling, quality suspension and brakes that were like shoving a scaffolding pole through the wheel's spokes.

Jack Valentine was a renowned tuner and previously one half of the TT-winning V&M race team. For 2003, he set up a new outfit called ValMoto and raced the new Daytona in the British Supersport championship. With a tuned engine and heavily altered injection, the engine made 130hp, and the Daytonas were ridden by trusted hand Jim Moodie and young sensation Craig Jones. The bikes did well, eventually getting a podium finish at the final round of the season. But ValMoto underlined the Triumph's potential and its road prowess at the Isle of Man TT. New Zealand rider Bruce Anstey skipped around the island at a record-breaking average speed of 120.36mph to win the Junior TT – bringing Triumph their first victory on the Isle of Man since way back in 1975. With Anstey's teammates John McGuinness and Moodie finishing in the top ten, they secured the manufacturers' award too. Triumph could stick their tongue out at the opposition and blow a big fat raspberry: with grit, determination and an ability to spot when things weren't up to scratch (and yet more of Mr Bloor's fortune), they had become a headline force in racing again.

BLAZE OF GLORY

Success on the track was only a part of Triumph's plan to stride boldly into the new century. The cunning plan for securing their future involved looking at the past.

The bestselling Thunderbird had amply demonstrated the power of the brand's heritage. That's why in 2000 they'd slapped a paint scheme that echoed the 1966 T120 Bonneville all over the Thunderbird Sport. After trying hard to shake off the lingering whiff of Meriden when they'd first fired up the Hinckley plant, the restored firm had built up such a solid reputation that they could now highlight their past without people starting to worry about porous cylinder heads and industrial action.

The time had come to reinstate the most famous model name in motorcycling. For 2001, the Bonneville was back.

Way back when, the Bonneville was the sportiest bike that Meriden made, a machine that was bought for its handling and excitement. The new Bonnie wasn't. The design brief for the new model required it to be agile and manageable, sure, but it was to be no road-burner. This was unashamed playing on the success of the original, replicating what it had offered all those decades earlier – which was, by modern standards, old fashioned and sedate.

Which was entirely the point, of course. In fact, Triumph got hold of a restored 1969 T120 Bonnie to use as a template for the new bike's riding position, feel and styling. Using a parallel-twin engine was a given. But while the new 790cc motor was a modern design with double overhead camshafts, four valves per pot and twin balance shafts, it was also air cooled. Its crank gave 360-degree firing intervals, the pistons rising and falling as a pair for that authentic old bike rumble and shake. Triumph also broke with modern convention to put the clutch cover on the left of the engine and the chain final drive on the right, and even shaped the engine covers to give the vague impression of having a separate gearbox. A steel tube frame, raked-out steering head angle and a 480mm (19in) front wheel continued the retro theme. Offering the two-tone scarlet red and silver paint of the legendary 1969 model was a given.

Japan's 'big four' factories had all dabbled with retro models. Their domestic market snapped up anything with a throwback feel, but for the wider world scene they'd mainly created four-cylinder machines that echoed the superbikes of the 1970s. Bikes like the Honda CB1000 and Yamaha XJR1200 had butch lines and enough torque to win a tug-of-war with a steam locomotive. Kawasaki had tried the hardest: the Zephyr models had been offered in a variety of sizes through the 1990s and you could sense that the bikes had their roots back in the 1970s (mainly because the air-cooled engine was verging on being an antique). Kawasaki had also been the first of the Japanese companies to look further back in time; in 1999, they released the W650, an air-cooled 676cc parallel twin with an old-fashioned bevel drive to the overhead camshaft and a proper 1960s image. It was basically a replica of their W models from the sixties, which, as we know, were copies of old BSAs ...

The all-new Bonneville took the concept and ran with it. Triumph's 61hp, 205kg (452lb) twin was gruntier and lighter than the W650 – its only direct rival. It was also smoother, classier and, crucially, had an illustrious British brand name stuck on its petrol tank. But the biggie was that it was a Bonneville: the most recognizable model name in the whole of motorcycling.

Triumph's timing also coincided perfectly with a global boom in the sales of cruisers – laid-back bikes that were all about style and enjoying the ride, rather than tearing around like your underpants were on fire. The Bonneville worked perfectly for this market, as well as giving a hefty twang to the heartstrings of people who still had leather jackets with 'Triumph' painted on the back. Reviving the model brought fresh glory for Triumph and restarted a product line that would significantly shape their future.

Feeling understandably puffed up and confident at their growing success, Triumph celebrated by opening another factory. Not in Hinckley. And not in Coventry, or Birmingham, or even in the UK. The new facility opened in Thailand. Several other major brands already had plants there: Honda had set up its Thai factory way back in 1965, followed by Yamaha the next year, then Suzuki, and Kawasaki in 1976. Brought to life in May 2002, the flash new Triumph premises manufactured parts including frames and swingarms, petrol tanks, exhausts and chrome trinkets. They'd open a second factory there in 2006 for squirting on paint and today have three sites in Thailand and build complete bikes there, not just components. The country has become a hub for bike building, with Ducati, BMW and Harley-Davidson established there as well.

Having this extra manufacturing capacity was useful back in 2002. Two months before cutting the ribbon on the sparkly new site, the T1 factory at Hinckley burnt down.

Starting on Friday 15 March 2002, the blaze completely swallowed the massive building. It was caused by leaking petrol in the assembly area, and the fire spread so quickly that the factory's automatic fire doors didn't have time to close and contain it to one area. At its peak on the Friday night, there were 120 firemen from three different counties fighting to bring the blaze under control, and they had to pump water from a nearby canal. Triumph lost their main assembly line as well as the engine assembly area, plus a day's worth of finished production – at least 100 bikes. 'It's gutted,' said a representative from Leicestershire Fire and Rescue. 'Around 75 per cent of the building has been destroyed. We have been struggling to put it out because the walls have partially collapsed inside. The whole thing could come down any minute.'

Thankfully, nobody was seriously injured. Triumph started rebuilding the factory almost exactly a month later, on 16 April, and the work took five months. This obviously created a sizeable gap in the middle of the year's production. They had enough parts in stock to carry on bundling bikes together for a couple of months, but the fire had a massive impact on what Triumph made. They'd intended to screw together 37,000 shiny new bikes that year, but the inferno slashed the figure in half. It also meant that the new Speed Four model, a naked pared-back TT600, would have its release delayed until the following year.

The fire did something else. Something unexpected. It gave an opportunity to draw a line in the sand and refresh the brand for the future. In a surprising move, John Bloor would bring in fresh blood and sanction bold new designs that would tread new ground – not just for Triumph, but the whole of motorcycling.

CHAPTER 10

ANYONE WHO'S ANYONE . . .

BACK IN THE BIG TIME

Imagine an alien race from far across the universe has landed on Earth back in the 1930s (go with me on this). They start conducting secret experiments and mucking about with various weapons, and in the mid-1940s set off a nuclear device out in the desert. This huge explosion forms a trans-dimensional wormhole – obviously – which is known as the Vortex. It excretes wondrous energy that gives numerous humans a variety of superpowers. This leads to numerous American civil wars, lots of disruption and assorted misery, and cities riddled with drugs, crime and gang wars, all under a thick layer of pollution. And, thanks to the aliens and the Vortex and all that, there's a rapid advancement of technology too.

This not-at-all far-fetched scenario is the plot behind a comic released in 1993 called *Barb Wire*. This is the nickname of the lead character, Barbara Kopetski, who runs a notorious bar in a grotty city and works as a vigilante. As you'd expect, she's a dab hand at fighting, weaponry and military tactics – it's what comes from running a bar, brawling in gang fights involving folk with superhuman powers and dealing with cyborgs. Oh, and she's an expert on two wheels as well.

In 1996, this vision of an alternative world was made into a film starring famous American coastguard actress Pamela Anderson. It was a catastrophic flop. However, Barb Wire rides a motorcycle in the movie, and so the high-glitz and very Hollywood promotional pictures featured a pouting Anderson draped over a Triumph Thunderbird. The publicity was huge.

There was more to follow. Much more, in fact. With their distinct engineering, growing reputation and defined style (and immense heritage), Triumph machines rapidly regained their position as the movie producer's motorbike of choice.

In 1999, cult classic *The Matrix* was released, in which a computer hacker discovers the world isn't in fact the world, but some huge-scale digital deception created by a nasty cyber-intelligence. Or something like that. Winning several Oscars and numerous other awards, the boundary-pushing film starred bike-loving Keanu Reeves along with Laurence Fishburne and Carrie-Anne Moss. Its numerous iconic moments include the slow-motion bit where Reeves arches his back and dodges bullets, which influenced action movies for years. And, more importantly, *The Matrix* also contains a Triumph. It's a fleeting appearance, however there's a scene where Moss's character is on a black 1998 Speed Triple.

Based around the 1966 television series, the movie *Mission: Impossible* had starred US actor Tom Cruise as an agent for the Impossible Missions Force and been an enormous box-office success. So, it was followed up in 2000 by *Mission: Impossible II*. This has a very Hollywood plot, with Cruise's character getting involved with a professional thief while trying to stop a rogue agent who, of course, turns out to be the thief's ex-lover. Happens to all of us. The highest-grossing movie of the year, it pulled in almost $550 million from the packed cinemas around the world – which means literally millions of people witnessed Triumph motorcycles front and centre.

The film's climax involves an all-action chase with lots of explosions and impressive stunts, with Cruise's character riding a black Speed Triple. And the bad guy is also suddenly on a bike from Hinckley, appearing on a red Daytona 955i (maybe there was a dealer just up the street). Some of the action scenes defy both physics and belief, and the tyres on the bikes magically sprout knobbles for the off-road scenes at the culmination. It matters not a jot. There is loads of two-wheel action, lots of enjoyable stunts (anyone fancy skiing off the side of a bike?) and, crucially, it's often very clearly stunt-loving and bike-owning Cruise doing the riding. With promotional images showing Tom bursting through a wall of fire on an unmistakable Speed Triple, the publicity and boost in status for Triumph was off the scale.

Keen to have their brand-defining supernaked in the best form and to keep Cruise-wannabe customers streaming into dealers, Triumph gave their movie-star model a shakeup. Already having been treated to the 955cc version of the stout three-cylinder engine at the end of the 1990s, the Speed Triple got further enhancement for the 2002 model year. There was more power and less weight, which is always a tantalizing combination, while faster steering geometry and a shorter wheelbase brought greater agility. It also received redrawn bodywork, more compact headlamps, a digital display and lost the muddled T509 bit from its name. I tested the new bike for a magazine in the South of France at the start of the year, against the established Suzuki Bandit 1200 and the all-new Honda CB900F Hornet, and it was riding the muscular Brit that left the lasting impression.

Obviously, it'd be the wheels of choice for any discerning British secret agent, then. The revised Speed Triple was used in its new Nuclear Red colour scheme – actually, a lurid shimmering pink – in the 2003 spoof spy flick *Johnny English* starring Rowan Atkinson. It was ridden by his co-star, Australian actress and singer Natalie Imbruglia. She's clearly seen pulling away on the bike, although the traffic-dodging action bits are by a stunt rider. If you happen to have a pinky-red Triumph with the registration number KU02 WUT tucked away in your shed, you own a genuine movie star.

The Bonneville was back on the screen in 2003 in *How to Lose a Guy in 10 Days*, starring Kate Hudson and Matthew McConaughey.

The lightly customized silver Bonnie makes several appearances and is integral to the plot of the classic Hollywood romcom.

There was a blip in Triumph's movie career the following year, mind. The film *Torque* had a dubious plot, terrible speeded-up action scenes and questionable acting. One of the stars was rapper Ice Cube – not his given name, he's actually O'Shea Jackson Sr – and unfortunately Mr Cube's skills in front of a camera didn't match his musical ability. His character's silver Triumph Daytona 995i is the lone highlight.

Thankfully, the dependable Tom Cruise was standing by to put everything back in order. For 2006, there was a new off-road flavoured version of the reintroduced Bonneville. Called the Scrambler, it featured high-level exhausts and more than a hint of the TR6 Trophy so loved by Steve McQueen and his desert-tearing buddies. And a Scrambler was used for a third film in the big-buck *Mission: Impossible* series, released the same year as the bike. This silver machine wore twin custom exhausts, with one exiting desert sled-style on either side of the bike, plus a single seat, a classic-style longer front mudguard with 1960s-style stays over off-road-ready chunky tyres and an old-fashioned front numberplate. It doesn't play an all-action role and the bike only has a minor appearance, but paparazzi snaps of superstar Cruise on the bike taken during filming ensured plenty of coverage nonetheless. Believed to be based on a pre-production development model, the ex-movie Triumph sold at auction for £22,760 in November 2006.

Bikes would return to a more prominent role in the many lucrative sequels that followed, with a Speed Triple making a reappearance in the 2018 film *Mission: Impossible Fallout*. Clearly a favourite with Tom and his celebrity mates.

As the noughties progressed, so did Triumph's film career. A classic model was rolled into action for *The Curious Case of Benjamin Button* in 2008, with evergreen Brad Pitt thrumming around on a 649cc T110

Tiger. In one scene, Pitt's riding the bike dressed in a light-coloured jacket and his pillion passenger is wearing a headscarf – they're replicating how Mr and Mrs McQueen appeared in a picture on the front cover of the 12 July 1963 issue of *Life* magazine.

Pitt's then-partner Angelina Jolie rode a Triumph in the 2010 action thriller *Salt*, and there's one in the 2014 science-fiction action movie *Edge of Tomorrow* (which stars Mr T. Cruise, so using the legendary British brand was surely a given). Actor Chris Pratt swings around on a Hinckley product in 2015's *Jurassic World* as well ...

And there were more. Other bike brands made silver-screen appearances, with BMW and Ducati models notably slipped into big-hit flicks – but it was Triumph that became the go-to brand for the biggest celebs and the blockbuster productions.

The fact that Triumph once again ruled the silver screen was written in massive capital letters and surrounded by flashing lights in 2021 when Triumph models took starring roles in the biggest movie franchise of them all: James Bond. In the 2021 smash-hit *No Time to Die*, the twenty-fifth Bond film, two Triumph models were given starring roles. Tigers and Bonneville-based Scramblers are used by gun-toting bad guys throughout an epic chase scene, but it's the wild jump that Bond does on a Scrambler that's the highlight of the movie. The stunt bike used for the gravity-defying leap was sold at auction the following year. As ridden by Bond actor Daniel Craig and stunt riders Paul Edmondson and Martin Craven, it was a star lot at a Christie's event to celebrate 60 years of Bond – and it fetched a staggering £138,600 for charity.

Combining the two iconic brands was what marketing executives call a win-win, and so the factory also produced a limited run of Bond edition models and a range of 'Triumph x 007' clothing, including leather jackets, T-shirts and toy bikes.

ME, ME, LOOK AT ME

Appearance and image are everything when you're the sort of person who has photographers hiding in the shrubbery outside their house and gets mobbed by adoring selfie-demanding fans when they pop to the supermarket. You need the right sunglasses – sorry, I mean 'eyewear'. You need to drape yourself in the right designer gear and have the correct breed of dog trotting along beside you (or tucked inside your ludicrously expensive handbag). And you are required to make sure your personal-trainer-improved backside is seen plonked on the right motorcycle as well.

James Dean, Steve McQueen, Bob Dylan and everyone else had made Triumph the brand of the discerning celebrity in the 1960s. But fast forward 40-odd years and the list of A-list stars choosing to ride the British brand's two-wheeled creations was longer than the wait for Christmas when you're a kid. Quite a few B-listers were on there, too.

Silver-haired charmer, Oscar-winning actor and coffee advertiser George Clooney had been regularly spotted rumbling around California on assorted Harley-Davidsons. But then Triumph introduced their 'sixty8' limited editions in 2006. The special custom line was a mildly curious mix of tradition and modernity – for example, the usually full-on retro Bonnevilles could be had with laptop bags and an iPod holder, rather than traditional panniers and tank bag. Mixing the luggage with a race-style single seat cowl was unconventional too. But no matter. It clearly rang Clooney's bell and the *Ocean's Eleven* star immediately switched brands.

He's not the only movie star to choose Triumph away from the cameras. British award-winning actor Daniel Day-Lewis is a life-long motorcyclist; he rode Harleys in his youth, is a fan of MotoGP and once took a ride on the back of Ducati's monstrous two-seat Grand Prix bike (with showboating American legend Randy Mamola at the controls). While Day-Lewis was filming *The Last of the Mohicans*, he was regularly snapped riding around on a classic T140 Bonneville and he has since been spotted many times aboard various Hinckley-era Bonnevilles and Scramblers.

His choice in machinery is shared by Hugh Laurie. Best known in the UK as part of the comedy duo Fry and Laurie, and for his eccentric characters in the iconic *Blackadder* comedy series, Laurie turned into a proper, serious, straight-faced actor when he took the lead in *House*, the runaway success medical drama, and became the world's highest-paid television star. Things you never expected to say ... Anyway, importantly, he's wisely spent some of his amassed fortune on motorcycles. He can be spotted around Los Angeles on Hondas and Yamahas, but most often on his Bonneville.

There could be a club for Bonnie-riding movie stars in the USA. It could be called 'Hollywood Hinckley Highway Stars'. They could have badges and stickers and appoint a secretary, and maybe they could get Bradley Cooper as treasurer. He owns a red Bonneville-based Thruxton café racer, and the multi-award-winning actor and filmmaker set the internet fizzing in 2012 when he was spotted riding around Paris, France, on a Bonneville. Seems he likes to arrange wheels for getting about when he's shooting on location. And you would, wouldn't you?

On their Tuesday evening meet at the lean-to clubhouse, the HHHS could talk to Ewan McGregor about customizing and fundraising too. The star of *Trainspotting* and *Star Wars* and many other big-hit flicks always had a soft spot for the products of Italian firm Moto Guzzi; however, when he did a commercial for Davidoff aftershave in 2007, he rode a Triumph Bonneville. The next year, to mark the fiftieth anniversary of the announcement of the original T120 Bonneville, Triumph roped McGregor into designing a special custom bike. His bike's fuel tank was copper plated and its seat and side panels were finished with waxed cotton supplied by legendary kit manufacturer Belstaff. 'I wanted to use a traditional waxed cotton material as it has such a resonance with the history of style in motorcycling and mix it with the tradition of coppering tanks,' said McGregor. Or at least the press release with his name on did. 'I am a huge fan of Steve McQueen and his films from the 1960s, and the font that I have chosen for the Triumph logo harks back to that golden era of biking.' The actor is an ambassador for the charity UNICEF and the bike was auctioned to raise money.

As well as Ewan's custom, there was also a black-with-gold-pinstripes bike designed by Belstaff. This was made in very limited numbers and displayed in their high-end stores around the world – the sort of places where if you need to enquire what something costs then you can't afford it. For the rest of us, Triumph kindly produced a limited run of 650 individually numbered Bonnevilles to mark the fiftieth anniversary. Each had a two-tone Meriden Blue and Exotic Orange paint scheme, chrome camshaft cover and a plaque on the handlebar showing which number of the examples you have. Plus a certificate signed by John Bloor to put on the mantelpiece.

CLAMBERING OVER EACH OTHER

Film producers and image-savvy movie stars weren't the only high-profile people captured by the reach of ever-expanding Triumph (and the attraction of the illustrious Bonneville in particular). Reestablished as style icons, Triumphs also attracted the attention of musicians, sports stars, adventurers and bona fide, crown-owning royalty.

Alecia Moore is better known as rock and pop singer Pink. She's used her powerful voice to shift 60 million albums worldwide and is married to Carey Hart, an ex-motocross racer and famous freestyle rider – where riders launch themselves into the air and do improbable things on twisting, rotating and often upside-down motorcycles. Hart was the first to try a BMX trick called the 'superman seat grab' on a motocross bike, and he came up with his own variation known as the 'Hart attack'. He was also the first rider to attempt a backflip – yes, rotating round backwards through 360 degrees while soaring through the air – in a freestyle competition.

Anyway, singer Pink proposed to Hart using his pit-board during a race and so it was only a matter of time until she was spotted on two wheels herself. Yes, you guessed it: a Triumph Bonneville, lightly customized and with a slightly lowered ride height (Pink might have a big presence on stage but she's a modest 5 feet, 4 inches tall).

As the guitarist for British rock beat-combo The Cult, Manchester-born Billy Duffy is best known for playing guitars by Gretsch and Gibson. And for playing around on Triumphs – he's owned several of the British twins and often fills his social media with pictures of him looking super-cool on a trendily customized twin. He rode one in a TV show too, when he was included in a documentary about guitarists called *Pursuit of Tone*. And in 2022, when Triumph built a special Gibson-inspired Bonneville as a prize for the Distinguished Gentleman's Ride (a huge world-wide fundraiser for prostate cancer and men's mental health), they also gave away three guitars signed by famous musicians – and the Epiphone 'Inspired by Gibson' 1959 Les Paul Standard was scribbled on by Duffy.

Towards the end of the Meriden days, the Triumph factory had a reputation for being a bit ... well, shall we say grubby? The perception was of a place that you'd stroll into and find blokes in dirty overalls beavering away covered in oil. There'd be a well-thumbed newspaper on a bench and perhaps a calendar packed with images of ladies who'd forgotten some of their clothes. New millenium Triumph was very different, however. This was a company that employed people with modern, word-salad job titles and who fully understood the power of celebrity and association.

Which is why they secured the services of British TV adventurer Bear Grylls to promote their new Tiger range at the end of 2014. Grylls is an ex-SAS soldier who'd set various records for doing extreme things in hostile environments and presented a show about wilderness and survival. And as he was also a motorcyclist, he rode the new bike in promotional videos. To the bemusement of the assembled world press, Edward Michael Grylls OBE was also unexpectedly present at the riding launch of the new bike. The swanky hotel, fine dining and gentle two-wheeled antics were probably less extreme than his normal activities, but I'm sure he had a very pleasant time.

There was more Triumph adventuring going on too, although the attention-grabbing star was someone less associated with living in tents on the side of a windswept craggy mountain or foraging for berries while lost in the tropics. David Beckham had been a super-high-profile footballer who'd played for England on 58 occasions, captained the team for six years and in 2013, was the highest-paid footballer (soccer player) in the world. He'd also married an ex-Spice Girl popstar and was consistently the focus of media attention. He had been spotted on Harley-Davidsons; however, having hung up his footie boots, Beckham went to Brazil on a riding holiday with three mates, which was documented for a BBC television programme called *Into the Unknown* – and the only machinery that such an image-conscious chap could choose was of course Triumph's Bonneville.

Heading into the Amazon, the bikes featured cut-down mudguards and chunky tyres to cope with unpaved roads. They had two-into-one exhausts so they sounded the part as well, plus different seats and handlebars, and lots of matt black paint. Old-style sleds and scramblers with flat brown seats and gloss-free paint were increasingly in vogue, and Mr Beckham was clearly keen to be on trend.

In 2015, Belstaff created a rather unusual short film and, as well as roping in actual movie stars – including award-winner Harvey Keitel – they cast Beckham as a Triumph-riding motorcycle stunt rider and drifter. *Outlaws* didn't catapult David Beckham into the glitzy world of movie superstardom, but it did help to yet again wheel the British bikes under the media spotlight.

BY ROYAL APPOINTMENT

When the Second World War was still raging in 1945, unmarried women under the age of 30 were required to either join the armed forces, work in industry or get a job on the land. So, in March that year, the Auxiliary Territorial Service (ATS) – the women's division of the army – was joined by an 18-year-old called Second Subaltern Elizabeth Alexandra Mary Windsor, better known to most as Princess Elizabeth.

Starting her training as a mechanic, the princess passed her driving and vehicle maintenance course on 14 April and was dubbed 'Princess Auto Mechanic' by the media. Catchy. The future Queen Elizabeth II also learnt how to ride a motorbike and was photographed negotiating a slalom on a 250cc single-cylinder BSA C10. Her future husband, Prince Phillip, was also into his bikes and often spotted at the TT on the Isle of Man.

Which is perhaps where Elizabeth's grandson, Prince William, caught the two-wheel bug from. After passing his test in 2002, when he was aged 19, William was frequently spotted carving to and from polo matches on a red Triumph Daytona 600, in race-style one-piece leathers, hiding inside a helmet with a dark visor. His father, then the Prince of Wales and now King Charles III, tasked one of his bodyguards with shadowing the bike-loving prince. Yet again, the newspapers were ready with a snappy headline: the Prince of Wheels.

William's younger brother, Harry, also got into biking. And, when the persistent paparazzi eventually caught up with him, he became the second prince to be snapped on a Triumph ...

CHAPTER 11

WORLD CLASS

REDEFINING THE BRAND

Let's politely overlook Triumph's slightly underwhelming efforts to wade into the profitable supersport market with the bothersome TT600. Let's also forgive them for the Daytona 600 that replaced it – sure, it won at the TT, but in the fast-changing sports market, it felt like it was slipping behind almost as soon as it had been launched. While there might have been some blushes in the design and engineering departments, in the grand scheme these can be glossed over. The Speed Triple and larger Daytona had made a substantial impression; Triumphs were (once again) turning up in big-buck movies and the company had successfully reintroduced the legendary Bonneville model name on a bike that had immediately become the thing to be seen on. The brand was finding its own new path – and, at last, returning a profit after all the millions invested.

Yet there was still more potential to be released. And it would be unlocked by the unlikely combination of the factory fire and a young Danish guy who knew nothing about motorcycles.

Ever the opportunist, John Bloor realized that the factory blaze could be a chance to rebuild Triumph differently; to refresh the brand and strengthen it within a churning, changing bike market. He brought in a consultancy firm called McKinsey. They went through the company's entire operation, its existing products and plans, looking at how to make the Triumph name more exciting, more alluring, more defined.

The review was handled by a chap called Tue Mantoni, who in July 2003 presented Bloor with his recommendations. Mantoni said that Triumph should only make two- and three-cylinder bikes and forget about inline-four engines – which meant cancelling a monstrously powerful 'hyperbike' that was already deep into development. The sacks of cash invested in it should just be written off. He reckoned the firm needed to embrace its heritage and revive the reputation for delicious-handling bikes that they'd had back in the 1960s, yet at the same time modernize the company's identity with a refreshed logo. Tue also thought Triumph needed its own slogan, one to underline the firm's individuality: 'Go your own way'.

Back in the Meriden era, the young Mantoni would have been frogmarched off the premises for such audacious recommendations. Bloor accepted them wholesale. Further than that, he gave the 28-year-old Swede the job of managing director. He may not have been an engineering pioneer or skilled designer, as Edward Turner had been, but Mantoni's effect on the company was arguably as great. And eight years later, he'd take over as CEO.

Refreshed, reinvigorated and having received a kick up the bum, the newly ambitious Hinckley outfit was ready to blow minds with some perception-shattering new creations. And they had something truly significant up their sleeve. Three things, in fact. Triumph rolled out a trio of showstopping new models over three consecutive years, with the first being the all-new Rocket III: the largest series-production motorcycle ever made.

Longer than a public-holiday traffic jam and heavy enough to create its own gravitational pull, the behemoth Rocket dominated the Milan Motorcycle Show when first wheeled out in September 2003. 'Power-cruisers' – long, low, laid-back bikes with serious presence and powerhouse engines – had been identified as 'a thing' within motorcycling in the late 1990s, and with the American market craving bikes with ever-bigger engines, Triumph created a whopper. Their plan was deliciously simple: build a bike with a ridiculously large engine and the fattest back tyre possible for maximum impact. This would be Triumph giving it full swagger. The firm's American colleagues and dealers were sending images of custom bikes with cartoon-style 240-section tyres and so the decision was made to go for this steam-roller rear rubber. If it's available, why not? With a biggest-yet version of their signature across-the-frame triple clearly differentiating the bike from the sizeable Harley-Davidson V-twins (and many Harley-esque twins knocked up by other firms) that defined the sector, it was what high-fiving marketing-types would undoubtedly tag a no-brainer.

'Let's have a look at a 1200cc triple – could we do that?' said Triumph's engineer Stuart Wood to *Bike* magazine. 'That grew very quickly into a 1500, and then talking with the American team to 1800cc. At 1800, we looked at turning the engine around so it would be in-line.'

The longitudinal engine in the machine making Milan's floors creak wasn't a paltry 1800, though. Oh no. Every time Triumph went back to talk to customers and their US colleagues, the displacement of the engine increased. When they told the Americans that the 1800 would be designed so that it could expand in size after three or four years to refresh the model, they said no – give it to us now. So, the motor became 2100cc. But when Triumph showed plans for this vast 2.1-litre device, the same thing happened again …

At a staggering 2294cc and using pistons the same size as those found in a Dodge Viper V10 supercar, the finished Rocket III made a mockery of what had previously been considered 'big'. Three times larger than the biggest engine ever made by 'old' Triumph – and out-cubing most cars as well – it was a third of a ton of proof that less definitely wasn't more. The 1,500 orders taken before the bike even got near a showroom showed that customers approved of Triumph's chest-out confidence too (and that they didn't care that the Rocket moniker had originally been slapped on the side of BSA's earlier triples, rather than Triumph's).

However, while the Rocket III was unexpected and headline-grabbing, perhaps the most important new Triumphs arrived in 2005. And by that I mean the most important of all time, not just the modern era.

Bold statement? Undoubtedly. But the new 1050cc three-cylinder engine in the revised Speed Triple supernaked and new Sprint ST sports-tourer was a massive milestone in the iconic brand's story. The widely held belief is that a three-cylinder motorcycle engine should mix the low-rev oomph of a twin and the high-rev power and fizz of an inline four, all delivered with the smoothness of a James Bond chat-up line, thanks to the natural balance of the layout's 120-degree firing intervals. Triumph's early 885cc engines had been strong. The 955cc unit had thrust the firm forwards, but never quite delivered the best-of-all-worlds promise – and it was already starting to show its age. But the new 1050 hit the mark. And then some.

BMW are renowned for their opposed-cylinder 'boxer' engines and Ducati for V-twins. The arrival of the 1050 was the moment that Triumph finally nailed the recipe, confirming the triple as truly their own – just as Mantoni wanted. The inline three may have been based on the previous 955cc engine, but with more cubic centimetres and significant changes to all the oily metal bits flying around inside, it felt and performed like a brand-new masterpiece. It gurgled and romped forwards with meaty low-rev stomp, surged on an unprecedentedly swollen midrange and had fireworks at the high end – in higher-tuned Speed Triple guise there was 128hp waiting at the top of the tachometer.

Magazine comparison tests put the two new models at the top of their respective classes. I remember riding the Speed Triple against established rivals from Aprilia, KTM and Kawasaki, and being bowled over by the sheer brilliance of its three-cylinder powerplant. The engine confirmed Triumph was back to their best, setting the foundations for the firm's future and its ongoing growth and success.

Of course, just as important was the fact these two new models looked glorious too. The Sprint ST ushered in contemporary, angular lines that were a clear step-change from the rounded edges and slightly fluffy appearance of Triumph's earlier fully faired models, and it boasted three headlights and three outlets for the under-seat exhaust pipe to remind the world that triples meant Triumph. But it was the Speed Triple that left the biggest impression. Its chassis might not have been that different to the earlier 955cc model but the bike's refresh gave it a bad-boy image. Its appearance was as subtle as a cricket bat to the forehead. The muscular stance with twin high-level exhausts and stumpy seat unit (not to mention the model's signature twin round headlamps) retained the streetfighter image and gave presence to back up the engine's potential, cementing its position as the bike that defined 'new' Triumph – something that continues even today.

One-hundred-and-twenty years after the company had been founded, Triumph had rediscovered their groove.

LEADING FROM THE FRONT

Every bike manufacturer has a 'moment' bike. A once-in-a-lifetime machine that's the benchmark against which all others are compared; a bike that becomes the emblem for a period of motorcycling, embodying the tastes and attitudes of the time. A nailed-on future classic.

They tend to be sportsbikes, as these are the models with the greatest performance and sexiest looks; the ones where you sense the passion of the designers captured in every gram of aluminium, every just-so contour of the close-fitting bodywork. Bikes like Yamaha's seminal

RD350 of 1980 and the game-changing Suzuki GSX-R750 of 1985, Honda's revolutionary 1992 CBR900RR FireBlade and the iconic 1994 Ducati 916. They're the two-wheeled equivalents of the E-type Jaguar or Supermarine Spitfire.

Triumph's moment bike came the following year, in 2006, with the Daytona 675. They'd already proved they could create models that were capable, effective, as good as anything the rest of the world could make and also distinct. Now they carried this momentum into creating a bike that was damn desirable too – and that once again moved Triumph ahead of the game.

The two-wheeled world knew something was bubbling away. Triumph had released the Daytona 650, a long-stroke version of the 600 that was an obvious stopgap while the final deep polish was applied to something fresh. Through the year leading up to this secret bike's announcement, the media was dotted with tantalizing grainy spy-shots of a new, lithe, striking Triumph mid-capacity sportsbike in development. And I knew for definite it was coming because I bumped into this new model being tested. Twice.

The first occasion was while carrying out a comparison test for a motorcycle magazine. The other riders and I had stopped alongside the A470 that scythes through Snowdonia in North Wales between Blaenau Ffestiniog and Betws-y-Coed. We were comparing notes, arguing over which bike was best and discussing pressing matters like what to have for dinner. One by one, our ears tuned in to the sound of a bike approaching on the climb between Ffestiniog's imposing slate mountains. The droning, soaring exhaust note confirmed it was a triple, but the clearly free-revving nature and crisp edge were unlike anything we could identify. And then it was passed and gone – a high-speed glimpse of sharp styling, miniscule build and hair-raising hubbub. Many expletives were uttered.

A few weeks later, I managed to get up close. My house was near a route used by Triumph's test riders at the time and heading home one night I caught up with a trim, focused sportsbike of unfamiliar form. Sneaking into the blind spot in the rider's mirrors, I trailed it for half a mile or so; despite the lack of badges and the dog-eared state of what was obviously a test mule, this was definitely the same bike I'd seen in Wales. And it was clearly *that* new Triumph. I was riding a Kawasaki ZZ-R1100, a bike not known for pedestrian performance, and when the test rider realized he was being ogled it also became very apparent that this new machine was also decidedly brisk.

When the groundbreaking Daytona 675 was eventually revealed, the whole of motorcycling recognized that this was one of those moments. Just as with the Rocket and Speed Triple, the new bike was a confident Triumph doing things their way rather than being steered by convention or the products of rivals.

Realizing they'd forever be playing catchup with the Japanese manufacturers when trying to emulate their 600cc inline-four sportsbikes, they reinvented the supersports category with a super-slim, light, high-spec chassis carrying an all-new 675cc triple. Styled in-house by Chris Hennegan, a factory technician who'd made the switch to shapes and colours, the new Daytona was unmistakably Triumph – and it was also staggeringly effective. Extra torque and more accessible power compared to higher-revving four-cylinder bikes made the 675 both faster and easier to ride – a heady combination. The flyweight chassis was accurate and filled you with confidence to explore the bike's highest-ever capabilities; the Triumph felt delicate and nimble when ridden back-to-back with rivals, with an up-on-its-toes eagerness. And the sensational noise chasing you between the hedgerows when you stretched the fabulous motor up to the 14,000rpm redline …

Journalists swooned. Bikes streamed out of showrooms (especially in the glorious Scorched Yellow paint scheme, like that used on the T595 back in 1997). Winning the 2006 International Bike of the Year award, as voted for by 15 magazines from around the world, was pretty much a given.

With the new Daytona, Triumph had put themselves back at the head of the table; for the first time in decades, it was the brand that was shaping motorcycling. And with their strongest model range since their 1990s rebirth, demand was strong – Triumph fired up their fourth factory in Thailand and production figures for 2006 soared to 37,400 bikes – an increase of 18 per cent over the record 'new Triumph' figure from the previous year. Crucially, for the first time in 40 years, Triumph was a headline, desirable, benchmark brand again.

When the company restarted manufacture under John Bloor, the modular models were not only easy and efficient to build, but also intentionally engineered to be safe and predictable. With an unsettled recent history, they couldn't risk flogging bikes that were anything but robust. Nothing wrong with that. But the resulting machines were on the sensible side of exciting and tended to attract a more ... well, let's say 'grown up' customer. With the tyre-slaying Rocket, imposing Speed Triple, dynamic Sprint ST and world-leading Daytona – not to mention an ever-expanding Classic range – there was a newfound energy and fizz. Now, having that famous scripted logo plastered across the front of your T-shirt or the back of a leather jacket was hip again. This made Triumph's own-brand clothing and official accessories a multi-million-pound business.

Stuart Wood and the rest of Triumph's designers and engineers were about to inject something else back into the brand too. Something that biking needed as a whole. They were going to crank back up the fun.

JOYOUS THINGS

Way back in black-and-white times, people bought motorcycles because they were cheap transport. This had changed somewhat by the early 2000s. Yes, folk were still buying small-capacity bikes for their commute and some customers bought a bike to be a workhorse;

however, the major chunk of the market – and the generous, well-heeled chunk that Triumph was aiming at – bought bikes for leisure. Through want, not need. And their reason for wanting a motorcycle was why most of us get onto two wheels in the first place: riding bikes is simply joyous.

The trouble was that the Japanese brands' development boom of the 1980s centred around performance. Racing shaped the showroom offerings and, as such, much of motorcycling had squeezed itself down a narrowly focused avenue. The motorcycle press didn't help – obsessions with saving a couple of grams, making half a horsepower more and shaving two-tenths of a second off an irrelevant lap time had made biking terribly serious.

In the UK, this made motorcycling curiously muddled. Through the late 1990s and into the 2000s, the 'bike meet' had become enormous. On summer evenings, you'd often be able to find a pub engulfed by literally thousands of riders all looking to share their passion, natter with like-minded enthusiasts and have a fine time with their bikes. But this feel-good movement was somewhat disconnected with the out-doing-each-other machines dominating the full car parks.

Triumph had the solution. The 2008 Street Triple: a bike designed for fun, not fractions of a second.

Back in 1996, Suzuki had shaken up the entire world of biking with their Bandit models. Straightforward, fuss-free, unpretentious, these bikes shunned the enclosing fairings and close-fitting plastic that had become the must-have feature during the 1980s and returned to traditional, unclothed, open-to-the-elements design. Accessible, perky and very keenly priced, these new 'nakeds' were a huge hit – especially the GSF600 variant – and spawned rival models from opposing companies, including the notable Honda CB600F Hornet.

Triumph dabbled a toe in the naked waters. Intended as a 2002 model, delayed by the factory fire and eventually released in 2003, the Speed Four was the stripped-down version of the TT600 sportsbike. It should have been a smaller four-cylinder take on the firm's consistently popular Speed Triple (it shared its twin round headlights), but its sporty focus and high-revving engine meant the Speed Four had a different flavour. Though intentional – it was supported by a marketing campaign that declared it was 'an extraordinary new take on the middleweight naked bike' and fanfares about 'the English Revolution' – it was a taste that didn't suit the palate of most potential customers. The Speed Four's situation wasn't helped by the lingering shadow cast by the so-so reputation of the sportsbike it was based on.

But the new Street Triple couldn't have been more on-point. With the glowing Daytona 675 as its base and with a modern stance that echoed the hugely respected 1050cc Speed Triple, this new model promised the engagement of the former and the attitude of the latter. However, its genius was that it delivered its performance and bold image with unprecedented accessibility, an easy-riding dynamic and – crucially – lashings of glorious old-fashioned fun.

For reasons best known to themselves, Triumph invited *Bike* magazine along to their Hinckley base for a sneaky ride on a pre-production example of the Street Triple in the middle of 2007. Obviously volunteering my services for this opportunity, I had the privilege of being one of the first people outside the factory to sample the model on the warm, sun-kissed B-roads of the British Midlands. And it wouldn't have mattered if I'd have been riding under a blanket of drizzle in a finger-nipping chill – the new Street Triple's perky engine, nimbleness, light-on-its-feet handling and breezy manner would have shone in the gloomiest of conditions. It was, and remains, one of those bikes that is simply 'right'; a just-so balance of excitement and cheekiness with usability and unfinicky ergonomics. Fine manners too: you could happily take it along to politely sip tea and nibble sandwiches with the local vicar.

It was easy to see how well Triumph had judged the new model by the vast amount of editorial space dedicated by the gushing media.

Or, far more importantly, by the number of Fusion White, Jet Black and Roulette Green (the best colour choice) Street Triples drawing crowds and raising smiles at bike meets across the country. Actually, no: make that wherever motorcyclists gathered almost anywhere in the world. With more than 7,500 examples built during its first year, this entertaining, exuberant, attention-grabbing machine played a significant role in helping Triumph become the fastest-growing bike company on the planet. Total production for 2008 reached 48,929 motorcycles, meaning that 'reborn' Triumph had at last passed the previous record of 46,700 bikes that had rolled out of the old Meriden plant back in 1969. Bigger than ever.

In the same year, Triumph also started properly kicking butt on the racetrack again too. Australian rider Glen Richards had started racing in the UK in 1998 and made a name for himself in British Superbike by constantly being a thorn in the side of title contenders – from 2002, the rules had allowed bikes up to 1000cc, but Richards was still a frontrunner on an outdated and outclassed 750cc Kawasaki in 2005. After switching to the more production-based Superstock class and winning the championship in 2007, he jumped classes again for 2008 and raced in British Supersport on a Triumph 675 Daytona run by the MAP Embassy team. Only finishing off the podium twice in the 13-round season and taking the top step four times, Richards claimed the title after a year-long scrap with Hudson 'Hurricane' Kennaugh on a Yamaha. It was Triumph's first British championship title since John Cooper won the 1972 MCN Superbikes on a Trident.

The crest-of-a-wave company also returned to the racing world stage. Stefano Caracchi, a former team manager for Ducati, oversaw official factory entries in the World Supersport and European Superstock 600 championships, with the team based in Bologna, Italy (the hometown of Ducati, funnily enough).

There was also some celebration at Hinckley. Along with the Ewan McGregor and Belstaff bikes created to mark the fiftieth anniversary of the original Bonneville's release, there was more Steve McQueen activity. Clearly believing you can't have too much of a good thing, an officially licenced vintage T-shirt was released on what would have been the king of cool's seventy-eighth birthday. Not his seventy-fifth or eightieth, but, er, his seventy-eighth. His old ISDT race number had been 278, if that helps at all …

ROMPING ONWARDS

Make hay while the sun shines, as your grandmother would say. Triumph certainly did. With the polite, throwback, air-cooled, parallel-twin engines and their burly, surging, boisterous inline threes firmly established as the blueprint for success, Triumph strode forth with the sort of assurance they'd not shown since self-confident Edward Turner was steering the ship.

Arriving alongside the fanfare for the Rocket III in 2004 came the Thruxton, a café racer version of the Bonneville. There'd been a limited-edition Thruxton Bonneville in 1965, named after the Hampshire race circuit where the old Bonnie had achieved production racing success, and the new model basked in this reflected glory. With a larger 865cc version of the motor, low clip-on handlebars and sportier chassis geometry, it immediately found an audience – and, as we know, was slipped into the garage of A-lister Bradley Cooper, among others. Two years later came the high-piped, knobbly-tyred, desert-sled-ish Scrambler variant that Mr Cruise used in his big-budget action film. There was a Rocket III Classic with US-style footboards instead of footpegs (less tiring for your booted foot and better for making sparks round long corners), followed by a Rocket III Touring with the necessary accoutrements for distance-swallowing ease. Also rolling out came a blinged-up SE version of the Daytona 675.

Come 2009 and it was time to deck the factory in streamers and set off a few party-poppers. To celebrate 15 years of the Speed Triple – their defining machine and most popular model of the period – there was an Anniversary Special Edition with a unique paint scheme and John Bloor's signature on the fuel tank, plus the fiftieth anniversary Bonneville in its old-style paint scheme. Much celebratory cake was eaten on the production line. Or I like to imagine it was.

All very lovely. But the Leicestershire factory had yet more big and bold plans for the second decade of the new millennium. You don't become the world's fastest-growing bike brand by just meandering along.

Delving into any sport, activity, hobby or pastime means caring about the details. Take football. For anyone on the outside, the ball is just a ball. But those who are passionate about kicking air-filled spheres around will point out that there are training balls, match balls and even professional match balls. And specific ones for street, turf, beach, indoor … in fact, for any other location or type of play that you might be able to dream up.

It's the same in pigeonhole-loving biking. We know that Triumph's traffic-worrying Rocket III fitted the power-cruiser mould. Excellent. But this obviously meant that, despite lots of visual, specification and ergonomic similarities, it was a different proposition to the bikes in the more established 'big cruiser' part of the market – even if your non-biking neighbour wouldn't be able to tell them apart. So, the Hinckley boffins needed to come up with something else to challenge the staggering quantity of large-capacity V-twin cruisers sold in the USA (if you're thinking Harley-Davidsons, you'd be right).

Thrust in the direction of Route 66 in the middle of 2009 as a new-for-2010 model came a spanking-fresh Thunderbird. Back in the rock 'n' rolling 1950s, the original bike with the motel-inspired name had been the machine behind Triumph's success in America. Then, the Thunderbird's 649cc engine had been the largest available with two pistons flailing about side-by-side. Sixty years later, the new Thunderbird replicated this – only now with a 1597cc liquid-cooled oversquare whopper. The mighty twin packed a tarmac-rippling 108 pound-feet of torque, served up at a super-lazy 2750rpm. Or, put another way, a knockout punch arriving just above tickover.

The engine layout fitted with the brand's heritage – Triumph being known for big parallel twins – and pleased US buyers who could remember the old days. But as the market was completely dominated by the V-twin configuration, Hinckley's engineers used a crankshaft with a 270-degree firing interval. Right, pay attention at the back: traditional British parallel twins used 360-degree cranks, which had the pistons rising and falling together and taking it in turn to fire. One was sucking and squeezing while the other was banging and blowing. Easy and cheap to make, and suited to using a single carburettor, the engines also vibrated like a faulty road drill and made your eyes rotate in their sockets. Some Japanese engines had introduced a 180-degree interval (measured as degrees of crank rotation), which helped with balance but caused a rocking couple – remember those? – which meant balance shafts, and cost, and complication. And a thinner, less impressive exhaust note, too. Triumph's 270-degree crank in the new Thunderbird still required balance shafts to counter its huge firing pulses, but the interval gave the feel, power delivery and character of a massive V-twin. Same meaty, rumbling, ground-shaking exhaust note too.

Tradition box ticked. Expectation box ticked. Packaged in a chassis that handled with the eager feel everyone had come to expect of a modern Triumph, and with bodywork that brought an elegance to trad cruiser shapes, the Thunderbird hit its mark. The American publication *Cycle World* voted the impressive new bike their Cruiser of the Year for two years in a row.

The Hinckley factory now offered highly acclaimed sportsbikes, cruisers, sports tourers, retros and, of course, power-cruisers. It was a range stuffed full of rather fine motorcycles. But what they didn't have was an adventure bike.

Back in 1980, German brand BMW had rolled out a new bike called the R80G/S. The name stood for Gelände/Strasse, which means 'terrain/street': a bike designed to be as happy heading through greenery as thrumming along the road. It was inspired by the ISDT. A few BMWs had competed in the 1950s and 1960s, and after an extended period away, the factory entered a works team into the 1979 event – and dominated. The bikes they used were 798cc prototypes with flat-twin boxer engines – the basis for the new R80G/S. As the largest dual-purpose bike available, the BMW caused a bit of a stir, including at the then-still-limping Meriden plant, which rustled up the TR7T in response.

BMW's factory racing versions of the G/S would record famous wins in the gruelling Paris-Dakar rally through the 1980s, and their success caused other factories to hurl large twin-cylinder bikes into the Dakar sand and to offer road versions. There was the Honda Africa Twin, Yamaha Super Ténéré and fabulously titled Cagiva Elefant. They became known as 'giant trailies'. It was always BMW who had the real giant, the GS losing the slash and growing to 1000cc, then 1100, and on to 1150. For 2004, they made it bigger again with the all-new R1200GS – and it was a pivotal moment. This bike turned the giant trailie into the adventure bike. Delivering tourer-like comfort, rugged capability in the muck, thumping twin-cylinder power and staggering usability, the R1200GS flipped a sportsbike-obsessed biking world on its head. In 2006, it became the UK's best-selling bike (over 500cc) – and the various evolutions have repeated this feat every year since. Genuinely staggering.

The Hinckley factory fancied a bit of this too. They'd previously waded into the area of the market: their early modular design had rolled up its sleeves, slipped on a pair of chunky wellington boots and strutted out into the giant trailie world as the Tiger 900. A success initially, its popularity had slipped over the years, so for 2007, it was completely reinvented as the Tiger 1050. Curiously classed as 'urban sports', it was effectively a high-rise Speed Triple with a fairing and a genuinely great bike – but ten years too soon. This style of upright, all-round sports tourer would later become a popular sector, but the road-only Tiger looked like an oddity as motorcycling went crazy for rugged, knobbly, go-anywhere, Swiss army-knife motorbikes with GS-style 'beak' front mudguards. Triumph had gone from playing catch-up to being too far ahead of the curve.

They corrected this product planning slip-up in 2011 with the suitably knobbled Tiger 800.

Using a long-stroke version of the 675cc triple from the Daytona, the new 799cc engine was tuned for flexibility and easy thrust. The tall chassis had a steel tube trellis frame that echoed the look of the Speed Triple. Using slightly different suspension and wheels gave two variants: the regular 'adventure touring' Tiger 800 with road bike-style cast 'mag' wheels; and the more dirt-biased Tiger 800XC with extended suspension travel for swallowing bumps and spoked wheels with a larger-diameter front to roll over obstacles more easily. Oh, and that all-important beak. With an adjustable seat height and a range of accessories aimed at adventurous folk, the functional-looking new Tiger not only did the famous model-name justice but was a perfectly timed counter to the increasingly big and heavy – and expensive – competition.

LEADING FROM THE FRONT

Tue Mantoni left Triumph at the start of 2011 for upmarket Swedish electronics company Bang & Olufsen. The role of CEO at Hinckley was taken by Nick Bloor, son of John, who'd previously worked as export manager and purchasing manager. Nick and his team understood that 'new' was always important on the showroom floor, and fresh and revised models started tumbling out of Hinckley in unprecedented numbers. There were probably plenty of Triumph dealers looking at their stuffed showroom floors and wondering if they needed to apply for planning permission for a sizeable extension.

Wedging the two new Tigers into their line-up gave the Hinckley firm a vast 22-bike range. This included a lighter, sportier, jazzed-up and modernized Speed Triple; they'd shifted over 65,000 of the things since the original spine-framed bike in 1994 and were keen to maintain its appeal. The hot-rodded Daytona 675R appeared to provide racers with an even stronger starting point, and there were additions and updates to the cruiser line-up. There was a new tourist for 2011 as well, in the form of the Sprint GT. This was based on the 1050cc Sprint ST but with colour-coded hard luggage as standard and new suspension, which included a longer swingarm for composure when loaded with gear and a hefty pillion. We'll talk about it quietly because the GT's chassis changes made the handling feel lazy. Deflated journalists trudged back from its press launch grumbling about how the bike behaved, saying it felt as though it had been launched before the development riders had quite finished with it.

More world-shrinking touring bikes followed in short order. The 2012 Tiger Explorer was a big adventure-tourer with a freshly designed 1215cc inline-three engine with pleasingly infrequent 10,000-mile service intervals. The rear suspension used a single-sided swingarm containing Triumph's first ever low-maintenance shaft drive, rather than the rear wheel being turned by a conventional chain, and their first ride-by-wire throttle too. Rather than you yanking the twistgrip and a cable opening the fuel injection's throttle to let air into the engine, it was all done with wires and black boxes. Sensors measured your hand movement and sent the signal to the bike's electronic brain, which looked at other things like engine revs, gear selected, road speed and the phase of the moon, and decided how much to open the throttle. The system meant the Tiger Explorer could also feature traction control (cutting power if it detected the rear tyre had lost grip) and cruise control (set your speed, release the twistgrip, daydream about cake).

Shaft drive and a single-sided swingarm were also highlight features of the omnipresent BMW R1200GS, and the new adventure-tourer Explorer was an unashamed attempt to make a GS with a Triumph badge. This was a bike they hoped could muscle into the German firm's territory and start throwing its weight around (tipping the scales at a considerable 259kg, it had plenty to throw – that's 571lb in old money, or over a quarter of a ton). There was even more brazen BMW bashing for 2013 when the Explorer's engine and drivetrain were used for the return of the Trophy as a luxurious full-loaded tourer. This trod even more new ground for Triumph, featuring fancy electronically controlled suspension, a windscreen that moved at the touch of a button, and an options list that included heated grips, heated seat, tyre pressure monitoring, USB sockets for plugging in your phone and a stereo. And it felt remarkably like the BMW R1200RT that defined the touring sector. It even looked like the BMW ...

The Trophy's press launch involved riding from St Andrews on the east coast of Scotland back to the Triumph factory right in the middle of the UK. I remember whirring along with hands and bum toasty warm and my dubious taste in music streaming out the stereo, thinking it was just like a three-cylinder RT. Which was good, as it meant the new model was clearly very capable indeed ... but it was also something of a slip-up. Making bikes that mirrored the bestselling BMWs so closely was a mistake. Anyone who wanted a GS or RT still bought one of those, rather than settling for the nearest thing with an Explorer or Trophy. Triumph shot themselves in the foot.

However, at the same time as all this, something shifted inside Hinckley. Their bikes were decently made, reliable, performed well, all of that – but their presentation could lack that final bit of polish.

It was in the details. For example, the sidestands would be attached with big, ugly fasteners – 'gutter bolts' as we called them. The rubber for the handlebar grips could feel cheap. And so on. Small details, but important ones, as an owner. From 2013, there was a step change: an updated Daytona 675 and new Tiger 1050 Sport shimmered with a newfound depth of finish and were neatly detailed to the final point. Triumph had been renowned for quality during their formative years and now they'd channelled their inner Bettmann.

Factory bosses had plenty to distract them from the lacklustre sales of their BMW-a-likes. Firstly, ongoing aggressive expansion meant that Triumph was ... well, enormous. By 2014, the company employed more than 1,600 people at six factories around the world: two at Hinckley, three in Thailand, plus a set-up in Brazil for CKD bikes (it stands for 'completely knocked down' and is where bikes arrive in lumps of parts and are assembled at the destination; for certain countries, it's a cunning way of avoiding customs tariffs and import taxes). Edward Turner would have been astounded and overjoyed at their global presence. And secondly, Triumph decided to once again get to the front of the racing world by ramping up factory support.

Over in the USA, a man called Danny Eslick raced a Daytona 675R during 2014. He entered the iconic Daytona 200 in March, put his Triumph on pole position and, after a race-long skirmish with the two Yamahas of Jake Lewis and Jake Gagne, crossed the line first. He'd secured Triumph's first victory at the legendary event since Gary Nixon had won way back in 1967 (you could argue the BSA that won in 1971 was technically a Triumph as well, but let's not get bogged down). The Daytona had won at Daytona. Triumph America was so pleased that they did a limited run of 675R Eslick Editions.

Back in the UK, Lincolnshire rider Gary Johnson had started road racing – as in, on closed public roads, rather than purpose-made tracks – in 2007. Immediately getting himself towards the sharp end at events like the Ulster Grand Prix and North West 200, his debut at the Isle of Man TT saw him become the third fastest ever newcomer. Riding a Yamaha R1 in the Superstock race, he did a blistering lap of 122.859mph. Let's take a moment to get our heads round that: Johnson turned up at the 37.7-mile course having never raced there before, with all its kerbs and walls and bumps and drain covers and nerve-jingling status, and he *averaged* almost 123mph. For the 2014 event, he had a Daytona 675R for the Supersport TT, and his average speed on the Triumph for the entire race – including setting off from a standing start and making pit stops – was a scintillating 124.5mph. In a desperately close skirmish with Bruce Anstey on a Honda, Johnson took the victory after four laps of the Isle of Man course – that's over 150 flat-out, full-concentration miles – with a winning margin of just 1.5 seconds. Eleven years after Anstey's victory, Triumph was back on the top step of the podium at the toughest road race in the world.

There was another great, big, shiny British championship trophy too. Riding for the Smiths Racing team, Australian Billy McConnell clinched the British Supersport title at the final round of the season at Brands Hatch, after a season-long showdown with teammate Graeme Gowland. There was more silverware to polish over on the other side of the Atlantic too, as Kenny Riedman won the Canadian Pro Sport Bike series. Yet another prize for the Daytona.

Clearly, bikes designed in Hinckley could scurry across the face of the planet quite briskly. They therefore decided it was time to again focus on going very fast indeed. How does 400mph sound?

Apart from for a few weeks in 1956 when German company NSU had briefly nicked their title, Triumph had been able to proudly declare that they were the world's fastest motorcycle all the way from 1955 to 1970. Scary-looking streamliners powered by the British firm's engines and boasting bonkers horsepower, torturous riding positions and terrifying exhaust notes had held the record continually. Now they wanted to be the world's fastest all over again.

In 2014, the record stood at a crazy 376mph over a two-run average, set on the Bonneville salt flats in September 2010 by the Ack Attack team. The gaggle of speed-obsessed folk is run by Mike Akatiff, who'd designed and built the Top 1 streamliner powered by two 1299cc Suzuki Hayabusa engines with a turbocharger and an intercooler that used dry ice. Ridden by Rocky Robinson (great name), the bike had officially hit 394mph on one of its runs. That's swift enough to blast from London all the way to Edinburgh in about an hour.

With their sights set on being the first two-wheeler to break 400mph, Triumph teamed up with oil company Castrol to create the 'Rocket Castrol'. Its carbon-fibre and Kevlar monocoque construction measuring over 7.5m (25 feet) was designed and built by Hot Rod Conspiracy, an American company run by engineer, aerodynamicist and Bonneville regular Matt Markstaller. Power came from not one but two Rocket III engines. Having double motors provided a bit of weight that would help the wild creation find traction on the salt, but as the capacity limit for the two-wheel record is 3000cc the engines had to be shrunk. Triumph entrusted Bob Carpenter at tuning firm Carpenter Racing to shorten the stroke of the motors, making them displace 1485cc each. As this also lowered the mean piston speed, it let Carpenter rev the engines higher. And revs bring power: with turbochargers and running on methanol, the pair of Rocket units gave over 1000hp. Over 330 times more power than that first-ever Triumph engine way back in 1905 …

Ridden by Daytona 200-winner Jason Di Salvo, the bike's initial runs at Bonneville encountered poor weather and a small fire caused by a broken camshaft chain. There was also an issue with the salt flats themselves, due to the gradual deterioration of their condition over recent years. Triumph returned to the salt in 2016, this time with TT racer, daredevil, TV star and famous Lincolnshire lad Guy Martin. Conditions were good at a private test in August and after a few days getting to grips with the bike, Martin hit 274.2mph. Conditions weren't as good for the official speed week in September, though, the softness of the salt preventing the Rocket Castrol from having a stab at the record – and conditions haven't allowed a proper attempt anytime since.

There was one consolation. Guy's 274.2mph was quicker than any of the British firm's old records, making it the world's fastest-ever Triumph.

UNSTOPPABLE

While Guy Martin was getting his boots all salty, Triumph was going from strength to strength where it really mattered: making motorcyclists feel all gooey and excited, and prompting them to get their wallets out.

Sportsbikes were in decline. Actually, no, that's underselling it – the market was in freefall, caused by the huge adventure-bike shake-up generated by BMW's pervasive GS and by the changing tastes of riders. Triumph's own Daytona 675 was discontinued in 2016 and the race-winning R version would only survive for another 24 months. Nick Bloor and his squad were probably rubbing their hands together as the shape of the market shifted, however – Triumph's funky, engaging, thrilling Speed Triple and Street Triple had become the wheels of choice for those still after motorbikes with an edge. The Tiger 800 adventurers had evolved into a six-bike range of their own, and the cruiser cupboard was very well stocked with assorted Rocket III, Thunderbird and Speedmaster variants.

Triumph also had something else waiting in the wings. Yet again, it was something significant: a fresh, new Bonneville. Not just one bike, in fact, but an entire model range built around an all-new platform.

Embracing everything they'd learnt from Tue Mantoni at the start of the century and responding to the market's demand for throwback-style motorcycles, this was Triumph reminding the world that nobody did – or could – do retro quite like them. Fifteen years after the 790cc Bonnie had relaunched the legendary name and kickstarted an entire part of the market, the new bike reset the standard. Other European brands with proper heritage had strutted onto the scene dressed in old-fashioned clothes: BMW had their convincing R nineT, and Moto Guzzi were pretty much being kept afloat by their charming and compelling 1970s-style V7. Some Japanese factories were dabbling too, most notably Kawasaki, who had the W800 which had evolved from their 650. With the new-from-the-ground-up Bonnie platform, Triumph was restamping their authority and holding their head high.

There was also a hefty dollop of early Hinckley modular thinking in the new machine, as the bike's designers had come up with a dependable recipe that could be seasoned to give a variety of different dishes. A new liquid-cooled parallel twin with a rumbling 270-degree crank gave three different configurations: all used the same 80mm stroke but there was a 900cc motor with slimmer (84.6mm) pistons; a 1200cc version with fatter (97.6mm) pistons and also a 1200 in 'high power' format, with a higher compression ratio, lighter crankshaft and various other alterations to its insides. The engines would all go into the same steel tube frame, but with the suspension, geometry, ergonomics and overall set-up configured differently in each of the five new Bonnies.

Yes, that's right. Five. Kicking off the family was the 900cc Street Twin, with 54hp and a five-speed gearbox, easy bend-swinging handling, and a bit of a flare-tastic seventies vibe thanks to its cast wheels. Next up was the Bonneville T120 with a 79hp version of the 1200cc motor, six gears to choose from and a full-on 1960s trad' Bonnie look, plus a T120 Black that had pretty much every single component painted … well, you can guess. There was a Thruxton, with the 1200 unit in a 96hp tune and the sportier, stubbier, high-bum, lower-handlebar stance necessary for racing between cafés. And at the top of the tree came the Thruxton R, with modern sportsbike-spec brakes and suspension, and a serious sense of premium.

The line-up was an instant hit. Triumph's detailing was exquisite: the spark plug caps were designed to look like old NGK ones, and the fuel injection's throttle bodies were styled to look like Amal carburettors from way back when. The finish throughout the bikes was a noticeable step up. Best of all, they were great to ride. I was fortunate enough to be invited to Spain for the riding launch of the Street Twin and let out an involuntary whoop the first time I wrenched the twistgrip with gusto – its rich bottom-end torque made the previous Bonnies feel like a wet flannel. The chassis pivoted about beneath you with composure and breeziness. The exhaust note bounced back off hillsides and made the hairs on my neck stick up. The ride quality and action of all the controls were tip-top for the bike's positioning and price. Triumph had built a bike with modern manners, technology and capabilities, convincingly fused with authentic period style and sensations – and, crucially, that was just damn good old-fashioned fun. It was an unprecedented mix of then and now.

The other models lived up to the standard set by the Street Twin. The T120 provided the laid-back thrumming vibe with newfound ease and pothole-swallowing comfort, while the Thruxton R was like a wheelie-popping modern thrill-seeker in a tweed jacket. Each of the Bonnevilles gathered rave reviews and won magazine comparison tests, and they flooded out of dealers. The new 'modern classic' models accounted for a third of all Triumph's sales in 2016.

Clearly buoyed by the success of the new range, Triumph jumped in with both feet. And both legs and much of their torso too. They doubled the Bonnie family the following year with another *five* models. The Street Twin was given a desert sled makeover to create the

Street Scrambler, and treated to the café racer treatment for the Street Cup. The 900cc engine was slipped into the T120 chassis to give it a smaller, more affordable T100 sibling – and a T100 Black, of course. But the biggest surprise was the Bonneville Bobber. This followed the custom scene's trend for low-slung, stripped back, single-seat bikes that replicated the 'bobbers' made by returning American soldiers in the late 1940s. And it was clever: the bike's new bespoke frame neatly concealed the rear suspension to give the appearance of a period hard-tail chassis, and yet handled in a manner completely at odds with its snake's belly stance and wide-barred cruiser looks.

The Bobber was a revelation. With dealers shifting 250 per cent more examples than anticipated in 2017 and bringing a 15 per cent increase of US sales, it was the quickest-selling model in the firm's history. Realizing that the potential of the whole retro and heritage thing was even greater than they'd thought, Triumph would add yet more modern classics over the next few years. Most notable were the Speed Twin, essentially a naked Thruxton with flat handlebars and effectively a B-road-devouring modern supernaked in period costume, and the Scrambler 1200, a chunky, trail-happy tool with clear vintage ISDT inspiration.

You can get a feel for the size of Triumph's operation and the level they'd reached by the fact that all 2017's standard-setting retro models were just a part of their activity that year. It was a huge 12 months, Triumph romping onwards and branching out in a way that no British manufacturer ever had.

After starting at Hinckley back in the 1980s, Stuart Wood had worked his way up to chief engineer and led a team that injected the Street Triple with even more fizz. The model had become the factory's most popular and so got a little of what sharp-dressed product planners would call future-proofing. The previous 675cc engine was stuffed full of new parts and stretched out to 765cc, boosting power but also unleashing lashings more of what the brand was known for: surging, shoving, feel-good torque. A new chassis had a more aggressive nose-down stance, the styling was modernized and young people who understood things like 'apps' and 'interfaces' festooned the bike with the latest electronic trinkets and baubles. There were three versions, starting with the entry-level 111hp Street Triple S and going via the blingier R model to the bells-and-whistles 121hp RS, with its trackday-ready chassis goodies and steal-your-lunch-money attitude.

Having turned heads with these new Street Triples, Triumph then opened eyes wide by announcing they would supply its 765cc engine in tuned-up, race-ready, 130hp form to the FIM Moto2 World Championship. During the first few years of this century, Grand Prix racing had moved from the traditional 125, 250 and 500cc categories. These were dominated by two-strokes, but the engine type had all but vanished from showrooms, so they'd moved to new classifications with four-stroke power. Moto3 sat at the bottom with 250cc singles and MotoGP was at the top with spaceship-like 1000cc madness. In the middle was Moto2, which had a control engine used across the class – and Hinckley signed a three-year deal to replace the existing Honda four-cylinder engines from 2019. Triumph had never won a Grand Prix; now it was guaranteed.

Fans of the Leicestershire-based brand could learn all about this new venture – along with all Triumph's history, successes and legendary status – at the swanky new Factory Visitor Experience. Opening its doors in November 2017, the £4 million facility allowed you to take a guided tour of the factory and facilities and gawp at some serious bikes. How about Johnny Allen's land-speed record 'Texas Ceegar' from 1956, Tom Cruise's Speed Triple from *Mission Impossible: 2* and the original TR6 as used for the world's most famous motorcycle movie scene – the Bud Ekins jump in *The Great Escape*?

As if all this wasn't enough, for one 12-month period, visitors could also learn all about Triumph's other 2017 news: their partnership with humungous Indian automotive company Bajaj. They were going to joint-develop a range of small and mid-capacity machines to allow the Hinckley company to break into the vast Indian market, where literally millions of powered two-wheelers are sold every year. (For some context, the Indian two-wheeler market consumed a staggering 13,600,000 machines in 2019. In one country, in one year. Bewildering. And in October 2024, Royal Enfield sold over 100,000 bikes in India – all from one brand, all in one month.)

Triumph was no longer 'that British bike' brand. They were a world force.

CHAPTER 12

TO THE FUTURE

CAN DO NO WRONG

After four years of planning and negotiation, in 2019, a film crew pitched up in the rolling bucolic splendour near Füssen, on the border between Germany and Austria. You might not know the name, but you'll know the location. It's where Bud Ekins got himself dressed up as his mate Steve McQueen and popped a TR6 Trophy over a fence. Fifty-six years later, Guy Martin was going to replicate the leap.

There were a few differences. Martin would be riding a lightly modified Scrambler 1200 with a far more jump-ready chassis and about four times as much torque as the old TR6. He wouldn't have to pretend he was being chased by angry Nazis. And, unlike Ekins, he didn't have any off-road riding skills. Zip, nada, none. In the lead-up to the event, Martin said, 'When I climb on an off-road bike, I can smell hospital.' So he spent many months being taught what to do by movie stuntman Andy Godbold.

Two 8-feet-high fences replicating the movie originals were built in the same location. The training, very many practice jumps, entire build-up and final nail-biting leaps were all broadcast in a two-hour documentary in December 2019 on Channel 4. Martin even wore a jumper with the sleeves rolled up, just like in the film, rather than modern protective clobber. He was made to wear a crash helmet, though. They didn't have as much health and safety back in Ekins' day.

Around the same time as Guy's leap, Triumph invented something unique. The oh-so-popular Tiger 800 line-up had been upgraded and updated to make a new Tiger 900, and it featured something nobody had seen before: a T-plane crank. If you imagine looking at the crankshaft end-on, the bits that mount the connecting rods for the pistons are traditionally evenly spaced on a triple, which means 120 degrees between them. This gives fabulous balance, a turbine-smooth engine and distinct wailing exhaust note. All Triumph's previous triples had been thus. View the end of the crank on the new 900, however, and the bits to attach the con-rods had unequal spacing and made a sort-of T shape. Hence the name.

Also introducing an unusual firing order (the sequence in which the cylinders ignite fuel), Triumph claimed this bold engineering was to make the new Tiger better in off-road situations as the power delivery helped with traction. All very good. Part of the huge appeal of adventure bikes is their promise of being able to take you anywhere, and extra off-road potential would obviously be a selling point. Some vocal and opinionated people didn't like the T-plane engine, however. Me, for example. The motor had the exhaust sound and vibrations of a twin, meaning Triumph had sacrificed their unique selling point – the glorious, luxurious experience of an inline three-cylinder engine. It all smacked of eager marketing types getting giddy at the prospect of the crank layout making a T for Triumph.

What did I know? The grumbly new Tiger 900 was a sales success and awarded 'bike of the year' by the UK press (although a couple of years later, Triumph would alter the engine to bring back some of that syrupy goodness). With their reputation, engineering nous and high quality – and the fact that every bike they made was so dynamically excellent – Triumph was on an all-time high.

Speaking of all-time highs, they also launched a ground-up redesign of the Rocket with – unbelievably – an even larger engine. The previous

Rocket III had run into problems with tightening emission regulations, so rather than redesign the existing 2294cc triple, Triumph took the opportunity for an all-new version displacing a truly whopping 2458cc. Resetting the record for the biggest production engine, and with 180hp and a bulldozer-shaming 166 pound-feet of torque, the new Rocket 3 (name altered to differentiate it from the previous Rocket III) was a monster – especially as its balloon-like 150mm (6in) wide front tyre gave an almost caricature appearance.

There was wizardry inside the new bike's chassis, though. It may have looked monstrous but that certainly wasn't how it rode. The previous model had felt as sizeable at it was and had traditional cruiser handling traits. Its dynamic matched the looks. But the new Rocket 3 was stiff, taut, composed and eminently manageable – more pumped-up, oversize Speed Triple than laid-back power-cruiser. It was utterly remarkable. Available in roadster R form and more practical GT guise with a pillion back rest and small screen, the new bike's designed-from-scratch engine, frame and running gear were specific to this model – a clear indication of the factory's belief in their product and a bit of a two-fingered salute to rival brands.

With the company's approach as far from the head-in-the-sand tactics of Meriden's final days as it was possible to get, in late 2020 they responded to a change that had occurred with middleweight machines. Back in 2014, there'd been a bit of another 'Bandit' moment when Yamaha introduced a bike called the MT-07. Powered by a 689cc parallel-twin engine and with a gloriously accessible feel, the Japanese factory's tactic with the new bike was stack 'em high, sell 'em cheap. As the MT was also brilliant to ride, it was a showroom phenomenon and completely altered public expectations for naked middleweights. Rivals were forced to not only make their bikes better but lower their prices. For Triumph, this was a headache. Their Street Triple models had become ever-more powerful and high-tech, as is the way – whether it's bikes, cars, smartphones or televisions, everything always evolves to become bigger and flashier. The relentless popularity of Street Triple RS confirmed demand, but Hinckley's designers really did need to tackle the impact of the irksome MT across Europe.

After 'teasing' with mock-up bikes and conveniently leaked 'spy shots' of barely camouflaged test mules, the new Trident 660 was officially wheeled out on 30 October 2020. Just as they had with the original 675cc Street Triple, Triumph strutted in with a benchmark new bike. In fact, the new Trident had more than a little of the original Street Trip' in its DNA: Stuart Wood and his cunning engineers had based the new 660cc motor heavily on the 675, but thanks to a lower state of tune – and because they now knew the unit inside out – it could have standard-setting service intervals. Simple yet fabulously effective, quality without being excessively priced, and crucially capturing the essence of modern Triumph, the new 660 was a ginormous hit. By the end of the following year, the Trident had overtaken the rumbling Tiger 900 GT Pro to become Triumph's bestselling model in the UK. It was also Britain's most popular bike in the 501–750cc category, the most popular naked bike (if you exclude commuter-friendly 125s and scooters) and the year's second biggest seller overall.

It seemed the Hinckley concern could do no wrong.

EYES ON THE HORIZON

Thick and fast. Not a poorly educated racer but how the next barrage of new motorcycles came spilling through the Hinckley gates. Hang on, that's not quite right. Production at the Leicestershire site was dialled down in the early 2020s. Triumph was now making around 65,000 machines a year but only 4,000 or so of these would be assembled in Britain, and they would be mainly limited editions. The rest would be made all over the world, the Triumph empire now including operations in North America, France, Germany, Spain, Italy, Japan, Sweden and Benelux. And of course the manufacturer hotspot of Thailand, not to mention the CKD carry-on happening in Brazil and now also India. Employing over 2,000 people around the world, the famous British brand had become a worldwide wonder. Imagine what Siegfried Bettmann might have made of it all when he was thinking of selling a few bicycles alongside his sewing machines.

Now larger than ever before, Triumph's range was full to bursting with modern classic, roadster and adventure models – all standard-setting, test-winning and class-defining metal. And there were more to come. A stream of them, in fact.

The Speed Triple got the largest shake-up in almost three decades of production. Monstrously powerful supernakeds from rival (mainly European) factories were stealing headlines, dominating the press and making motorcyclists decidedly weak in their lower limbs, so the designers at Hinckley started from scratch. The new version featured a 1200cc triple with enough torque to accidentally speed up the rotation of the Earth and a monumental 180hp, making it by far the quickest version of the model ever made. Weighing just 198kg (437lb) with its tank brimming with unleaded, the new Speed Triple RS was lighter, sharper and more 'grrr' than ever – and it was followed by an RR version with a Thruxton-ish semi-retro fairing and lower handlebars. A full-on superbike for a modern heritage-loving market.

Long after Triumph had wandered off down a blind alleyway with the Tiger 1050, the hybrid of adventure bike and roadster – neatly categorized as 'adventure sports' – had very much become a thing. Spotting an opportunity, they gave the Trident a light adventure-ish makeover, whacked on a half-fairing and called it the Tiger Sport 660. Released in 2022, it immediately became the bestselling model in its class and Triumph's most popular bike in the UK. See, told you they could do no wrong.

Two years later, the evergreen Trident platform would get another reworking too, with a full fairing, sporty stance and a name on the side guaranteed to cause fluttering inside riders of a certain vintage and inkling: Daytona 660. The various Tiger 900s evolved and were joined by a trinkets-and-baubles Tiger 1200 with the same engine as the Speed Triple (in June 2023, Iván Cervantes, a five-time world enduro champion, thrashed this larger Tiger around the Nardò Ring in Italy and did 2493.3 miles in a day, setting a new world record for the distance covered in 24 hours). And the many modern classics developed and became even more desirable.

Since their reinvention, Triumph clearly hadn't let themselves gather dust. The business model involved constant newness and progression, and it worked – as well as chart-topping sales, the firm was making a fortune, with annual turnover passing £750 million and pre-tax profits topping £90 million. Yes, as in a nine and then seven zeroes. Now, with one eye on the horizon and to make sure they remained a rolling stone and moss-free, they stuffed a bike full of batteries.

The planet's oil reserves won't last forever. Fossil fuels are a finite recourse – there were only so many dead dinosaurs – and there's also the problem with all the muck that spills out of exhaust pipes, global warming and air quality. With the planet's total obsession with private transport (bikes and cars), we'll need alternative fuels; boffins with massive foreheads and letters after their names are looking at how to decarbonize petrol and there's much research into synthetic and renewable fuel. But a major part of future mobility will come from electricity.

Started in 2022, Project Triumph TE-1 was a joint exercise with Williams Advanced Engineering – the company that's won lots of Formula 1 championships – and Warwickshire University. Electrification is something all the big bike brands were (and are) investing in, and Triumph's angle was to build a research bike based around chassis measurements and ergonomics of their existing petrol-fuelled roadsters. Don't think that electric bike means wimpy two-wheeled mobile phone. With 175hp and a torque delivery that replicated the tyre-testing Speed Triple 1200 RS, the TE-1 whistled from standstill to 100mph in just six seconds. It had a realistic range of 100 miles and could be plugged in and recharged from flat to 80 per cent full in just 20 minutes (the final bit of charge needs to be done slowly on any electric vehicle, to help maintain battery health). This charge rate was quicker than the electric bikes appearing on the market, and, at 220kg (485lb), the battery-powered Triumph was as much as 25kg (55lb) lighter too. If you dropped that on your toe you'd know about it.

There was no production plan ... or not yet. This was the Hinckley outfit readying itself for what might come next. But while the development of a battery-packed Triumph was only to be expected, their other news caused rather more 'I'm sorry, they're doing what?' – in 2023, Triumph announced they were going motocross racing.

This was like Ferrari deciding to build a tractor or Nike moving into footwear for the allotment. Yes, Triumph had a long and illustrious history with off-road machinery, but back in the time of flat caps and sepia-tone, the bikes were tweaked roadsters. So were all those iconic 1960s desert sleds. Motocross had become very different, with ultra-specialist machines all made to a proven template and, because of this, having like-for-like specification and performance. Triumph had no experience but tramped in anyway. They roped in American off-road specialist Ricky Carmichael – considered one of the greatest motocross riders of all time and with a roll of career victories that would require another book to list – to help develop the bike. The all-new TF 250-X was revealed in December 2023.

Packing a 250cc single-cylinder motor, lightweight aluminium frame and components from all the big-name, go-to dirt bike brands, the TF 250-X boasted the best power-to-weight ratio in its class. It wowed the press with the quality of its suspension. Dirt bike racing is huge in the USA, particularly supercross (like motocross but raced in stadiums in front of huge baying crowds and with intentionally huge jumps), and Triumph entered the TF 250-X in the ridiculously competitive 2024 AMA 250 Supercross Championship with rider Jalek Swoll. They finished the season in seventh place. New bike? First attempt? That'll do.

IN THE FABRIC

A name that has meant so much to so many people, at the start of 2025, the Triumph brand is in greater shape than ever before in its long, famous, intriguing history.

Appearing in 2024, the new Speed 400 and Scrambler 400 X were the first fruits of Triumph's partnership with Bajaj. Smaller capacity bikes were making a comeback in the UK, with machines from Royal Enfield selling by the boatload and displacing the traditional big sellers from the registration results, and the Asian market continued to gulp down bikes at an inconceivable rate. Triumph's response was a pair of new, retro-style bikes sharing a made-from-scratch engine and new frame, with the Speed a traditional roadster and the Scrambler configured exactly as its name suggests. Both had the specification and features – and, crucially, the price – to rival the bestsellers. But what made them really stand out was that these weren't simplified, pared-down, built-to-a-price, entry-level bikes. Oh goodness no. These were proper Triumphs, with all the quality, presence and butterfly-bringing feel of their larger siblings.

Designed to attract younger European riders, the Speed 400 and Scrambler 400 X also proved a huge hit with established riders in the UK. They were a whirlwind success, becoming the year's bestselling retro, the chart-topping naked and most popular smaller-capacity bike. In some months, the Speed was even the bestselling motorcycle overall. Astounding. Crucially the 400s also hit their mark in the huge Indian market, with 29,736 bikes sold – and this impressive figure played a part in Triumph's global sales passing 100,000 for the first time ever. And they didn't just edge past the landmark figure. Compared to the previous year 2024's global sales were up by a staggering 64 per cent, allowing Triumph to shift a total of 134,635 motorcycles. Almost three times what the bustling Meriden plant ever churned out in a year.

For 2025, these game-changing 400s are joined by another bike perfectly pitched for the evolving marketplace. The attention-grabbing new Tiger Sport 800 is the inspired and tantalizing combination of the Tiger Sport 660 all-rounder with a souped-up 113hp 798cc engine. Whoever came up with the concept deserves a massive bonus. Perfectly conceived, planned and executed, the Tiger Sport 800 is an absolutely nailed-on showroom sensation – it's like Triumph's greatest hits in one package.

One-hundred-and-forty years after being founded and 120 years after the first true Triumph motorcycle – the 1905 Triumph 3hp Motor Bicycle, the inaugural machine completely created in-house – the world's most famous motorcycle company is the strongest it's ever been. Wider-reaching and forward-looking, they're touching more riders than ever and creating bestselling motorcycles. The name embedded in biking folklore is so, so much more than merely intact.

After setting records, being a cinema star, helping win two world wars, dominating races, overcoming adversity, becoming a style icon and influencing generation after generation – and, of course, thrilling and engaging thousands of us riders with their standard-setting machines – Triumph is pumped up, celebrated, striding onwards. Integral to the very fabric of motorcycling, the iconic British marque is building on its legend, model after model, year by year.

I wonder what the next 140 years will bring?

Acknowledgements

Writing this book would not have been possible without John Westlake and Damon I'Anson, who took a gamble on the unqualified wannabe and gave me a start in motorcycle journalism. Huge thanks to them, Tim Thompson, Hugo Wilson, and all the other influential journalists and editors who I've been fortunate enough to work with over almost a quarter of a century – your shared knowledge, insight and enthusiasm let me make it look like I know what I'm doing. Thank you also to the brand experts and historians whose existing work allowed this all-inclusive story to be compiled, and to Louise Dixon and Gabby Nemeth at Michael O'Mara Books for entrusting me not to make a hash of it.

Packing 140 years of history into one book has been hugely enjoyable but not without some head scratching. Facts become blurred with time, and opinions turn into truths. Our digital age gives access to historical documents, data and guidance like never before, but can also present alternative versions of the same story. Where differing accounts exist, I've followed the widest-held belief and deployed my own knowledge and judgement. Any factual errors or misquotes within these pages are down to my own foolishness. And with my own recollections, I apologize if my memory has become foggy.

Select Bibliography

In addition to the massive stack of dusty old magazines in my house, I recommend the following books:

Edward Turner: The Man Behind the Motorcycles, Jeff Clew, Veloce, 2006
McQueen's Motorcycles, Matt Stone, Quarto, 2017
The Complete Book of Classic and Modern Triumph Motorcycles: 1937–Today, Ian Falloon, Quarto, 2019
The Ultimate History of Fast Bikes, Roland Brown, Parragon, 2004
The Classic Bike Buying Guide, Bauer Media, 2018
Jupiter's Travels, Ted Simon, Hamilton, 1980
Triumph 1915-1924, Peter Cornelius, self-published, 2002

Websites

Triumph Owners' Motor Cycle Club: tomcc.org
Pre-1941 Triumph Motorcycle Pages: triumph.gen.nz
The History of Triumph: ianchadwick.com /motorcycles/triumph
World's Fastest Motorcycle: gyronautx1.com
Sheldon's EMU: cybermotorcycle.com
Sweet Triumph: money.cnn.com/magazines/fsb/ fsbarchive/2002/04/01/320994/
Isle of Man TT database: iomtt.com
Col. Holbrook and the Early Triumph Days: triumphworks.co.uk
ISDT history: speedtracktales.com
Why Brand Positioning Matters: Chris Bullick, thepullagency.com

Picture Credits

The publisher would like to thank the following sources for their kind permission to reproduce the pictures in this book.

Plate Section One in order of appearance:

1: RW Ayton, 1905 3hp. Photo by Mortons Media Group
2: 1925 Triumph 494cc Model P. Photo by Malcolm Haines/Alamy Stock Photo
3: Siegfried Bettman premises plaque on Priory Street, Coventry. Photo by Colin Underhill/Alamy Stock Photo
4: Riders of Britain's new almost 100mph motorcycle, the Triumph Thunderbird meeting with the designer, Edward Turner. Photo by Smith Archive/Alamy Stock Photo
5: Early advertisement for Triumph Cycles. Photo by Universal History Archive/Universal Images Group via Getty Images.
6: The Gyronaut X-1 driven by Bob Leppan. Photo by Eric Rickman/ The Enthusiast Network via Getty Images/Getty Images
7: Poster for the celebrated British motorcycle. Photo by Michael Nicholson/Corbis via Getty Images
8: Despatch riders for the Women's Royal Naval Service (WRNS). Photo by Eric Harlow/Keystone/Hulton Archive/Getty Images
9: Steve McQueen in the 'Olympics of Motorcycling', the Motocross World Championship. Photo by Francois Gragnon/Paris Match via Getty Images
10: American motorcyclist Johnny Allen shows off his Triumph. Photo by © Hulton-Deutsch Collection/CORBIS/Corbis via Getty Images
11: The police in France rode Triumph motorbikes. Photo by Keystone-France/Gamma-Rapho via Getty Images
12: Marlon Brando on the set of *The Wild One*. Photo by Pictorial Press/ Alamy Stock Photo

13: Stuntman Bud Ekins on motorcycle doubling for Steve McQueen in *The Great Escape*. Photo by Everett Collection Inc/Alamy Stock Photo
14: The 557cc Triumph model H motor bicycle. Photo by Bonhams Motorcycle Dept.
15: Production line at the Meriden motorcycle factory in Solihull. Photo by Brian Bould/ANL/Shutterstock
16: Manufacturing at Norton Villers. Photo by PA Images/Alamy Stock Photo

Plate Section Two in order of appearance:

1: Triumph TSS motorcycle. Photo by Author
2: 1968 Triumph Bonneville T120R. Photo by National Motor Museum/ Heritage Images/Getty Images
3: *Happy Days* with Henry Winkler. Photo by ABC/Everett/Shutterstock
4: Triumph 1938 Triumph Speed Twin. Photo By Reading Eagle/Tim Leedy/MediaNews Group/Reading Eagle via Getty Images
5: Daniel Craig in *No Time to Die*. Photo by Landmark Media/Alamy Stock Photo
6: Triumph Rocket III. Photo by Associated Press/Alamy Stock Photo
7: Triumph Speed 400 motorcycle. Photo by Raimo Bergroth/Alamy Stock Photo
8: 1990 Triumph Daytona 1000 motorcycle. Photo by Adrian Turner/ Alamy Stock Photo
9: 1997 Speed Triple T509. Photo by Richard Brown/Alamy Stock Photo
10: Triumph TE-1. Photo by Pier Marco Tacca/Getty Images
11: Guy Martin rides the Triumph Infor Rocket Streamliner. Photo by PA Images/Alamy Stock Photo
12: Álex Márquez in action. Photo by David Ramos/Getty Images
13: Tiger Sport 660. Photo by Zoran Karapancev/Shutterstock
14: 1996 Triumph Daytona T595. Photo by Heritage Image Partnership Ltd/Alami Stock Photo

Every effort has been made to acknowledge correctly and contact the source and/or copyright holder of each picture and the publisher apologises for any unintentional errors or omissions, which will be corrected in future editions of this book.

Index